Cover Design: Norman Goodwin
Edited By: Kendra Newton

A Notion Outgrown

Norman Goodwin

1

The crew was somewhere near the coast of Iran when Rusty raced to assume the midnight watch. It had been ninety days since the ship's last port call in Egypt, and the Persian Gulf seascapes replaced those of the fabled Red Sea.

Long, hurried strides carried Rusty through the lower decks to relieve the forward lookout. Exiting a watertight door, he emerged topside, appearing to a moonless night; an evening soddened by briny salt spray, chilled winds, and indigo starlight. Rusty stood on the weather deck, gripping the cold, metal life-rail. Blinking to adjust his eyes, he waited as the dim outlines of the ship's metal hull faded into view, developing like a fresh Polaroid. "Darken Ship" condition meant no white light emanated from the destroyer's interior, preventing vessels from spotting the nocturnal ship.

The cosmic explosion of a trillion stars peppered the night sky, and their glow cast a soft, omni-directional aura, making the world seem more expansive. With starlight, there were no shadows to constrain objects, therefore everything seemed larger from the silver light of countless celestial bodies.

Being topside was dangerous, but walking on the bow could be fatal. Under the right conditions, if the wind didn't carry a sailor overboard a rogue wave could. However, the choice was never up to Rusty, as life burdened him with a duty not of his own volition. Punctuality was a collective obsession instilled in everyone since birth, and no one showed more devotion to meeting at an appointed time in space than a watch-stander waiting to be relieved. Rusty had better not be late or Connelly would have his ass reported.

With a bounce and a shrug, Rusty's mechanic's coat rode higher on his shoulders and the seafarer found the new looseness of his sleeves more agreeable. He stuffed his thermos under his arm and slid his hands deep into his pockets, psyching himself up for the extremes ahead. Pulling his elbows close, he stepped onto the focsle. The large, one-hundred foot long, bullet-shaped deck held the VLS Tomahawk missile launcher, and the Mark 45 cannon turret. Dark silhouettes from these weapons of mass destruction helped the unsteady sailor chart his way through the veiled darkness.

Strong winds swept across the deck. His hands shivered as he removed his hat to comb wavering fingers through his hair. After surveying the scene, he placed his white cap back on his head and sighed, cursing in defiance of the bracing wind. *This is bullshit.*

The swash of the ship's stem slicing its way through the ocean's wake, mixed with howling gusts, created an audible white noise that seemed to originate everywhere. The ship's pitching motions were stronger on the bow than at the midship. Turbulent seas heaved, but not as hard as the largest oceans he'd sailed, and any sailor would attest that the Arabian Gulf was far less hostile than the aerated seas of the North Atlantic. The mild conditions Rusty faced this night were only a minor annoyance.

Like a drunken sailor, Rusty staggered his way around the various obstacles laid out on the focsle. He placed purposed steps on the deck, one foot in front of the other, taking nothing for granted when the cost of a mistake exceeded the value of his life.

When the ship slid down the backside of massive swells, it felt like she would pull herself from under his feet, tossing Rusty into places far worse than a rough deck. If Rusty tripped, the non-skid floor would shred his palms. And what would he do on a four-hour watch with shredded, blood-caked palms?

He slalomed the large missile launcher and the tall mount of the forward cannon before approaching the nose of the massive warship, stopping ten feet behind Petty Officer Connelly.

Facing oncoming winds, Connelly stared at the open water, oblivious to Rusty's presence as he clocked the sea for mines. Rusty cupped his hands and raised them to his mouth, amplifying his voice over the boisterous groan of the elements. "Hey!"

Connelly turned to Rusty, but said nothing. Large, oversized night-vision goggles weighed his head down, exaggerating his movements with jerky imprecision. His sluggish hands fumbled with his cord as he climbed down from his chair, gripping the handrail to aid his descent from the towering seat.

The tall chair resembled an airboat seat, or a lifeguard station on a busy beach. The only way to get to the tower was via a ladder which was welded to the deck. It was a sturdy tower, even though it was not a permanent fixture. Sailors could rest easy knowing it would not break off during rough seas.

With his feet planted on the deck, Connelly lifted his goggles, eager to hand them to Rusty. Connelly's clumsy fingers dropped the sound-powered phones, but he snagged the cord before the earpiece connected with the deck. After situating himself, the tired sailor stood half-assed erect and raised his chin to meet Rusty's gaze.

Rusty saluted the watchman. "I'm here to relieve you."

Connelly returned the salute with his elbow held low. "I stand relieved." With his other hand, he cradled the large clump of electronic components, and soon it would be Rusty's turn to babysit the laughable bundle of gear.

"Cold?" Rusty asked.

"Freezing my ass off." Marching in place, Connelly looked past Rusty's shoulder, staring at the ship's superstructure.

"Who's on the bridge?" Rusty asked.

Connelly stopped stomping to better answer Rusty. "Chief Gilmore."

"All right, thanks... Oh, I saw some 'Mid-Rats' in the mess hall." Rusty was in no hurry to assume the watch and he figured involving Connelly in a conversation would make the four-hour shift go by faster.

"What is it?" Connelly asked. He'd started marching again.

"Roast beef." Rusty said.

Connelly sighed, tilting his head back. "Eh, again? We have roast beef every night."

"I think it's real beef this time."

"No thanks. I'll wait till breakfast. Catch ya later." Connelly handed the night-vision goggles and sound-powered phones to Rusty before hobbling toward the ship's superstructure.

Connelly failed to swing his arms or bend his knees. His gait was off and he moved like a wooden nutcracker. Although he willed his body to move, his muscles refused to comply with his mind's requests. *The wind froze the poor bastard stiff.*

Tapped out as he was, the weary shipmate made his way around the tall gun turret and entered the same door Rusty had exited.

Rusty sighed and turned, looking in the direction the ship sailed to conduct a quick situational analysis of his surroundings. Starlight reflected on the ocean's uneven surface, hinting at tranquil seas which were not as rough as he'd assumed.

The swells ran at a three to four-foot chop, and the ship's speed was thirty-five knots. The USS John Adams hauled ass, and Rusty was about to become her new hood ornament.

Over eight thousand tons of steel pitched up and down on an endless loop. With each wave, Rusty's weight alternated from heavy to light as her massive nose see-sawed in a calming rhythm. The soothing pitch was more likely to lull Rusty to sleep than toss him overboard, and if it were not for the chilly wind, Rusty *would* fall asleep sitting in the chair. Snoozing in a cushy bed would be great, whereas dozing on the forward lookout would be fatal. To fall asleep, and land in the ocean, only to have a fast-moving Navy destroyer run you over, under, and through the screws would be a damn tragedy.

He climbed the ladder and sat on the seat. A few minutes of exposure to the brisk night air already cooled the metal to the atmosphere's ambient temperature. It wouldn't be long before Rusty's rear grew numb.

The three by three-foot piece of sheet metal was hard, flat, and smooth like polished stainless steel. Engineers cut the slippery sheet too wide to be called a seat in any actual sense of the word. Rusty resembled a toddler on a patio chair, and the armrests were too far apart, preventing him from resting both arms at the same time. It lacked safety straps to keep sailors from coasting straight into the water. Hell, the only safety device Rusty had was his grip on the armrest and the minuscule friction of his denim pants. Had the engineers not welded the footrest at the proper height, Rusty would have been able to swing his legs.

Rusty folded and stowed his hat in his back pocket before prepping his night-vision goggles. With the straps adjusted and secured, he donned the sound-powered phones. They gripped like a pair of traditional headphones except for a strap-mounted microphone that hung around his neck, positioning its diaphragm near his mouth.

A quick look at the ocean revealed merchant ships sailing on the horizon, casting faint glows like distant green cities, as viewed from the rural outskirts of any midwestern town back home. Rolling green clouds littered the night sky, obscuring large swaths of bright stars. Although he'd stood mine-watch for weeks, the unobstructed view of the ocean and its vast openness still unnerved him.

Rusty's watch had begun. He fumbled for the tiny button on the glossy black microphone. "Pilothouse. Mine-watch. Manned and ready," Rusty said.

The Officer of the Deck replied over the headset. "Mine-watch. Pilothouse. Very well."

Rusty glanced over his shoulder. The scale of the ship's superstructure seemed odd. The massive structure appeared small and distant. Its long bow dwarfed the ship's primary structure, making the decks above the hull look too small by comparison. From his vantage point, it seemed Rusty was over-extended, pushed forward to the farthest point of the bow. With snuffed panic, he turned his face back into the endless inflow of oncoming headwinds. *Hood ornament indeed.*

A fishy odor of salted jelly polyps and plankton embedded itself in the lining of his nose. Rusty licked his lips, and salt melted on the tip of his tongue.

He peered through the night-vision goggles, squinting at its bright green LED display. It took time for him to acclimate to their obnoxious light.

When sailing at sea, the ocean extended to meet the horizon in all directions; whereas visiting the beach during summer vacation only provided half the experience. The land-locked feeling from a day at the beach did not compare to the openness of being underway in the middle of the naked ocean, and nothing could ever compare to flying on the front end of a fast-moving ship.

Rusty's primary duty was to spot mines. He was a lookout, tasked with locating hazards placed in the ship's path. The situation was absurd, because although he had never seen a photograph of a mine, if he saw anything resembling one, he was to report its range and bearing to the Officer of the Deck standing watch on the bridge. If a floating bomb endangered the ship, it was to be destroyed.

Rusty gripped his thermos between both legs and unscrewed the lid. Steam rose as he poured coffee into the lid. Even in the heavy wind, the savory aroma of blueberries filled the air as he lifted his cup and sipped the hot beverage, relishing the small pleasure it brought.

The helmsman turned to port, forcing the ship to lean precipitously. Rusty seized the rail in one hand, eyeing his coffee cup in the other, all the while hoping it would not spill. He remained in his fixed position for the duration of the maneuver. Once the ship righted herself, he downed the cup of coffee and secured the half-filled thermos inside his coat, fearing another random course correction might surprise him.

Frontal wind speed increased with the ship's new heading. Rusty clenched his coat's breast, taking up the garment's slack, pulling the fabric tighter around his chest, bringing his warm thermos closer to his body. With his free hand, he flipped his collar to shelter his neck. With four hours until his relief showed, Rusty did his best to settle in for the long shift ahead.

In twelve minutes, it will be my birthday. Of all the ways I could have imagined spending my twenty-first birthday, seated on mine-watch in the Persian Gulf, was one scenario I never expected.

Saddening nostalgia overcame Rusty.

What are my friends doing for their birthdays?

Halfway through his watch, as most bored people do, Rusty contemplated the mundane nature of his situation.

What does a mine look like? A ball with flat protrusions or spikes? Do they look like an Everlasting Gobb-Stopper? Do they float, or are they submerged? How could someone spot a submerged mine if the mine is underwater?

The sea's wake mirrored the vibrating reflection of a billion stars, from the brightest to the faintest. Rusty's eyes traced the dense band of the Milky Way that swept across the sky before fixating his stare on the constellation of Orion and Orion's top right shoulder, Betelgeuse. He scanned the sky for more familiar patterns, testing his ability to identify other constellations and celestial bodies, but he could only name a few. Ursa Major, the Big Dipper, and the Little Dipper were constellations the amateur astronomer could name.

As far as light pollution, there were no artificial lights in the middle of the ocean; nothing but natural darkness for hundreds of miles, allowing the dimmest of stars to shine. With nothing but time and his imagination to keep him company, Rusty pondered the scale of the universe. The billions of years the universe took to develop, and the random emergence of intelligent life, seemed paradoxical to the truth of human existence. How could the universe, and all its beauty, constrain the shortness of a person's experience? It wasn't right that life was so short in the universal scale.

At 2:45 a.m., loud slapping sounds interrupted the monotonous rumble of the ship's splashing, pulling Rusty from his tranced state. He jerked his head to the right, expecting a sea monster to emerge and drag him to his death, or a missed hazard seconds away from blowing the ship in half. However, reality offered something far more interesting than anything Rusty could imagine from his limited experience.

At first, the slapping sounded like jumping fish, but their pitch was much deeper, much lower, and much… larger. His focused attention made the sounds seem louder. Decisive strikes on the ocean punctuated a series of rapid clicking noises.

The commotion originated from the starboard side, at his three o'clock position, just below his tower. He looked over his right shoulder, to the water. He leaned over, way too far and way too fast! Panicked hands gripped the armrest, and he flung his body back. Heavy heartbeats thumped in his chest and echoed in his temples as he counted the ways he almost died.

A tragedy indeed.

Motivated to mind his center of gravity, he lowered his goggles to view the dark, shaded water, looking a second too late. He saw nothing but the fast-moving surf as waves sped past the ship. Perplexed, he sat upright, and again he heard a loud slap.

Time seemed to slow as he waited. Determination fixed his stare, and after a dozen seconds, the source of the commotion revealed itself.

Dolphins, longer than canoes, emerged from the water, superimposing their green glowing forms against the ocean's black surface. Giant green dolphins hovered four feet in the air. From the top, they seemed to fly with the ship, remaining motionless for upwards of three seconds until smacking the water's surface with a loud glunking.

Green-glowing streams of bubbles followed the descending dolphins, resembling diving torpedoes. Turbulence of the one-ton mammals radiated in the agitation, and the trails faded as the dolphins dove deeper.

It took a second for the event to register in Rusty's mind, and for a moment, nothing else in the universe existed. Wide eyes stared as dolphins performed aquabatics, surfing the stem's wake.

He glanced at the rear of the ship, expecting witnesses — but he was alone.

Alternating turns, dolphins leapt from the water and slapped back into the sea, diving deep into the black abyss. Dolphins jumped twenty feet across the surface. The ship cruised at thirty-five knots, but the pod maintained their pace with minimal effort.

Many people have watched dolphins skim the bow of a ship, but this was different. Rusty experienced something few people on Earth had ever seen, illuminated dolphins viewed through night-vision goggles with blazing bubbles.

One after another, the dolphins jumped. Hurdling like racers, they leaped and plunged, moving in long repeating sine waves. In mid-flight, one dolphin twisted and corkscrewed to its left, locking stares with Rusty. Its black dot of an eyeball appeared in the green, glowing froth. Night-vision goggles amplified the phosphorescence created in the ocean water, highlighting its black bead. It was a tiny orb resembling a single raisin on glowing lime jello.

As the frequency of their jumping decreased, the dolphin's aquabatics subsided. As quickly as it began, the spectacle stopped. Saddened to be alone, Rusty continued looking at the water for much longer, hoping the dolphins would resume frolicking in the swells. But minutes went by with nothing. He sat upright and stared ahead, his head filled with the enchanted memories of the dolphins.

Looking back at the horizon, he resumed his watch.

Perhaps it was the unusual spectacle, or more likely, it was the intimate nature of the personal event, but the tiny electric whales were among the most exciting things Rusty had ever recalled seeing. It was a sight few people were privileged to see, and it was a scene seldom duplicated.

2

Two hours later, in the lower berthing compartment, ET2 Palmer shouted in Rusty's bunk, tapping his keyring on the metal locker next to Rusty's head. The tiny man's voice was much too whiney. Years earlier, Palmer practiced speaking like Thurston Howell III and found he couldn't stop. "Rusty, get up. Mr. Kistner wants you in the Shop. He wants you and Mux," Palmer said. He pleaded as he pushed Rusty's shoulder, rocking him. Palmer's shouting drew the annoyance of men from other divisions who were still sleeping in their racks, and it was clear to those in berthing that Palmer was power-mad.

Rusty's pulse quickened as he squinted at the bright lights. "Shit man, I didn't go to sleep until six-thirty. What time is it, anyway?"

"It's seven-fifteen.'"

"Are you serious? I stood the mid-watch last night." Rusty fumbled under his blanket, struggling to untangle his arm. With a flip of the wrist, he peered at his old Submariner wristwatch. He closed his eyes, pulled his blanket over his head and rolled away from Palmer, blocking the blinding light invading his bunk. It seemed that the only way around Palmer's intrusion was cocooning himself to shut the world out.

Palmer told Rusty he understood what time the mid-watch was over, but the point was moot. "Mr. Kistner asked me to come down here and wake you. He's got something important to pass along. Get up or get written up. Reveille - reveille bitches."

Palmer smiled with teeth which were too dense for flossing and Rusty wanted to know if they hurt, being as compressed as they were.

There was no getting around the disturbance, so Rusty flipped the blanket off his head. His crewcut wild hair pointed in all directions.

"Couldn't you just take notes? Damn, man."

Instead of looking into Rusty's eyes, Palmer stared at Rusty's forehead as he rejoiced in relaying the message. "He wants you in the Shop. Don't forget to wake Mux."

Palmer's brass keys clinked around his belt loop as he scurried out of berthing and ascended the ladder well, stomping his boots on the ladder's stainless steel rungs, to make as much noise as possible.

Rusty rolled his head to loosen his neck muscles. He stretched his arms and gripped the curtain, pulling it aside enough to roll out of the top bunk. His bare feet slammed onto the cold terrazzo deck with a heavy thump. The blue floor was freezing. Standing in his white boxers, coveting the warmth of his wool blanket, he wedged his feet into his shower slippers. A violent shiver cascaded his body, urging him to cross his arms to insulate his exposed chest. His warm hands rubbed over his shoulders, generating friction as he scanned the compartment, allowing himself time to adjust to the berthing's harsh conditions.

To the left of his stand-up locker hung his well-worn, soft denim dungaree pants. Faded by salt water and countless washings, the bell-bottomed jeans were close to retirement. Replacing the jeans was not an option. The cardboard, starchy feel of new denim made Rusty itch. He exhausted considerable effort to keep his cultured denim devoid of holes and stains. Rusty was a sailor who liked his uniform cleaned by the ocean air. He was a bluejacket of the highest caliber — an old salty, as they say.

After stepping into his dungaree trousers, Rusty hobbled to Mux's rack. He buttoned his pants, then leaned forward to knock on his best friend's bunk.

Mux gripped the curtain and slid it aside, smiling with one eye closed. "What's up?"

"Mr. Kistner wants us in the Shop." Rusty grabbed his shirt from a nearby hook.

Mux wiped his eyes, trying to adjust to the brightness. He squinted at Rusty, who loomed above him, buttoning his light blue cotton shirt. "Damn," Mux said.

He rolled out of the bottom bunk and started dressing beside Rusty. Both shipmates had been awakened for important meetings before and were used to dressing while half awake. Still, any unexpected reveilles were aggravating, and no sane person relished waking a tired sailor who'd only received half an hour's rest.

"Rusty. Who told you we needed to be at the Shop?"

"Palmer," Rusty said, sliding his hand into his waistband, tucking in his shirt. He stared at his crotch and adjusted his belt buckle, ensuring his gig line was straight.

Mux raised his arm to spray deodorant. "Did he say why?"

Residual fumes from Mux's deodorant floated into Rusty's mouth, leaving a bitter aftertaste. "Mr. Kistner wants us all to be there. Palmer seemed to enjoy blasting me out of my rack. Bitch has Crow Fever or something."

"I know. Right?"

As Rusty unlocked his stand-up locker, a thought crossed his mind. "I wonder what humans invented first? The wheel or the key?"

Mux stopped dressing and gave Rusty a quizzed look. "I would think the wheel."

"I don't know. Seems like humans have been stealing since they discovered work." Rusty smiled. "Anyway. Palmer always looks at my forehead when he talks."

"Like those people who talk with their eyes closed?" Mux asked, smirking.

"Yeah. Just like that. I don't trust people who talk with their eyes closed." Rusty slipped on his black boon-docker boots — boots he kept as shiny as a polished eight ball. "It's weird," he said.

Rusty was ill-prepared for the day, and it showed. His short-cropped, sandy-brown hair pointed in wild directions, conditioned by the ocean's sticky sea salt. There was no time to calm it with a comb, so the best he could manage was dousing it with cold sink water.

It will have to ride.

He tossed his towel on his bunk and met Mux at the door just as his best friend started up the steep ladder.

Mux was from Dallas, Texas. His father was on the job the day someone assassinated Kennedy at Dealey Plaza, and Mux knew how JFK's assassination went down. His father was a retired homicide detective in his hometown, and he held a solid theory about the assassination. The more Rusty thought about his dad's theory, the more it made sense.

Mux was supposed to enter the academy to be a police officer like his dad, but joined the Navy to earn a degree and pursue a career in mechanical engineering.

Rusty met Mux's dad once at their graduation in Chicago. The police detective was an intimidating person, and Rusty remembered how practiced the man's handshake was. He imagined Mux's father perfected his handshake over countless hours, portraying the "good cop" in grimy interrogation rooms.

The Electronic Technician's repair Shop was located four floors up, a few spaces aft of the Bridge. It was a central hub for the nerdy science types, who enlisted with higher-than-average ASVAB test scores. The brainy group of tech-nerds was part of "Combat Systems Central" and the division's name sounded way cooler than its members deserved.

Rusty and Mux raced up ladder wells and through the dense chow-line of men waiting to be fed.

"Make a hole!" Mux shouted.

Sailors stepped aside, allowing them to pass without paying much attention. It was not unusual to see men running around the ship, as every division had its occasional urgent meetings, or dilemma in need of immediate resolution.

Mess Specialists served the usual breakfast menu, filling the passageway with the smell of fresh bacon. The morning menu also comprised steaming eggs, buttered grits, and fluffy blueberry pancakes. Mess cooks provided everyone with their choice of scrambled eggs or custom omelets. They laid an assortment of pastries and muffins at the end of the line, arranged on a large tray, for the crew to help themselves.

Rusty grabbed a strawberry danish as they passed the line. The aroma whet Rusty's appetite. "I'm gonna have to come back and get me a mushroom omelet. I'm starved." He bit into the pastry as they rounded the ship's store, holding it in his mouth to climb the ladder.

Mux pulled away, sprinting down the hall before turning to ascend the next set of steps.

During Rusty's struggle to keep pace, he slipped, busting his shin on the top rung, dropping the last bite of his danish. "Shit!"

"You okay?" Mux asked.

"Hurts like hell, but I'll live. Jelly is all over the ladder."

"Then move your ass." Mux said.

Being the first to reach the Shop, Mux stopped to enter the four-digit combination that released the cypher lock.

Still racing, Rusty ran at him, sprinting too fast to stop. While trying to break his own momentum, he slammed into Mux, pushing him off the lock. Laughing, Rusty backed away to allow Mux space to key in the cryptic code.

Typing the code into the lock was like playing a piano with four keys. Keying in "2241" produced a popping sound, hinting the lock released. It was a standing contest to see who could enter the code the quickest. So far, Palmer had the fastest fingers. His record was less than one second, and many members of the crew often tested their skill, but to no avail. Palmer was so fast, he could approach the door, pop the combo, and open the door without breaking his stride. On one occasion, where the lock failed to disengage, Palmer's face slammed into the three-hundred-pound metal door, making an awful thud. It was a sound Rusty found amusing.

Mux and Rusty burst into the electronics repair shop. Barging in at the same pace they held getting there, the pair infiltrated the Shop like agents busting up a brothel. They roistered like teenagers, arms entangled, blocking each other's attempts to lead, and although their enthusiasm was well-intentioned, they irritated the rest of the morning crew with their early morning antics.

Lunging to a stop, both sailors nearly fell, their heavy boots slammed down on the deck in loud slaps, and the two almost crashed into Mr. Kistner who stood in the middle of the room.

Mr. Kistner was a taller-than-average, medium-build Lieutenant with distinguished dark hair that didn't match his maturity. He wore a khaki-colored uniform, adorned with two bright shiny gold bars on his collar. He grinned and locked eyes with Rusty. "Easy boys, we aren't at GQ."

Rusty could never be sure if it was the looks or the accent, but something about Mr. Kistner reminded him of James Stewart. After many years of outstanding performance, Mr. Kistner worked his way through the enlisted ranks and earned his commission. He'd competed with thousands of other enlisted sailors and received accelerated advancements as a trophy reward for his exemplary service record. It was more prestigious to gain a commission, having trudged through the enlisted sludge, than to earn college credits and join the fleet straight out of Officer Candidate School. Mr. Kistner was the coolest and most likely oldest Lieutenant in the entire Destroyer Squadron.

Crew members exchanged puzzled glances, and a crossfire of contempt bounced around the room as everyone waited for Mr. Kistner to begin the meeting. Having had to wait so long, everyone scorned the tardy interlopers.

"Good morning, gentlemen," Mr. Kistner said. "Now that everyone is here, I want you all to know we are pulling into Bahrain tomorrow.

We will be there for fourteen days."

The over-crowded Shop cheered, as twelve men whistled and clapped. Their level of ovation was too loud for such a small venue.

Rusty crossed his arms, rolling his eyes at Mux. The crewmen acted too dramatically and their reaction felt awkward, canned even. Being immersed in so much faux exuberance embarrassed Rusty, as everyone reacted too grindy to be cool.

Mr. Kistner waved his clipboard in the air. "Okay, settle down. To remind you, the Navy takes your health seriously, and I am instructed to show you, ladies, these photos. The Navy has invested a lot of money in your training, and it doesn't want you laid out with medical issues. If any of you come crying to me about having crotch crickets, I will write letters to your mothers explaining in *exact detail* why I busted your ass down a rank and took away ninety days of your paychecks."

Mr Kistner held up a medical photo of a male with an STD infection. The oversized photo was explicit and vulgar.

"I would like to call your attention to this unfortunate bastard," Mr. Kistner said.

Mux stood with his arms crossed, squinting at the photo. "What is that?" he asked.

"Ew," Palmer said. Some in the division made faces, some shook their head, and some joked.

Rusty was indifferent to the photos, but found his shipmate's comments unrefined. Leaning against the desk with his arms and legs crossed, he watched the other's reactions. Having seen the photo before, the sensational photo didn't bother Rusty. He suspected Mr. Kistner didn't like showing the photos, but the officer was under orders to scare the division into abstinence. The Navy showed those types of photos as a deterrent. The repetition of showing the photos seemed to be the reason someone laminated them like a Denny's menu, strengthening their demonstrative quality, while compounding the ridiculousness of the situation.

Mr. Kistner scrutinized everyone and asked if anyone had ever seen this person.

"Palmer has!" Jones said, convoluting the meeting by inciting group laughter.

Palmer's cold eyes locked with Jones. "Hardy har -har."

"Nice comeback," Jones said.

"Stow it. This shit is serious," Mr. Kistner said, suppressing his own laughter. He repositioned his glasses, tucking them higher onto the bridge of his nose as he shook his head. His arm waved the stack of obscene photos in the air, as if to toss them, before tucking them under his arm. With a lowered chin, he peeked above his reading glasses, studying the group while taking mental bets on who'd break his orders.

Mr. Kistner didn't need to show the photos, as most of the geeks in the division didn't know how to talk to a girl, let alone pick up a one-night stand or hire a local sex worker. Hell, half of the division was married. The entire exercise of showing the offensive photos was redundant.

The Division Officer concluded by going over the basic protocols and rules for their visit to Bahrain. "Here are some rules. Write them on paper, tattoo them on your arm if you have to, but the list is important and you don't want to forget it. Do not do any of the following:

1. Two thumbs up means "Fuck You." That is all you need to know about thumbs.

2. Do not point. Someone might think you're talking about them and it's rude.

3. Crossing your legs is disrespectful.

4. Greeting with your left hand is a sign of rudeness.

5. Checking your watch during a conversation is rude.

6. Showing the bottom of your foot is rude. The sole of your shoe is foul, so don't show the bottom of your foot to anyone.

7. If you see someone drop to their knees, they are praying. Do not stand in front of them."

"Are there questions? No? Good. Meeting adjourned," Mr. Kistner said. He chopped his clipboard under his arm and turned to the door. Petty Officer Jones called for "attention on deck!" as Mr. Kistner left the space.

"Carry on," the officer ordered. Stepping over the threshold, he closed and bolted the watertight door behind him.

With his shoulders slumped, Mux leaned onto the workbench. "Bahrain? Ninety days at sea and they take us to a damn sand-dune?"

"I have an old buddy from school, stationed there," Rusty said.

"Does he live off base?" This news excited Mux.

Spending time in bars did not fit Rusty's idea of seeing the world, but visiting a fellow shipmate might provide a local's perspective and bring some culture to an otherwise bleak port visit. Having a friend in Bahrain gave Rusty the edge his fellow crew members lacked.

"I don't know. But I know he's stationed there. When we pull in, I'll look him up."

Mux looked at his boon-dockers. "Great, I hope they don't put us in different duty sections."

"Palmer won't switch up the watch bill. It would require too much planning," Rusty said.

"Why couldn't we go somewhere better?" Mux asked.

Rusty smiled and placed a hand on his friend's shoulders, while sweeping his other as if showcasing imagined landscapes. "Picture this and look at the bright side. Bahrain is like a huge beach, and besides, we can't afford liberty somewhere nicer. Bahrain is cheap, so think of all the money we'll save."

Mux chuckled and smiled in agreement.

The friends gambled breakfast was still being served. Since there was no urgency to go back to their racks and seeing how the morning meeting made them too wired to sleep, they figured breakfast was the obvious choice.

As everyone exited the Shop, Rusty followed Palmer out of the space. He studied the back of Palmer's tiny head, noticing his thick sandy blonde hair and how perfect his trimmed neckline was.

Rusty never understood why married men would select to ride out their tour with sea duty. Being stationed on a Navy Destroyer was not an ideal place for a family man, and Palmer was the most married of all married men. He had two small girls, and this only seemed to compound Rusty's confusion. Geography separated Palmer from his family for eight or nine months a year, yet he talked about them ad nauseam.

Thinking of the dreadful goodbyes could depress a man into drinking. With all their sobbing and desperate waving of handkerchiefs, it was mental torment and self-abuse. The hardest thing imaginable was leaving loved ones — all those wives and kids crying on the pier.

Even if it was temporary, what was it like having to say goodbye, knowing it would be half a year or more before Palmer would see his wife again? Would his wife still be the same person? Would their relationship stagnate?

Letters helped, or so it seemed, because Palmer wrote daily. But what did he write about, being stationed on a ship of monotonous repetition? How many ways could you tell someone you miss them before it loses effect?

Looking at the married sailor incited pity. But Rusty knew Palmer would never cheat on his wife. Palmer's faithful dedication was commendable even if Rusty hated the man. He annoyed the hell out of Rusty while exemplifying profound morality, thus broadening the paradox. The question nagged. *Did Palmer have more grit than Rusty?*

Testing the question proved improbable, as there was no way any girl was ever going to pinch Rusty — at least not while he was stuck on the "USS Underway."

Tucked in Rusty's sock was a pocket-sized leather journal. Rusty removed his journal and pulled his fancy ballpoint pen from his breast pocket. Opening the binder to reveal dozens of poems, philosophical musings, and notes he'd written over the past few months, he flipped the soft edges of paper across his thumb, fanning air on his face, before stopping on the last page filled with writing. At the bottom was a space just large enough for him to scribble the words: "Do not get married!"

He folded the small book and tucked it into his sock.

Mux and Rusty waited in the food line with empty trays in hand. Boredom pressed Rusty to fan Mux with his tray as they waited for a dawdling crew member to decide how he wanted his eggs cooked. His morale hinged on the tantamount decision between fried eggs; pre-scrambled or not.

Rusty just wished he'd decide, because the breakfast smells stoked his appetite and made his stomach growl. He swallowed as he craned over the indecisive man's shoulder, inventorying what remained of the morning's menu, as most of the crew had already made their way through the line.

Steam slipped from below the large trays of food that lay behind glass panels, spanning the length of the serving line. Excessive heat caused sweat to drip from the foreheads of the Mess Specialists. Their salty perspiration landed on the food trays, "seasoning the meals," or so the story goes.

Rusty received his omelets and headed to the table. He stopped to fill his plastic cup with orange bug juice from the chilled beverage dispenser. The scent of citrus concentrate fixed itself in his nose; smelling more like Tang than real, unadulterated fruit.

Before leaving the beverage area, Rusty grabbed a thin stack of napkins and wet them. He tightened his fist to squeeze the excess water from the wad. Tinkles ran through his clenched knuckles, dripping into the catcher. With a quick shake of his fist, the excess water flew free, and he set the large moistened napkin wad on his tray.

He spotted Mux. After steering his way through the tables littering the mess hall, he placed his tray at the opposite end of Mux's table. Sitting down, he un-wrinkled the wet wad of paper and folded the towels in fourths, placing them on the light blue tabletop. Mux watched as Rusty centered his tray on the wet, folded square.

Urged by gravity and the rolling ship, Rusty's plastic cup slid across the small table's slick surface. He caught it before spilling the orange-flavored sugar water on his friend's lap. Rusty repeated the "wet square" procedure with the remaining towel, placing it under his cup before grabbing his fork to eat.

When securing for rough seas, friction can be a sailor's best friend.

Thinking back to the day he arrived onboard, a sailor's first day was always his best. The Navy built the USS John Adams in 1978. The crew nicknamed her the "USS Underway" because the ship was always out at sea. Her Captain's chair had a high turnover rate, and the aspiring officers worked her hard. The Navy made her a stepping stone for Commissioned Officers eager for advancement. Overzealous Captains ran exercises non-stop, volunteering her to do every evolution that came their way.

Rusty had spent two weeks land-locked in Mayport before the ship pulled in. Once the day came, he packed his bags and headed to the docks. Spotting the tall masts from a mile away, he walked to the moored fleet of ships and eyed ten destroyers tied to the two-mile long pier. Dozens of towering steel masts stood poised to defy those gale-forced winds and rain, if the need arose.

An armada of destroyers and frigates lined the pier like soldiers awaiting inspection. The only means of differentiating the ships was to inspect the various numbers painted on their noses. Rusty searched for number eighty-three, and after traversing the lengthy pier, he spotted her parked near the inlet. Her gray-painted signature appeared dark against the sunny backdrop, as enormous clouds swam in the blue sky behind her.

Built for speed and maneuverability, her keel was long, and her beam was narrow. Her prow pointed to the open inlet, arched toward the sky, ready to carry Rusty into parts unknown. Rusty's first step on her deck felt uneven. She moved, even though she was moored — she was alive. Powered by four DC-10 turbine engines, she sounded similar to commercial airliners from inside just before takeoff. Not loud enough to be deafening, but for crew members to communicate, it was necessary to shout above the ship's ambient drone. It was a half-whistle, half-hum that Rusty found calming.

Above the ship's primary structure, blurry air vented from hot stacks as heat-filled exhaust plumes radiated upward, floating into the cool afternoon sky. Radar antennas quivered in the clear thermal drafts. Rusty recognized the black antenna of his radar. He'd studied one like it in school, but it was the first time he'd seen one in its natural setting. His radar was real and no longer something he saw in classroom textbooks.

Over the following weeks, qualifications forced Rusty to learn advanced surface warfare and all other facets of ship-wide operations; locations of the Damage Control Stations; knowing how to read the large yellow and black "Bullseyes" painted in every space. The stencils displayed coordinates which helped the crew find any point of the ship by listing the deck, frame number from the bow, odd or even numbers from the centerline of the ship, and letters listing the purpose of the space. Rusty's shop was located at "02-106-1-L"

Months later, the newness of the ship's routine became less interesting, mundane even. Rusty wanted excitement and sought the enthusiasm he felt during his first weeks onboard. He wanted to see what his ship could do under real-life combat, although not in any murderous sense. Rusty was the opposite of a warmonger. He was a conscientious objector — a man of science and physics who sought amazement — not war and death.

However, instead of excitement, Rusty did nothing but stand his watch, practice drills, mop, and paint. There were times he worked on his radar, but he had it so tuned it ran itself without asking much of him. As a result, Rusty spent most of his time standing watch or polishing the decks of the hall leading to the Captain's inshore stateroom.

A mere twelve months separated him from his re-enlistment. But the daily monotony convinced Rusty that when the time came to re-enlist, he was getting out.

3

While both shipmates ate breakfast in the mess hall, Mux brought up the meeting. "Whatcha think about Mr. Kistner's pic?"

"I'm eating." Rusty held his fork like a pen, making swirling gestures above his omelet.

Mux looked up from Rusty's plate. "So?" His hazel eyes locked with Rusty's.

"It was gross. Can we talk about something else?"

The appalling image was one Rusty did not want ingrained in his memory. On an informational level, it was important, but it was an unnecessary distraction, and a sensational one — bordering on mental scarring.

"I'm trying not to think about it, and I'd appreciate it if you never brought it up again."

The ship leaned hard to Port. Rusty kicked his leg out to brace himself, preventing his ass from sliding out of his seat. Everyone in the galley gripped their drinks and trays, riding out the maneuver until the ship righted herself and they could resume their meals.

"Mr. Kistner said 'Crotch Crickets,'" Mux said.

Rusty fought to maintain his grumpy morning disposition, but he felt Mux's facetious eyes glaring at his lowered head.

Mux joked about the morning meeting, which forced Rusty's scowl to morph into a contained smile. One which grew larger, the harder he tried to suppress it.

Rusty took a drink of his orange juice and slammed the cup on the table. "Derpies."

"Booty Cooties."

This started a naming war that lasted a solid minute. The battle escalated, becoming more distasteful as the list grew.

Sailors expressed profanity. It's just what they did. To cuss like a sailor was fact, not fiction. On a ship composed of men, the words spoken could make mortal people cry. Navy swearing was a licensed tradition, rooted in rich history. It wasn't the actual obscenity that caused civilians to cringe; it was context. A sailor could say "moist, shaft, or tug" with the correct inflection, and make virgin ears weep.

"Okay, we have a grip on what to look for. I'll stay away from the red-light districts," Rusty said, berating the truth with sarcasm.

Sailors made jokes. It's what they did when contesting boredom. Rusty liked Mux because he grounded Rusty from his dark thoughts. Rusty over-analyzed far too often, and Mux knew this. Mux urged Rusty to keep his philosophies simple, and not "nuking" every situation he experienced. Sometimes it worked, and other times, not so much.

Rusty was a nihilist, and the morals he held conflicted with the unjustness of the world. It appeared he suffered from owning a surplus of ethics in a world fed by immorality. In Rusty's opinion, he disliked people because he felt the general population was shortsighted. People trampled one another to consume things — nouns — with the least amount of effort. In a world perverted by takers, Rusty was an involuntary participant. He'd never gripped the concept of "domination and conquest" with any real proficiency. There were many facets to greed, and Rusty seemed to lack them all.

Alarms disrupted Rusty's breakfast. It seemed the Duke wanted to run a "General Quarters Drill."

BONG! BONG! BONG! **"General Quarters, General Quarters, all hands man your battle stations. Set condition Zebra through the ship. This is a drill."** *Sh-click.*

The alarm repeated.

BONG! BONG! BONG! **"General Quarters, General Quarters, all hands man your battle stations. Set condition Zebra through the ship. This is a drill."** *Sh-click.*

"Oh, great," Mux said. "See ya."

Rusty got up and dropped his tray without scraping it clean. Activity in the passageways increased as men ran in all directions, scattering in coordinated chaos.

When a "GQ" alarm went off, the entire crew had two minutes to "make ready" their assigned battle stations, regardless of personal circumstances. The goal of running GQ drills was to measure the proficiency of the crew by measuring the time taken to establish an "all manned and ready" status, instilling a fast response by the crew. Through repetition and practice, the ship developed a systemic muscle memory, which enabled her to face any oncoming threat with an autopilot-like response.

A Marine clad in desert fatigues blew toward Rusty. The hulk sprinted at full speed, his face contorted to look like a mad comic villain plowing his way through weak superheroes. His tight, olive-green shirt complemented his tall, flat-topped hair. With the locked arms of a defensive linebacker, he mowed a path through the busy passageway.

To the Jarhead, the GQ drill was a football game and sailors were the offensive line. He crashed into a lost Seaman Apprentice, who was trying to make his way through the rushing crowd. The Marine threw the young sailor into the bulkhead, having never looked back to see the trauma he betrothed his helpless victim. On a Navy ship, few things equate to the terror instilled by a berserker-crazed Marine. It was a ridiculous domestic arrangement.

Rusty made his way to his assigned post. He keyed in the code to open the door to Radar 2. Inside, cool air hit him like an industrial freezer. The small room held four large cabinets. Each cabinet measured three feet wide and four feet tall. These were the key components of the ship's air search radar. Along with tool boxes and a small desk, most of the space was used to house large cables that came into the bulkhead and passed through to the other spaces throughout the ship.

He grabbed his coat, which hung just inside the door, and flipped on the light switch. After securing the door's latch, he reached for his sound-powered headphones to check-in. "Combat Systems. Radar two. Manned and ready," he said, while pressing the microphone's button.

"Radar 2. Manned and ready, aye." Senior Chief said. His voice sounded muffled, distant.

Navy policy posted Mr. Kistner and Senior Chief in the Shop. Senior Chief spoke into the headset and ordered every station to check-in. Their call sign was "Combat Systems" and they acknowledged every station as each one sounded off.

Rusty listened as the other guys announced their state of readiness into his headset.

"Combat Systems. Tacan. Manned and ready," Palmer said.

"Combat Systems. Transmitters. Manned and ready," Mux said.

"Combat Systems. Data Systems. Manned and ready," Chase said.

After all stations reported in, the chatter fell silent.

Thirty seconds later, the 1MC blasted the announcement over the ship's speakers. **"'Condition Zebra' is set throughout the ship."** *Sh-click.*

The crew was at GQ for forty-five minutes before the first cannon fired, booming like distant thunder. The ship rocked. Severe vibrations shuttered through the enormous metal hull, in fast wavelike tremors.

Shooting from both the rear and forward cannons, the entire ship shimmied with each volley, reverberating as the cannon's recoil rocked her hull. Seventy pounds of high explosive propelled the fifty-pound bullet hard enough blow a transit bus off a bridge.

A deafening buzzing accompanied the loud five-inch cannon booms. It was the rear CWIS Gatling gun. The gun sounded like someone drilled into the ship with a hammer drill the size of a dump truck.

The chorus of artillery would sound off in intermittent gunfire. The CWIS would cease fire for extended periods, while at other times it filled the silence with the sustained humming of 3,000 bullets a minute. Streams of heavy metal projectiles ejected from the CWIS gatling guns. Although the turning of the ship forced moments of unpredictability, its cannons maintained a barrage of devastation. Undeterred by the erratic movement of the ship, its gun barrels remained committed — steady as the bill of a stalking heron before snatching a lizard.

Being the ship's captain, the Duke also liked to push himself to his breaking point. Sometimes, the ship would find herself in seas so rough, the entire crew might have succumbed to seasickness, and it was then the ship's captain would call for a GQ drill. The Duke, sick from motion, would continue issuing orders even as he vomited over the railing. No matter how nauseated he might have been, the Duke never once stopped an exercise. How could he ever command a ship afterward? — the entire fleet would think he was a "pamby." Leaders led by example, and his bravado was the reason the crew called him "The Duke."

The cannon's volleys ceased. After five minutes of silence, they passed the order throughout the 1MC. **"All hands secure from General Quarters!"** *Sh-click!*

Rusty stowed his headphones and opened the door to leave Radar 2. He exited the space to loiter in the main hall. Outside the chilled confines of Radar 2, the relative temperature was much higher, and

Rusty felt himself blanketed by the warmth. As he stood in the hall, he heard a friendly voice.

"Hey bro, let's go play some chess in the mess hall and discuss plans for Bahrain," Mux said.

"I'll race you down." Rusty smiled as he turned to face his best friend.

"You can try."

Later that evening, Rusty ventured to Engineering to get his final five signatures for his ESWS qualification. On his way, Rusty thought of the upcoming trip to Bahrain and wondered if the Navy still had his old buddy Blume stationed there. They met in electronic's school and spent countless hours studying the rigorous course material together. They spent many school nights listening to music while eating Chinese takeout.

Everyone in their class picked orders based on their GPA, and Rusty held the second-highest grade. Of all the duty packets he could have picked, he elected to spend the rest of his enlistment on the USS John Adams. Passing up some of the best shore stations in the world, he chose orders to be the only radar technician on a destroyer.

Blume, with a GPA near the bottom of the class, had to choose between a shore duty in Bahrain or San Diego.

Last time Rusty saw Blume was shortly after graduation. Blume stood on a curb at the Greyhound bus station, waving just before he boarded a bus to Baton Rouge.

Below decks, on the ship's main level behind the mess hall, was Chief's Berthing. A tiny window, in the middle of a watertight door, offered a view of the senior enlisted's sleeping quarters. Rusty peeked into the round six-inch glass and watched as a Chief Petty Officer struggled to climb into his top rack. The man only wore two articles of clothing — his boxer skivvies and knee-high black dress socks.

Weird.

Farther down the hall, slippery ladders led to the lower decks and Engineering. Cold ocean water rubbed against the ship's warmed hull, combining with stagnant air to dampen the metal surfaces of the lower decks with condensed moisture. The space felt clammy and chilled — two of the most uninviting feelings in the world.

Far below decks, and far below the waterline, dark red lamps replaced the sterile fluorescents found on the higher decks, and the floor's blue tile appeared black in the morose light. No sailors moved around the lower decks, as was a common occurrence on the upper decks. Being so far below the waterline after normal working hours, Rusty would find no one but the skeleton crew wandering the dead-end halls of Engineering.

Rusty made his way deeper still, to the lowest to the lowest decks, to the heart of "Snipe Country" — an alien world. Venturing into the bizarre realm of the obnoxious E-Gang filled Rusty with apprehension. His best chance of success was to infiltrate the Propulsion Control Room, where he could find Master Chief Machinist Mate Greeley who might sign Rusty's qualification book.

Because of the added pressure of the ship's water displacement pressing in on Rusty's ears, the turbines were much louder. Cold humidity added to his tension as the ambient sounds increased in pitch.

Like driving through a deep tunnel.

Rusty faced the door of the Propulsion Control Room. After a last-second pep talk, he wiped the sweat off his forehead and knocked on the metal door. The sound of his knock was faint, tinny. He rubbed his knuckles, where they itched from striking solid steel, and waited for a response.

Machinist Mate Third Class Burke opened the door to find Rusty staring back at him. "Is Master Chief Greeley here? I wanted to see if he would sign my ESWS book," Rusty said.

Burke glanced behind his shoulder, glancing into the well-lit space. He backed away and widened the door, inviting Rusty to step inside.

Waves of cologne, starched cotton shirts, and strong cups of coffee embedded their aromas in Rusty's nose. He surveyed the layout. One would think Engineering would be dimly lit, but the room's ambiance felt clinical. The vast array of esoteric dials and control consoles were flooded with intense white lights. All the assorted gizmos were as perplexing to Rusty as the radar screens of the CIC room looked to a Third Class Signalman. It was all so confusing: Damage Control Status Boards, Fuel System Controls, Propulsion, and Electrical Consoles littered the compartment. It was more complex than Rusty imagined, never having visited the control room.

Snipes ran the heart of the ship. The distinction between the ship being the "Wolf of the Sea," or a glorified weather buoy depended on the engineer's ability to keep the motors cleaned, tuned, and running at all times. Without mobility and the ability to maneuver, the ship was useless. A lump of steel an enemy ship might use for target practice —

flotsam.

Any sounds made by the E-gang were drowned out by loud whining hums of the ship's turbines. If ever there was a place on the ship with noise hazards, Snipe Country would be it.

Rusty swallowed and closed the door behind him. A large man in a swiveling chair sat in the middle of the space. The chair was the same style of command chair used by the Duke, in the Pilothouse. Ambient lighting made the Master Chief extremely pink.

Mustering the confidence needed to address the Master Chief, Rusty approached. "Hi, Master Chief. Do you have a few minutes to help me with my ESWS qualification?"

The Master Chief was stern. "Do I look busy?" His inflection was too dramatic for the setting, and under the circumstances, his act suggested a rehearsal on his part.

Rusty knew he must stand up to the Master Chief, or he would never get the needed signatures. "When are you not?" Rusty chuckled to lighten the mood.

The Master Chief's pensive eyes stared at Rusty. Extending his hand, he snapped meaty fingers which resembled fat sausages, requesting the paperback ESWS book. Rusty reached into his back pocket and removed the rolled-up book. Underestimating his strength, he slapped the roll into Master Chief Greeley's hand with a loud smack.

The Master Chief opened the book, searching for the unsigned engineering sections. His slow and deliberate manner intimidated Rusty. The bear of a man thumbed through the booklet, licking his finger with the turning of each page.

Greeley looked like his name suggested. He was a large, bullish brute who lacked a high degree of useless intellect — book smarts. But common sense offset his shortage of higher education.

Previous occasions that Rusty'd spent with Greeley were ripe with cheap insults and backhanded innuendos. Those insults fueled morale boosts to the E-Gang, and everyone loves to work when the laughter isn't at their own expense.

The wide man placed his sweaty hand on the book. He ran the heel of his palm down the inside spine, making a series of sounds like popping knuckles, attempting to dominate the book's binder into submission. The Master Chief removed his ballpoint pen and licked the tip while running his finger down the page, tracing his finger to the Engineering questions with blank signature lines.

"What type of fire systems are used to extinguish oil fires, and where are they located?" Greeley asked.

"CO2 and halon. You can find halon in the kitchen of the mess hall and carbon dioxide extinguishers are everywhere."

Master Chief Greeley signed off on a line in the book. The ink was dry, motivating him to draw blank circles all across the page.

Rusty glared at the ceiling and placed his hands in his pockets, waiting for Master Chief Greeley to troubleshoot his pen.

"How many PKP extinguishers are onboard and where are they located?" The Master Chief asked.

"Two. Anchor Windlass and Aft Windlass."

"Last question. What does 'A Triple F' stand for and what is its use?"

"**A**queous **F**ilm **F**orming **F**oam. It's used to smother fuel fires," Rusty said.

"Very well, Petty Officer Russell." Having signed the last spot, he rolled the book into a tight baton and handed it to Rusty.

"Thank You, Master Chief." Rusty tightened the rolled book and placed it in his back pocket. He ambled to the door, hoping he would never have to set foot in Engineering ever again.

Just before exiting, the Master Chief shouted, "Good job getting your qualification, kid."

"Thank you, Master Chief."

Rusty was surprised by the Master Chief's change in demeanor and he couldn't wait to tell Mux all about his little side quest.

4

After escaping Snipe Country, Rusty sought sanctuary and the refuge his comfortable bed provided. Only a few brief hours separated him from his watch and he wanted to make the most of the time he had left, getting as much rest as possible.

On his way to berthing, he replayed conversations he'd held with Palmer. The Petty Officer should be Rusty's friend, and truth be told, Rusty spent more time with Palmer than he did with Mux.

Will I ever get along with Palmer? Hell, Master Chief Greeley was even more agreeable than Palmer, relatively speaking, and he dislikes twidgets. But Palmer is part of my group, so what would make a person want to be so irritable to be around?

The philosopher in Rusty convinced him he was justified in his assessment, and Palmer antagonized Rusty for no other reason than his own pleasure; at least from Rusty's perspective.

Truth was, Rusty's personal dilemma with Palmer was so distracting that he was unaware his personal perspective was askew. Rusty was no superstar who'd lived long enough to accomplish a thing of worth. His moral insights held him back, restraining him because he lacked the wisdom to scale his understanding against reality. His talent rested with the number of books he had read, not the lessons learned from personal trials. Reality was relative, and to Rusty, Palmer was the antagonist. However, in more ways than one, Rusty was his own worst foe, but he was too self-involved to spot his own shortcomings.

While on watch, sitting on the ship's bow, Rusty looked west. An ominous glow lit low in the night sky. The aura emanated from over the horizon, originating from the port of Bahrain. If it weren't for the amplified illumination of his night-vision goggles, displaying the sky like a radioactive green sunset leaking over Earth, the light would have been undetectable.

To his right, north of the crew's position, was the bright dot of a merchant's cargo ship. It was nothing unusual, and Rusty'd seen many like it before. The faint hint of the merchant ship was visible in the distance — maybe an oil tanker leaving Saudi Arabia or Iraq, or a Taiwanese container ship headed out of the gulf, returning to its home port in the Far East.

High-flying planes on the horizon flew through the jade-colored clouds. Each plane carried hundreds of passengers, and each passenger held a different story; dramas, tragedies, and comedies.

The irony was not knowing which of the passengers were living the tragedies and who lived the comedies.

Years earlier, the news broke of a Navy officer who downed a civilian airliner by mistake. A mistake with the communication and IFF code, a procedural error which scuttled the lives of two hundred and nine people, sacrificing their futures to a Sea Sparrow surface-to-air missile. Passengers never knew what hit them. One second they flew in the plane, oblivious to the danger, traveling home, planning to reunite with loved ones, when out of nowhere a wall of fire scuttled the plane's interior. 700 mile per hour flames sterilized the cabin of every living thing larger than a virus, rendering the fuselage as barren as an industrial autoclave.

A loud voice over his headset startled Rusty. He was in mid-yawn when the loud sounds of the OOD's voice erupted inside his headset.

"Mine-watch. Pilothouse. Com check!" The voice was far too loud and far too obnoxious to be unintentional. The OOD must have suspected Rusty of sleeping while on watch and wanted to set an example.

Rusty licked his lips, hoping he wouldn't sound as raspy as he felt. Pure sea salt flowed across his tongue. He lowered his chin, pressed the tiny button, and spoke into the mic. "Pilothouse. Mine-watch. Aye," he said with blatant irritation in his voice. It took a few moments for his blood pressure to return to normal levels. After a minute, he sighed and settled back into to the meditative daydreams which carried him through long periods of immobilization.

Stellar scenes blanketed the sky. Now and then, shooting stars darted across the stratosphere, bridging the eastern and western horizons in less than a second. They blazed like lightning, only to fade out in the foreground of constellations; shapes of Greek champions, depicting epic moments during the pinnacle of their immortal lives.

On one occasion, in less than a second, a sizable piece of alien rock left a fiery trail hundreds of miles long. It vanished as fast as it appeared. The only evidence of the meteor's existence lived in Rusty's memory, but the ever-flowing future replaced those memories, and soon the meteor would cease to exist in any form, tangible or in.

You survived a billion years and died in front of me.

Rusty stared at the point where the rock vaporized, contemplating the spot for a long time before other events in the night sky distracted him.

A weather satellite vaulted the Earth's inner orbit. Its flashing lights appeared dotted, trailing patterns in the green goggles as the object circled the planet, strobing and disappearing behind the horizon. As with every satellite, Rusty waited for the unidentified flying object to change course, defying physics, announcing to the world that alien life existed. But like all the other satellites, it never did.

The immobility of the Mine-watch made Rusty's ass sore. Standing guard as the roving patrol, he could move and stay alert through activity. Besides bruising one's own butt, sitting in the chair for almost four hours provided the added torture of struggling to remaining awake.

The sea calmed as the night wore on. Cool air of the early morning hours tamed the usual rough chop to a glassy, smooth surface water. Reflections of sparkling stars blanketed the glassy ocean, and although it was beautiful to behold, calm seas made locating hazards difficult.

Calm conditions also made it harder for Rusty to stay alert. He traded the urge to sleep for the energy to stand. It was a dangerous stunt, standing up half-tired, but he wanted to get his blood circulating.

At 3:46 a.m., Rusty glanced aft, hoping to catch sight of his relief. But the ship's deck was absent of any human activity and her dark silhouette stared back with statuesque coldness. He hoped his relief would show up soon. He yawned and climbed off the tall chair, paying special attention as he negotiated the steep ladder.

Halfway down, the armrest snagged the cord of the sound-powered phones, yanking his head back as he jumped the last two rungs. This resulted in a rude thumping and harsh banging in his ears, both of which hurt like hell.

"Damn!" He lifted the phones and rubbed his hands over his ears to soothe the pain.

Rusty flipped the cord, dislodging it from the metal obstruction. He repositioned the headphones and stood near the tower, stretching his legs.

His yawn, loud and deep, bellowed with a gargling wail. But the gulp of oxygen refreshed his body with energy and renewed vigor. Had he been asleep for the past hour?

Maybe half asleep, operating on autopilot. Shit! He shuddered at the thought.

Someone shouted above the wind. Standing ten feet behind Rusty was a young Boatswain's Mate, who for unknown reasons everyone called "Booger."

Booger joined the crew while they anchored the ship in Egypt. He'd been on the Adams for three months, and after spending those ninety days scraping away at the ship's gray paint, Booger now relieved his first watch.

"I'm sorry for being late, Petty Officer Russell," the kid said. "Petty Officer Connelly woke me to fill in for him."

"It's okay. Call me Rusty. Are you ready?"

"Yes, sir," Booger saluted. "I am here to relieve you."

"I stand relieved. Also, you don't need to call me sir. I'm enlisted," Rusty said.

"Yes, sir. But why do I salute you then?" Booger asked.

Rusty shrugged as he looked behind Booger's shoulder to the Pilothouse. "Don't know. That is an excellent question," he said, removing his gear to hand it over to the young Seaman Apprentice. "Look at the sky and move your eyes around like you are reading a book — line by line as you scan the area. Look in the water and do the same thing. If you see anything, report it to the Officer of the Deck. Point and tell them the approximate range and bearing."

"I got it. I mean, aye-aye."

Rusty patted the young man on his arm. "I'm sure you do. Be careful of the chair. It's slippery and you don't need a swim."

The young sailor chortled and shifted his stance. "Yes sir. That water would be cold."

The Junior Seaman struggled with the night-vision goggles, fussing with its straps. Rusty pointed to the strap and provided instructions to tighten the band.

Booger owned an unusual wristwatch. It was a solid white G-shock. The bright and tacky clock seemed to glow in the darkness of the early morning sky.

"That's quite the watch," Rusty said, pointing.

"Thank you, Mr. Rusty. My mom gave it to me when I graduated from boot camp. It's waterproof and digital, so it tells me the time in twenty-four hours. Military time."

"Well, it looks great, and I'm sure you'll never lose it."

"Are you kidding? I never take it off." The young sailor brimmed with zeal. It made Rusty wonder if he himself had become too cynical for Navy life.

During his shift, Rusty'd daydreamed for almost four hours. In contrast, Booger stood straight, holding his arms tucked close to his sides at attention, ready to undertake the task with gusto. He was, as the Zen masters say, "being in the moment with a learner's focus."

Rusty snapped out of his thoughts and watched as Booger made last-minute adjustments. "That's great. I wish I owned one just like it," Rusty said.

"It's the best watch in the world."

"I bet it is. Now mount up and mind your step." Rusty placed a hand on the backrest of the chair and gestured with his open palm, pointing to the vacant seat.

Booger climbed the ladder with unsteady feet and Rusty feared he'd slip. The cold air made even the most seasoned fingers numb. Darkness hindered visibility, and the wet surfaces provided little traction for the bottom of Booger's rubber soles. But the enthused Seamen Apprentice made his way to the chair. He peered down to center his ass on the flat seat and placed his arm on the rest, straightening his posture with the stiffened poise of a pianist.

The young sailor stared at Rusty. "Wow. How do I look?"

Rusty smiled. "You look like a badass from the future. Can you see alright?"

"I can see everything." Booger surveyed the ship, inspecting everything with his new vision, seeing an altered world for the first time.

With his back to Rusty, Booger lifted his head, shaking to gauge the stability of the gear. He pressed his hands to his earphones, pressing inwards, probing for gaps in the muffled seals. Once satisfied, he scanned the open sea to begin his duty.

Rusty tapped Booger on his knee. "Press the button and say the following, 'Pilothouse. Mine-watch. Manned and ready!' That will let them know who's boss out here."

Booger pressed the microphone button and shouted the exact words into the mouthpiece. The young boy yelled so loud, even the harsh wind did little to mute the kid's enthusiasm. To make matters worse, he held the microphone so close to his mouth that he telegraphed loud breaths to the recipients of his transmission.

Rusty cupped a hand to his mouth and shouted. "Let off the button when you're finished talking and don't scream into the mic!"

Booger gave Rusty a thumbs up and released the button. His posture waned as he listened to the headset, fidgeting with the cable, twirling it around his pointy finger. With a hushed voice, Booger replied into the microphone. "Yes, sir. I'm sorry. Aye-aye. I won't do that again."

Rusty performed an about-face and meandered to the starboard break room. He paused and glanced at the red lights of the bridge. Crewmen's shadows beamed from the window. The whole bridge just received one hell of a wake-up call from the screaming sailor who'd just blasted everyone with deafening shouts and at four o'clock in the morning, no less.

Imagining the scene in the Pilothouse, Rusty's smile turned into chuckles. Chuckles turned into laughter as Rusty made his way into the ship's interior. Eyes watery from hysterics, he clutched his gut and struggled for air while leaning against the nearest bulkhead. The situation was not funny enough to warrant his uncontrolled response, but it was 4:00 a.m. and he was slap-happy.

Later, reflections on Booger's enthusiasm with his new watch assignment made Rusty ashamed when thinking of his own sated outlook towards watch-standing. To Booger, the responsibility was of great significance and the young man faced the challenge with all the enthusiasm of a child learning to surf. It was a "first experience" and one of many, as he continued on his long journey through life. Booger cherished the moment, and he recognized it as a tremendous memory. The pollywog would re-live his first night on duty, and the humor of it all, for the rest of his life. The night was an ingredient of his many fabled sea stories.

To Rusty, Booger's excitement was a gift to the world, and Rusty acknowledged it as being what it was — a vicarious moment providing Rusty with a morsel of his long-abandoned appreciation for new experiences.

The Junior Seaman Apprentice spent ninety days scraping rust, cleaning shit, swabbing decks, and there he sat with an untroubled smile so grand it was discernible with his back to the world. As far as anyone was concerned, for the next four hours, Booger was the most important person onboard the ship.

Grit? Damn, Booger brimmed with it.

A profound clarity entered Rusty's thoughts, dampening his vicarious feeling of happiness. The notion hinted the Boatswain Mate was stronger-willed than he, and Rusty vowed to appreciate his responsibility of being on a Mine-watch and to appreciate the splendid view it afforded, all in the name of self-improvement.

However, fate would not permit him to follow through with the promise he made to himself that evening. In fact, that night would be Rusty's last night on Mine-watch, and had he known, he may have appreciated the moment all the more.

Inside the darkened ship, the red lights cast their usual sullen glow. There was no one to engage in idle banter, no one to roam the halls in search of meaningless activity, and no one to complain to about trivial gossip. The crew was asleep, and Rusty would soon join them.

He perused the Mess Hall, looking for weary stragglers who might have been sitting ready for a good game of chess. But nothing. The ship seemed deserted, forsaken maybe.

The crew's absence compelled Rusty to Berthing. The soles of his feet chirped on the shiny vinyl tile as he made his way down the hall toward the open hatch. Because of Rusty's groggy vision, the steps of the ladder appeared far steeper than usual.

A giant leap for mankind, as Armstrong would have said.

Rusty concentrated on the steps to avoid being shunted to the lower deck by gravity. Berthing was dark, and ninety of his fellow crew members slept in veiled beds. Behind their curtains, some men lay in lit bunks, and Rusty wondered why there were so many of them awake at four in the morning.

After brushing his teeth, he undressed and hung his clothes on his hook and slid his boots against his locker.

Palmer slept in the middle bunk and although it was the most convenient bunk for accessing his belongings, it was also the most heavily trafficked of the three-tiered bunk system. For Rusty to clamber to his top bunk, he needed to step on Palmer's, leaving dirt no matter how much he wiped his feet beforehand.

"Get your feet off my mattress," Palmer whispered in a sort of hushed yell. As much as he wanted to shout, he couldn't for fear of the received reprisals of a roused Berthing compartment.

"How do you propose I get to my rack?"

Rusty welcomed the chance to discuss the impossibility of levitation at the inconvenient hour of 4:17 in the morning, all while basking in the light of vindication, yet again. He half-expected Palmer would be foolish enough to oblige him in debating who had the right of way where bunks were concerned.

"Eh," Palmer said. His condemnation receded to a mere whisper as he rolled over to resume snoring.

With his hands tucked behind his head, Rusty laid in his rack, staring at the overhead of his bunk, wondering if Palmer would remember the encounter later on. It would take a good long while for Rusty to curb his thoughts enough to sleep, as memories of the watch turnover were inescapable.

He rolled toward the bulkhead. Tucking his arm under the flat, military-issued pillow, he stared at the wall. It was early morning and Rusty should have welcomed the rest, but insomnia gnawed at him to get up and move about the ship, almost daring him.

Above his head was his Sony Walkman. He placed the foam-covered headphones over his ears, situated the thin speaker wires around his chin, and pressed the large play button. A dynamic chorus of cellos broke the static-filled silence as polyester tape floated across the magnetic head of the cassette player.

On most occasions, Rusty preferred hard rock or new wave, but where sleep and relaxation was concerned, only classical music could calm him enough to rest. Tonight, it was Bach. A chorus of vibrating strings quieted Rusty's mind. Soft notes faded in and out, while soothing oscillations lightened his mood. It made him feel like floating on a warm cloud. His head relaxed as comforting paralysis undulated throughout his body, cradling him toward sleep.

It did not take long. His jaw relaxed and his clenched muscles eased. His chest... His arms... His legs... His body grew heavy as it drifted. Random notions replaced coherence and ideas no longer made sense. Awareness streamed in non-linear order, struggling to be experienced, and it wasn't long before Rusty had no thoughts at all, not even dreams.

5

The day arrived for the crew to make port in Bahrain. A small group of hyper-squared-away nerds huddled in the small confines of the Shop. Being this was the day the crew would make landfall, all hands were required to attend the morning briefing. Rusty operated on 3 hours of sleep again.

He tolerated the men he served with, and hell, even though they were complete geeks, he appreciated the camaraderie, as long as no one wanted conversations so early in the morning. If there was one thing Rusty disliked about the morning meetings, it was ugly chattering and annoying morning laughter which echoed around the small room.

He wiped sleepy grit from the corner of his eye and looked into his ceramic mug, watching swirls of heat perform pirouettes across the surface of his coffee. Tiny wisps of steam climbed the air above his cup, which read, "Sorry I'm Late. I didn't want to be here."

Heat equals time. Thermal equilibrium means my coffee experiences time faster than the cooler air filling the room. Everything wants to reach absolute zero, where time and energy transfer stops.

Morning laughter was a reflex Rusty lacked. Groggy hilarity was something only weirdos did to wake up. People who operated in different dimensions never needed caffeine. To Rusty, early morning meetings were a waste, a distraction from more important things. The crew would repeat anything that needed to be shared a dozen times throughout the day, as there was nothing else to talk about, anyway.

Rusty's coffee permeated the room. He sipped at first, but soon after, timid sips of his French Vanilla black coffee turned into chugs as he rolled his eyes.

Will Jones ever shut the hell up?

At 7:05 a.m., Mr. Kistner entered the space, and someone called for "attention on deck."

Mr. Kistner tossed his clipboard on the desk and paced, pressing his palms on his hips. "As you were. Is everyone here?"

"Yes sir, all present and counted for," The Senior Chief said.

"I'm gonna make this real quick. We will run 'four duty sections while we're docked in Bahrain. I need all Division Heads to set up a roster and have it on my desk by oh-nine hundred. You ladies need to remember to be on your best behavior while we are in Bahrain. We are ambassadors and we need to set a great example."

Mr. Kistner turned to leave and ordered the crew to 'carry on' before anyone could announce his departure.

His morning itinerary must be tight.

ET1 Jones stood, holding the watch list and duty roster. It seemed he had them prepared before the meeting began.

"I have the roster. Who is going to stand OOD watch?" Jones asked, looking at the older Petty Officers.

Stunned looks crossed their faces as they scanned the room, looking at one another. Jones handed everyone a copy of the list. There were a few blank spaces which needed filling in.

"The Operations Division stands the OOD watch. Why are we doing it?" Palmer asked, sounding like a whining millionaire.

"The Ops Division is short-staffed. Chief Reid said we need to pull the slack," Jones said.

Rusty decided not to loiter with a bunch of entitled Petty Officers. He despised listening to the senior enlisted sailors squabble between 'who gets what,' especially when he was assigned the worst shift on the list. Rusty turned toward the door, seeking cover from the inevitable fallout of their bitching.

The 'Saturday morning mid-watch' was the least desired slot of the two-week-long port. It ate into the overnight weekend, and Palmer was nice enough to award it to Rusty. Rusty could have offered Palmer condolences for having to stand duty as OOD, but he didn't.

It was a burning day, in the middle of August, when the ship prepared to pull into Bahrain and the Adams began docking procedures. Calm seas reflected the rays of sunlight beaming through cracks in the clouds, blasting webbed strips of light across the ocean. The water's crystalline surface was dotted with large islands of shade from a hundred random cloud formations. The atmosphere was unusually still, and for the first time in weeks, the glassy ocean felt more sublime than depressing.

Boatswain Mates descended into the eighteen-inch-wide hatch below, to the storage space holding a few hundred yards of mooring lines. The thick lines were heavy enough when dry, but weighed a ton when saturated with saltwater. The deckhands fished the lines out and readied them on the fantail. Giant white mounds of polyester lay coiled on the decks, available for deployment at a moment's notice.

The ship steamed close to the flat sandy island. Its shoreline lacked distinguishing features. Beset with miles and miles of boring greige colored desert sand, the desert resembled the barren landscapes of the Sahara.

The Adams had seen nothing but thousands of miles of sandy shoreline and Bahrain was nowhere near kinky enough to write home about.

With interlocked hands held together, tucked into the small of his back, Rusty stood ready at the rail, spreading his feet to match his shoulder's width. Dressed in his summer white Cracker Jacks, his black neckerchief blew in the wind. The group of sailors formed a line along the starboard rail, making a human fence along the side of the ship.

Rusty spoke before he turned to look at the man standing beside him. "Why are we wearing our dress uniforms for this dump? It's not like we are pulling into Boston or New York..." As he turned, he realized who he was talking to.

Booger's smile beamed as his eager eyes searched the desolate-looking island. Being this was only Booger's second port call. The young sailor bounced on his toes as he looked along the shore, surveying the landscape, eager for the fun-filled adventures awaiting his discovery. Booger's positive outlook shamed Rusty in spreading so much negativity.

Tying off to a tug was a straightforward, but dangerous, procedure; tossing a line and looping it over a cleat. But, the intense strain on the lines could snap the heavy rope and send it back to the handlers with more ferocity than any man could tame. The immense power of such tension could cut a sailor in half. All crewmen saw the boot camp training videos of legs being amputated by snapping mooring lines. Worse yet were the stories of men who found their legs tangled in runaway lines, only to be squeezed and pulled through a sixteen-inch closed-chock, leg first by a million pounds of tugging pressure. The effect of which noodled their bodies and caused a fatal case of the splits. No sane sailor would ever think of testing their resolve against such violence.

Sailors watched as the tug pulled at the lines. The fat rope stretched, crackled, and groaned as it tightened. Its five-inch diameter vibrated and contracted to three inches from the intense strain. The potential energy manifested itself as the massive ropes stretched from eighty tons of stress. Like all things under pressure, the lines sought the path of least resistance. Popping with tension, the line re-adjusted itself against the contact points, telegraphing through the cleat, over the steel deck, and through Rusty's boots. Gripping both hands on Booger's shoulders, Rusty took three enormous steps back from the heavy line, pulling Booger with him.

Tug boats maneuvered the enormous ship and made it possible for the destroyer to dock in the tight confines of the busy pier. The powerful boats pushed the Adams in a lateral direction and positioned all 563 feet of her, next to a sister ship.

The USS Savannah was a twin ship to the Adams — the same in every way except her numerical designation. Rusty and the men tethered the Adams to her outboard side, allowing his crew access to the pier by crossing the Savannah's quarterdeck.

The crew of the Savannah received the mooring lines and tied them off to their cleats. Once secured, officers ordered the tugs released and everyone to stand down from line handling procedures.

The high-pitched whines of the gas turbines descended to a halt as their droning hum lowered in pitch at a steady pace. Turbines dipped below infrasonic, replacing the steady white-noise accompanying the crew for many long weeks, with an eerie silence. Rusty missed the constant groan of white noise which had accompanied him for so many weeks.

The Adam's bell rang. *Ding-Ding, Ding-Ding.* **"John Adams departing."** *Sh-click.* The announcement notified the crew that their Captain went ashore.

Seconds later, Rusty heard the same announcement on the Savannah as the Duke traversed their ship, making his way to the pier.

*Ding-Ding, Ding-Din***g. "John Adams, arriving."** *Sh-click.*

Ding-Ding, Ding-Ding. **"John Adams, departing."** *Sh-click.*

What would happen if the Captain forgot to grab his wallet?

Rusty stood on the fantail next to Petty Officer Ellis, looking over the railing into the water. Ellis wore his dungarees and smoked a Camel filterless cigarette. He was one of the ship's Yeoman, tasked with maintaining service records and performing various clerical duties for the crew.

"Man, they're wearing that bell out, and we just got moored," Rusty said.

"Yeah, that's gotta suck. Once, I heard the arrivals of a whole slew of Captains and Admirals. The Navy held a decommissioning ceremony on the Yosemite. The Admiral hired a 'rent-a-crowd' for the event, which messed everyone's shit up. Must have been two hundred high-ranked officers. That damn bell was going off for almost an hour, and the OOD kept fucking up the names of the ships," Ellis said.

"I would've liked to see that," Rusty said, looking along the shore. Everything was hot, hazy, and beige.

"It's a good thing us plep's never get announced or I would fuck with the OOD on purpose," Ellis said.

It seemed Ellis thought enough of Rusty to make light of the situation in his presence. Rusty chuckled, not because it was funny, but because he didn't want to appear rude, especially after being grouped into the same illustrious class of sailors as all the other plebs.

"Hey Ellis, if I wanted to look someone up here in Bahrain, where would I go?"

Ellis pondered the question as he kicked his toe on one of the railing's support poles. "I'd check to see if the Administration office was open. You might find someone there to help you out."

"Man. That is a great idea. Thank you."

Rusty slapped the top rail and did an about-face, heading off in the opposite direction to change into civilian clothing.

"Sure thing. I hope it helps," Ellis said. His voice followed Rusty through the opened door. Ellis tossed his butt into the bay and scratched his wrist before following Rusty. "Wait up. I got it," he said, just as Rusty attempted to close the door.

It was ten til four p.m. or 15:50 military time when Rusty opened his rack. He rummaged through his possessions, searching for the most important item he owned. After digging through bars of soap, wads of socks, and stacks of well-read paperbacks, he found what he had searched for — his soft leather wallet. Kneading fingers stroked the smoothness of the wallet's broken-in surface, brushing aside lint and dust, before opening it to ensure it still held his credentials. After not having carried the wallet in over three months, one could only imagine his delight at finding three crisp hundred-dollar bills tucked in its back compartment.

Beer Tickets!

Any shipmate not on duty got dressed for liberty. The problem with sailors wearing civilian attire was, regardless of how much they tried, they still resembled sailors. Some wore cotton t-shirts tucked in, and others wore their military-issue prescription glasses — "birth control devices" as sailors called them, because no squid could ever get laid while wearing them.

One guy wore a neon purple shirt with a tacky screen print design that read, "Sarah's Crab Shack." Each of the blue claws pinched a crab mallet and a cracker, implying the large shit-eater was a cannibal. The design made no sense.

Having never understood clothes, Rusty still wanted to dress nicely. High fashion was much harder to achieve than most people realized. He wore boot-cut jeans suspended by a genuine black leather belt, an ivory-colored, short-sleeved button-down dress shirt, and black Doc Marten boots, purchased in London a year earlier.

At 16:00, the OOD passed the word for liberty to begin — one second later and he would have faced a mob of insurrectionists. The officer's lips moved as he spoke into the 1MC, out of synch with a laggy delay. His voice blared over the speakers like a translated foreign movie.

"Liberty. Liberty. Liberty for sections two, three, and four. Liberty will expire at oh seven-hundred, Monday morning. Now liberty!" *Sh-click.* No sooner had he placed the mic on its hook, did sailors flood him with impatient requests to depart the ship.

The crab-shirt squid turned aft to salute the flag at the ship's stern. He then turned to face the OOD. "Request permission to go ashore." The screen-printed giant crab stretched along with the sailor's arm as he saluted.

The OOD replied, returning the salute. "Permission granted."

One by one, crew members requested permission to exit the ship, and one by one, the OOD granted permission for their requests, saluting every crew member as they left the quarterdeck.

The USS Savannah allowed the crew of the Adams to traverse their ship. As each crew member boarded the Savannah, Navy policy required the watch-standers and departing sailors to follow the same protocols for crossing the sister ship as they did their own.

The OOD on the Savannah acknowledged the sailors' requests. "Permission granted. Permission granted. Permission granted. Permission granted..." The enlisted officer ran on infinite repeat, saying the words as fast as he could, blurring his words, and sounding like a drunken tongue twister until the entire gang crossed the Savannah. Clumped like fire ants in floodwater, the rabble of sailors floated across the ship, spilling down the pier. They filed into waiting cabs before finally dissolving into Bahrain's opened bars and tourist traps.

After waiting for the rush to settle, Rusty crossed the Savannah and descended the gangway, scanning the pier for clues as to the whereabouts of the Admin building. But, just as he started toward the base, Booger came up and stood beside him.

"Rusty, why is the pier moving?" Booger asked.

Rusty recalled his first time walking down a pair after many days at sea. "It's not moving. You just have sea legs, phantom sensations like being at the beach all day. You'll get used to it."

"Oh cool. Want to share a cab?"

"No, thank you. I'm on a mission to find an old friend."

"Well, good luck. I need to find a pay phone and call my parents. I can't wait to talk to them."

Rusty waved as Booger climbed into one of the few remaining cabs.

The need for directions urged Rusty to approach the guard who stood in a small shack at the end of the pier. The shack looked more like an air-conditioned port-a-potty than a proper building, in any sense of the word. One strong wind and the small shack would topple.

"Hey, shipmate. Can you tell me where to find the Admin Office?" Rusty asked.

"Sure. Two blocks that way, then left. You can't miss it," he said as he pointed down the main road.

Rusty couldn't help but note just how unremarkable the base appeared. The dense confines of the utilitarian buildings yielded little variety. The interior of the installation was bland, displaying as much diversity as the stacked containers of a cargo ship.

If it was anything at all, the walk to the Admin Quarterdeck was uneventful. Admin was an enormous building that anyone would find hard to miss. Sailors and Marines arriving on base would need to check in with the office before reporting for duty, and the military's chain of command had zero tolerance for misplaced service members who'd gotten lost. The main road was like a funnel to the Admin's reception desk.

Rusty walked into the building and an attractive Petty Officer, wearing her Navy Dress-White uniform, was involved in an important phone conversation. She greeted him with a wink and a simper, pointing her index finger into the air so as not to be interrupted.

The Yeoman wore substantial quantities of copper hair pulled back into a tight bun. Full lips displayed a subtle shade of Mars Red lipstick. She toned her lips so discreetly Rusty had to look twice to see if she'd painted them at all.

As politely as she could, she held the phone to her ear, and instructed someone to where they could get a visitor's pass. "You need to contact the Vehicle Inspection facility," she said. After a brief pause, she ended the conversation. "Sure thing, ma'am. You are totally welcome."

The Yeoman hung up and threw a casual glance at Rusty, before propping her elbows on the desk, leaning forward to rest her chin on her bridged fingers. "Let me guess. You just pulled into port?" she said.

"What makes you say that?" Rusty asked.

She sniffed the air and said: "You smell like diesel."

"It's JP-5." Sweat dripped under his shirt, and he was suddenly more insecure about his body odor than he had ever been before.

"What is JP-5?" she asked, reaching for her pen.

"Jet fuel."

The scent of JP-5 pervaded the ship, embedding itself in every crack and crevice, garnishing everything with its pervasive stench. Regardless of how many washings, fresh clothing always smelled like a grimy jetway while boarding a commercial airliner.

The Yeoman perked up. "Wow! Jet fuel? I knew it. That must be so totally bitchin'."

"What's so bitchin'?"

"Being a pilot on an aircraft carrier," she said.

Rusty laughed. "Oh, I'm not a pilot. I wish. No, ma'am, I'm on a destroyer."

"Oh. A destroyer." She scrunched her nose and cocked her head, throwing a vacant stare at the wall, before pressing Rusty for more elaborate details. "Why would there be jet fuel on a destroyer?" she asked.

"The ship runs on jet fuel."

She gave Rusty a quizzical look. "Weird, I would have thought it ran on diesel or nuclear or something."

"Nope. It runs on jet fuel."

"You already said that," The Yeoman said. "You're funny."

Rusty micro-grimaced at her ditzy reply. "I was hoping you could help me track down an old friend from boot camp. I believe he's stationed here," he said.

"Fer sure. What's their name?"

The Yeoman seemed confident but far too immature for her age. She was spritely. Energetic like a child kicking puddles after an early morning rain. Yet there was something off about her behavior, as no one could be so damn positive given her boring duty position.

"ET2 Blume, he's a radio tech."

The young female perked up, almost springing from her chair. "Yeah. Like, I know Blume. Everyone on base, totally, knows Blume. He's the most famous person here. Wow, I think even the Commanding Officer has partied at his house before."

"You know Blume?" Rusty asked, astonished.

"Fer sure. Shit, that's what I just said, didn't I? This is a small base, and everyone knows everyone. Blume is a popular guy and loves to have all the cool people over to his house. It's a veritable nightclub at this point — a real righteous party palace, baby."

"That's great. Do you have his phone number?" Rusty asked.

She pursed her lips. "No. He doesn't own a phone. But he works just down the road, at the Maintenance Shop. They have a phone... Ah, but I think he's off today, though," she said, reaching for the receiver. "Let's try, anyway. Shall we?"

Her manicured fingers wrapped around the shiny phone receiver as she pressed it to her chest, dialing the three-digit rotary number.

The tawny-eyed Yeoman placed her hand over the mouthpiece. "It's ringing." After a few moments, the Yeoman spoke into the diaphragm. "ET2 Blume please, this is YN3 Fitzgerald....... Sure I'll hold."

Her soft, Nordic complexion was fair and untanned — no desert lines had yet cracked her smooth skin. Light freckles formed on the crest of her cheeks, highlighting the dark copper glow of her auburn eyebrows. Delicate peach-fuzz airbrushed the length of her un-blemished arms.

Her personality conveyed an extroverted quality. Her voice sounded mousy and if it weren't for her cheery attitude, it would sound whiney — annoying.

"Oh, okay. No, no message. Thank you," she said, hanging the receiver onto its cradle. She turned, biting her index fingernail in an obvious gesture of repentance. "Oops, I forgot to ask, but did you want to leave a message?"

"No, I can always try again later."

"What is your name?" she asked.

"Rick Russell, but everyone calls me 'Rusty,'" he said, scratching his chin. "Well, I appreciate you trying."

The Yeoman removed a pink legal pad from the top drawer of her desk and wrote Rusty's name on the top sheet.

"My name is Erica Fitzgerald, but everyone likes to call me 'Fitz' and it's been my pleasure to help. I am sorry he wasn't there." She reclined and rocked in her chair. Arms crossed over her stomach as she stared at Rusty. An awkward silence filled the room. Seconds passed and then the Yeoman tilted her head and studied Rusty with stern eyes, gauging his reaction to the bad news.

"Okay, well, thank you. Maybe I can try Sunday."

Petty Officer Fitzgerald leaned in. "No one works on Sunday, around here." Her voice inflected relished delight at conveying more bad news.

His smile waned. "Shit, of course not. Well, maybe in another life," he said. "I appreciate your help."

Rusty paused near the reception counter, re-charging his confidence. He glanced at the door and back at the Yeoman, seeming to weigh options.

I'm sure she gets asked out by every guy who walks in here.

Rusty knocked on the counter in a friendly gesture of finality and started for the door. "Well, thank you again. Please tell Blume I stopped by. It would have been fun catching up with an old buddy. And it was awesome to meet you, Fitz."

Fitz stood and looked at her watch. She raised her chin and addressed Rusty, who was halfway across the lobby. "I will tell you what. I get off in twenty-six minutes, and you can ride with me to his house."

"What's that?"

"His girlfriend is one of my best friends, but she's off today. I can take you to his house and we can both surprise them."

"Oh, that's a generous offer, but I couldn't impose."

YN3 Fitz laughed. "Impose? What are you like fifty or something? It's no imposition. I go there all the time." Fitz sat back in her seat, lowering her gaze.

Rusty reiterated that he felt bad for using her and asked where he lived. *It was impolite to ask for a ride from a lady.*

"Like, I'm sure. How cheesy is that? Besides, would using me be so bad?" Drawing with her pen, she doodled on her legal pad, making tiny loops resembling clovers. "Look. I get off work in twenty-five minutes. You can ride in my Jeep," she said. "Everybody's been to Blume's house. I go there on the weekends because there's nothing to do here. This entire island is dead. Driving you there is no big deal. Besides, I think it would be funny to see his expression when I show up with you as my date."

"A date?" Rusty asked.

"Don't you wish? You know what I meant," she said, smirking.

"Well thank you," Rusty said.

After some time listening to Fitz speak, Rusty placed her accent. Fitz's accent was a mix of California rich girl with a slow Texas drawl. Her valley slang seemed unnatural, forced even.

Perhaps she was born in the south and migrated to California?

"What ship are you on?" Fitz asked.

"The USS John Adams," he said. "How long have you been here?"

"Too long. I am due for re-enlistment in twelve months, but I'm thinking of getting out unless they can give me a better station," she said. "I am so tired of the desert."

Rusty cast a dismayed grin. "Wow, no shit. I am due for re-up in twelve months, too. When my time is up, I'm getting out."

Fitz stopped doodling. "Not even if they gave you twelve thousand dollars as a re-enlistment bonus?"

"Well, since you put it like that, we should re-enlist together."

"Wouldn't that be a hoot?" she said, laughing.

The phone rang, and Fitz flinched. The Navy designed the loud phone so anyone inside the office could hear the important calls from 200 yards away. Its bell was obnoxious. Fitz sat upright and stared at the phone with scornful eyes. "Shit. It never stops." She held her index finger up as she answered the phone. Her voice inflection changed to that of her polite phone receptionist. "Admin. Petty Officer Fitzgerald. How may I help you, sir or ma'am?"

Fitz pinched the phone between her shoulder and cheek, then typed on her keyboard. Her fingers were slow and deliberate.

With one eyebrow raised, Rusty watched her struggle with the computer keypad. He loitered in the lobby reception area, shuffling his shoes on the generic vinyl tile. But the phone conversation lasted longer than Rusty expected, motivating him to step outside.

Thirty minutes later, Fitz caught Rusty kneeling down, tying his boot, when she emerged from the admin door. Her arm waved her jingling keys high in the air. "Yay," she said. "I'm free and damn if it ain't Friday!"

She wore black Capri trousers with a black-and-white striped, long-sleeved cotton shirt. She resembled a French artist. Fitz possessed a fine understanding of clothes and her keen sense of deciphering "fashion-speak" blended well with civilian life. No one would mistake her for a squid.

"That's me," she said, pointing to the white Jeep backed into a corner spot near the far end of the empty parking lot.

"I like your Jeep. It looks nice," he said.

Fitz locked eyes with Rusty and chortled. "You must be kidding me? That thing's ragged as hell."

"I don't trust Jeeps that are immaculate," Rusty said. "The driver hasn't gained enough off-road time for my liking."

Fitz paused in the middle of the parking lot, looking at her Jeep. One hand rested on her hip as she spun her keys around her index finger. "Hmm. Maybe you're right."

Rusty climbed onto the sun-bleached seat. The desert winds had covered the floorboard with a fair amount of sand, preventing Rusty's feet from gaining traction on its gritty surface. The hot, dry breeze circulated the smells of unleaded gas mixed with leather throughout the Jeep.

Fitz wiggled the knob at the end of the stick shift, ensuring it was in neutral. She pressed the clutch and turned the key. Her long fingers wrapped around the wheel while her other hand grabbed the shifter. "You ready?"

"Let's." Rusty found it hard to look away from her painted, slender fingers. It seemed she'd spent idle time at work making sure her nails were flawless.

"Great, let's get rad," she said, her waggish grin hinting at the prospect of excitement. She popped the clutch and gassed the Jeep, squealing her tires on the sand-covered pavement.

She blew past the main gate and pulled out the rubber hairband holding her ponytail, freeing her hair. Long, cinnamon-hued locks set off in the wind.

"What music do you like?" she asked.

"I like a little of everything. Do you have anything upbeat?"

"Totally," she said, smiling. Fitz pushed in a preloaded cassette. 80's pop music blasted from the speakers as Fitz raised the volume. Dust trailed the white Jeep, while locals strained to watch the crazy Americans blaring pop music as they ripped through town.

The Jeep approached a yellow light, and Rusty expected her to slow down. Instead, she downshifted and floored the gas pedal, speeding through the empty intersection and drifting to the left. As they approached a restaurant, Fitz turned and zipped into the parking lot, screeching to a halt. She reached across to lower the radio's volume.

"We need dinner." Fitz clutched her keys and felt for her wallet under her seat, before exiting the Jeep. Rusty followed as they walked to the restaurant.

Inside, the overwhelming smell of mint and sage filled the air. The owners plastered photos of the menu on the wall behind the register. It all appeared delicious. Unable to decide, Rusty let Fitz do all the ordering for both of them.

"Two Mutton Karahi, for here," Fitz said, holding up the peace sign.

The proprietors were Arabs, and the friendly owner wore a long white thawb that almost swept the floor. A black rope wrapped around his agal, securing the white Kaffiyeh-turban on his head.

"Is there a bank around? I only have hundreds." Rusty said.

"Oh boy, that's awful. Sounds like a real first-world problem to me. But don't worry, you can pay me back later." Fitz removed a stack of currency and handed the store owner 14,000 dinars.

Rusty asked Fitz how much the dinner cost.

"Fourteen thousand dinars." Fitz looked at the man and grinned as he unfolded the wad of bills, placing them in the register.

"I meant how much is it in dollars?"

"Not sure. Ten dollars, maybe. I just give him money until he stops asking," Fitz said. She glared at Rusty and turned to the man, nodding her head.

Shifting his feet, Rusty expressed objections. "Seems iniquitous. Sounds sketchy. Is everyone in Bahrain a crook?" Almost before finishing his question, Rusty worried the proprietors might have been fluent in English.

Smiles faded as Fitz turned to Rusty with a contemptuous glare. "You try being a moralist with a house full of hungry kids," she said. "It's easy being honest when you're not responsible for others. Petty Officer Russell, you have the luxury of living onboard a ship, and you have all your needs handed to you. Besides, it's not like the food, here, is expensive or anything. Also, in fact, it's much healthier than the shit we're served on base."

Fitz placed an additional 6,000 BD tip in the large glass jar beside the register and waved at the man's wife.

Rusty realized how crass he'd sounded and wondered why he lacked empathy for the person behind the counter. He viewed the man as a shyster who stole money from foreign tourists, but it was obvious the proprietors knew Fitz. And since it was the only restaurant near the base, she might have frequented the place twice a week, at least. It should have been obvious they were all friends.

Rusty found himself outside the reality bubble, feeling alienated, seeing the world through warped goggles. It was strange for him to make snap appraisals on unfamiliar situations, judging the scene with a narrowed view of the facts, while wedging himself in matters which did not involve him. It was a rushed impression and one made with ignorance. Who was he to interject himself into a stranger's life, dictating morals where none were solicited? The entire situation proved emotive, and not in a good way. If nothing else, it was enlightening.

"I guess you're right. I didn't think it through," Rusty said.

"Shit happens. I'm sure you'll get over it." Fitz said as she opened the large glass door and removed a bottle of orange soda.

Rusty could not be sure if his hearing changed, or if Fitz's inflection changed, but her voice sounded lower. Much in the way a person sounds when they hang up after a business call.

"So, fourteen thousand dinars is about ten dollars, huh?" Rusty asked.

"Yeah. Sounds about right."

The first few days in every foreign port involved getting accustomed to the exchange rates of the individual country. Rusty could approximate the exchange rate of the British pound, the Norwegian Kroner, and the Greek Drachma. The Dinar was still new to him, but having just learned 14,000 dinars was about ten dollars, then he calculated he held about 420,000 dinars in his wallet.

Rusty was great at math, but he never understood money with any proficiency. It was a concept he neglected in his extra-curricular studies. Since no one taught business in public school and Dow Jones was not an important facet of radar repair, knowing how to accumulate wealth and stockpile money was a skill he'd never gained.

There was an art to financial success, and money was its own reward for the tenacity it took to gain it. Shrewd business dealings were an uncomfortable concept for a person as agreeable as Rusty. He never learned to compartmentalize himself, to disconnect his morals from the aggressive nature of financial competitiveness.

The proprietor wore a seemed smile as he handed Rusty the tray of exotic food. As Rusty turned to walk away, the man grabbed his arm and handed Rusty a small stack of paper towels, along with some extra condiments. Then he patted Rusty on his shoulder and shoved him off with a grin.

I guess In this part of the world, or any country with very few sources of income, a couple of extra dollars meant survival for the hardworking man and those family members who relied on him for support.

Rusty followed Fitz to a table overlooking the road. Outside, the view was about as dramatic as any open desert could be. The Eastern sky grew dark, as it crept closer to dusk.

Classical music floated from the back of the kitchen. It seemed the delightful owner put relaxing music on for Fitz and her guest.

Both of their plates comprised yellow rice, topped off with chunks of lamb, sautéed in a dark red curry seasoning. There were green peppers and minced parsley. It was one of the best dishes Rusty had eaten in months.

"Is this an Arabic recipe?"

Fitz waited until she finished chewing before answering. "Pakistani, I think."

"Well, it tastes great," Rusty said.

"It's pretty tubular. I stop here, like, all the time."

Rusty met Fitz's gaze. "Do you like Bahrain?"

"It's totally bonk. I don't know *how* I ended up here." She looked down, glaring at her dinner plate.

"How far is Blume's house?" Rusty looked outside into the darkening eastern sky.

"It's like thirty minutes that way." Fitz pointed south into the desert.

"Hmm." His voice trembled. "Is there a town out there?"

Fitz laughed. "I'm totally sure, but it's like a hundred miles past his house. I know what you're thinking, but you shouldn't freak out. You get used to the desolation. It can be so spooky, I'm sure." She placed her fork on the table and took a sip from her straw.

"I thought Bahrain was only like 60 miles long."

Fitz twirled a long strand of shiny auburn hair around her index finger and looked over Rusty's shoulder, staring out of the window behind him. "Don't be so pedantic. If you're going to err, why not err on the side of exaggeration? Or, as you hotshots might say, 'hyperbole?'" With that, she matched Rusty's stare; garnishing her expression with wide-eyed sarcasm.

Fitz had an easygoing nature about her. Rusty sought to define it, but he couldn't get an accurate read on her. She kept something back, and her occasional quip derailed Rusty almost as if she'd resolved herself to mislead him out of pure spite.

6

After eating, the two walked to the Jeep. Fitz started it up and they sped down the two-lane road, headed south out of town. She reached into her front pocket and removed a pack of gum and offered Rusty a piece. It was watermelon, Rusty's favorite.

A few miles down the road, Rusty paused his gum chewing, pinching it between his molars to inspect his mouth in the side-view mirror, seeking parsley which may have lodged itself between his teeth.

Pockets of hot and cold air fluctuated as they sped down the highway. It had been a long time since he last rode with open windows in anything moving faster than his ship. After three soggy months, the thrill of cool, dry air, was exhilarating.

Bahrain's green highway signs displayed the speed limit in kilometers. Ashamed to admit he did not know what one-hundred kilometers per hour was, Rusty asked Fitz an indirect question, hoping to side-step sounding ignorant. "How long did it take you to learn to drive here?" Rusty asked.

"What do you mean? Shit, I was stealing my mom's car when I was twelve," Fitz said.

That didn't go the way I planned.

"No, sorry. I meant the 'kilometers per hour' thing. How long did it take you to learn to convert kilometers to miles per hour?"

Fitz's quizzical expression faded. Her moment of clarity relieved Rusty. She smiled and said, "oh. I don't know what the conversion is. I just look at the speedometer." Eyeing the Jeep's gauges, she jerked her chin up, directing Rusty's attention to the instrument cluster.

Rusty peeked at the speedometer. Jeep manufacturers printed

numbers to show both miles per hour and kilometers per hour on the glass. He rolled his eyes and sneered, turning to his attention back to his passenger side window.

The long stretch of highway was uniform, and its desolation was overwhelming. Neglected power lines and the sandy highway seemed to be the only signs of human development. Rusty panicked when he realized there were no pay phones, fire stations, patrolling police, nor were there hospitals or ambulances. With no means of calling rescue, if something bad were to happen, it would take an ambulance too long to respond if they showed up at all. Onboard, he could always count on the Corpsman being two minutes away from any point on the ship. However, out in the open desert, he was at the mercy of fate.

I'd be dead before help even showed up.

Fitz paid no mind. She sang along with the music, oblivious to any self-conceived notions of danger. She chanted, bouncing in chorus and slapping her hands on the steering wheel in rhythm to the song's drumbeats.

They traveled twenty minutes before Fitz turned the volume down enough to shout above the wind. She pointed and yelled. "Land ho! Over there, ya scurvy dog!"

Rusty squinted in the direction Fitz pointed. A tall and unassuming cube stood above the western horizon. Developers placed the structure in the middle of a barren landscape. Illusionary water surrounded the lonely building, and it seemed to float in the middle of a vast, shimmering mirage.

To the west, the sky appeared golden as the sun dipped closer, almost touching the sand. The backdrop was dreamlike and if it were a photograph, Rusty would assume it was a manipulated landscape. For miles in all directions, the lone building stood in surreal contrast to the desolate nature of the featureless desert.

To the east, the environment seemed apocalyptic. In the late afternoon, a dark haze obscured the leeward side of Bahrain, shading the land in the fog of diminishing light as early dusk crawled across the sand.

"There it is," she said, shouting and pointing. "Blume's personal party palace. An oasis in the desert."

"Wow, he lives in the boonies," Rusty said.

Fitz jabbed Rusty's thigh, laughing. "Like fir sure. This whole place is the boonies. We are just east of 'Bum fuck, Egypt.'"

Miles later, Fitz turned off the main highway onto a long, paved driveway which led to Blume's condo building. The open expanse of the area dwarfed the building.

Fitz sped toward the tall, five-story structure. Light dust obscured the distant condo, but the air cleared as they drove closer, and the building's color darkened with the thinning of the haze. However, its size did not grow larger, as it should have according to the laws of perspective, remaining static until they drove within fifty yards.

As they approached, the building sprang up from the desert, almost as if being inflated to prepare for their arrival. The effect made Rusty dizzy, like viewing the advancing building through a fast-zooming, wide-angled lens.

There were three cars parked on the sand beside the building. An olive-colored 1975 Mercedes sedan, a white Toyota Four Runner, and a sky blue Nissan 4WD pickup. All vehicles were beat to shit, dirty, and sandblasted by years of wind exposure.

Fitz locked the brakes, sliding ten feet to a halt in the gritty parking lot. Sudden braking kicked dust into their faces, forcing Rusty to raise his hands and squint. The two locked eyes but said nothing. Unable to hide her mistake, the Yeoman wiped dust off of her painted lips. Laughing at her own miscalculation made Rusty laugh.

"Kickass," she said, wiggling the stick shifter before releasing the clutch and turning off the ignition. Then there was silence.

Looking at the strange building, it was apparent wind erosion took its toll on the concrete facade, reducing the bottom floors to support beams, cinder blocks, and broken windows — allowing the desert to reclaim the lowest parts of the building. Except for the lobby, the bottom floors were abandoned. Deserted. Sealed by reinforced walls, the lobby's insulation preserved its original design, shutting out most of the desert thanks to the double-thick windows installed along its shaded perimeter.

Remnants of concrete slabs and long sidewalks disappeared into a sea of beige sand. The condo was the start of an unfinished development project. Cement foundations intended for additional buildings that were never realized lay half-covered in sand. Plans of someone's long-abandoned dreams of wealth faded into the expanse, along with electrical boxes, parking bumpers, and wiggling signposts — rejecting the desert's attempts at assimilation.

The wind kicked dust into the air, following Rusty as he climbed out of the Jeep and walked to the main entrance, only pausing a moment to scope out his surroundings.

Fitz grabbed his arm. "Come on. We need to get inside before it gets dark or the boogie monsters will eat us."

The front door led to a grand entryway. At some earlier time, fine artisans tiled the lobby floors in high gloss red marble. But years of sandy foot traffic smeared scratches across the exquisite lobby floors. The lobby's decor was dated and ornate beyond measure.

Musty smells of old paperwork mixed with stale fabric. The embedded odors seeped from the back offices of the abandoned reception counter, mixing with undisturbed stacks of files, layered with the same dusty patina that coated everything. Rolodexes with important numbers sat undisturbed near dead rotary phones still plugged in behind ransacked file cabinets.

On the wall opposite of the main entryway, a long glass window spanned the full length of the lobby. A large pool sat empty outside the lobby's main windows, never completed beyond its framing stage. Instead of blue water, sand filled the large concrete pool, blanketing its surrounding cement deck, transitioning in and out of the pool like snow drifts crossing a road after a heavy blizzard. Random tile peeked through the drifts, hinting at the shape of the oversized public swimming hole.

Heavy breezes swept through the vacant building, blowing through its broken windows and snaking their way through the many abandoned rooms, while an occasional knocking of an open door echoed throughout the lower floors.

"Well, this is dramatic." Rusty had never seen such a surreal setting before.

"I'm sure. Wait until you see his place." Fitz said. Her grin was ravenous, and she appeared crazed, fanatical even. It was easy to read her expression, even in the darkened space. Her odd look spooked Rusty.

There was an elevator, and he stopped to stand in front of the door. "Does the elevator work?"

Fitz ignored the elevator and approached the door leading to the staircase. She swung around, looking back at Rusty. She propped her hand on the door above her head, and the other on her hip, like a sophisticated fashion model. "Why yes, it works. I wouldn't use it though. Like, could you imagine getting totally stuck in there? It would be weeks before they found your poor, dead little body. But by then there'd be nothing left of you but dry bones… You're better off coming with me," she said. She pointed at him and drew tiny circles in mid-air with her index finger, beckoning him to follow her up the stairs instead.

Claustrophobia stirred in Rusty. *What did she say about a dead body?*

With reservations, Rusty followed the Yeoman. Besides, there was nowhere for him to retreat, as he was far beyond the point of safe return.

"It's this way, sailor," Fitz said. Her smirk drew Rusty closer.

Staring at the lifeless elevator button, Rusty walked toward the door, where Fitz stood waiting.

"There aren't any locks?" he asked.

She threw Rusty a stern glance as if surprised by his ridiculous question. "Shit. If they catch you stealing out here, they'll cut your arm off. I saw them do it in the market. Cops around here, they walk around with these long-ass Scimitar swords. They totally chopped a man's arm off for stealing bread. It was gnarly as hell. Blood everywhere and no one bothered to help the dude get to the hospital." Her expression was stony. "I saw him bleed out all over the street."

In the darkened lobby, Rusty waited for a sign of jest. Instead, Fitz didn't say a word. She watched him with wide, unflinching eyes, nursing an expression only a logician could appreciate.

What the hell?

The Yeoman elbowed Rusty's bicep. She curled her arm around her belly and pointed at Rusty. Her body shook with violent laughter. "I'm so totally messing with you. Dude. Man, you should have seen your face. You looked like someone put country music on at your new-wave party. I flipped you out."

Rusty tried his best to fake a chuckle.

I don't even know this girl and where the hell is she taking me?

They started up the five flights of stairs. Their footsteps echoed throughout the concrete stairwell as rubber soles scraped across the gritty treads of the sandy steps.

At the top of the stairs, on the fifth floor, the door opened inward, leading to a large vestibule. The small space allowed access to the penthouse elevator door and a red door opposite the elevator. Numbers on the wall beside the large red door hinted of a domicile, and smack dab in the center of the door's panel was an ornate, shiny brass knob. Pretentious and campy, decorators intended the knob to imitate gold, amplifying the illusion of exotic wealth where none existed — faux precious metal.

The marble floor, colored blood red, resembled a giant piece of uncooked steak with long streaks of white fat for veins. Long ago, skilled artists polished the shine to a brilliant gloss, similar to the main lobby.

Fitz opened the wooden door to Blume's apartment. Rusty started in, but she pressed her palm on Rusty's chest, leaning close enough to whisper. The smell of fresh jasmine radiated from her flowing hair. With a hushed voice, she put her long, slender index finger to her puckered lips. "Shhh. I want to surprise them, so you wait here."

Rusty shrugged. "Whatever works," he said.

I sure hope it's the same Blume I know. This might get weird.

Fitz walked inside, closed the door, and left Rusty to the silence of the empty hall, where he waited two minutes before the tacky door opened. Fitz waved him in. "Come on," she said. She grabbed Rusty's arm and pulled him in, eager to present Blume with her latest find.

Rusty entered the darkened apartment. The dim room smelled of spicy food and expired beer. While looking around and getting acclimated to the darkened ambient light, he heard a familiar voice. "Well, fuck me runnin'. You gotta be shittin' me," the voice said. Rusty turned as Blume emerged from his bedroom and approached with open arms. The friends hugged, patting each other's back.

Blume backed up, still gripping Rusty's elbows, looking at the salty sailor from stem to stern. He grabbed Rusty to hug him again. "Wow, this is so crazy. How the hell are ya? What in the world are ya doing here?" Dewy-eyed, Blume inspected Rusty with an open smile. He could not believe Rusty was in Bahrain — in his home — with Fitz!

"I am in port for a few days and wanted to look you up," Rusty said, a grin of relief crossed his face. Anxiety left his body, replaced by a warm wave of comforting numbness. The moment left Rusty with a mix of happiness and relief for surviving the most unusual trip.

Blume grabbed Rusty's elbow and dragged him to a light, inspecting him for any signs of damage. "Shit, son. You ain't changed a bit."

"It's great to see you, Blume," Rusty said. "Thanks to Fitz. I owe her."

A dark-haired female reclined on the swanky couch. She stood and approached the group.

"This is Danielle," Blume said. "Dani, this is my best friend from school. His name's Rusty, the one I tol' ya about. He and I always found trouble."

"Hi, Rusty. It's nice to meet you," Dani said, extending her hand for

Rusty to shake. Her brown hair was long, sleek, and pulled into a tight ponytail.

"I told her about you," Blume said. "Like that night, we saw Rush in Wisconsin. Do you remember that?"

"How could anyone ever forget seeing a Rush concert?" Rusty placed his hand on Blume's shoulder, stepping past his old friend to get a better view of the condo. "Wow. You have a great place," he said.

The penthouse was commodious and sparsely adorned. The 3000 square foot penthouse held wide patio windows overlooking the desert. An intense western view of the setting sun pierced the large glass, throwing stretched shadows across the floor.

"What does this place cost you?" Rusty asked.

Blume cast a wry smile. "Three hundred dollars a month. Can ya believe that shit?"

Rusty folded his arms. "Get the fuck outta here. Three hundred a month? That's obscene," he shouted.

"I know, right? Das less than my per diem check. I think it was an old model unit for the building. Yeah. Some guys on base told me about it. The landlord only lets military people rent the place. I guess he thinks we are rich or something," Blume said.

Ruggers blanketed the entire floor in loud Bordeaux red shag carpeting — wall to wall. The fibers were stringier than the traditional napped carpet of the 70s and Rusty calculated the stringy fibers to be about two inches long. It resembled a deep red lamb's wool, laid across the floor.

"This carpet is crazy," Rusty said.

"Right? It's nice, but it takes forever to clean. It took me a month to figure out how to vacuum the damn thing. There's crumbs in there from the 'Nixon Era.'"

Kitschy trim bordered the walls, lining the room from all sides with gilded bands of imitation gold-leafing, while cheesy red paint held the walls hostage. The entire condo was red and gold.

"Rusty, would you like something to drink?" Dani asked.

"Thank you. A drink would be nice. Do you have any water?"

Dani walked to the large fridge. She opened the door and stood back, allowing Rusty to see its contents. Dani and Blume stocked it with beer, soda, and cases of bottled water. There was a gallon of milk, a bottle of Vodka, a six-pack of Sprite, and a pitcher of iced tea. Dani's complaisant nature reminded Rusty of his mother, when she would entertain guests, back in the 70s — the only things missing were a barbecue and Rod Stewart asking if the sugar ladies think he's sexy.

"Well, I suppose if you live in a desert, hydration is a priority," Rusty said. "May I have iced tea?"

Dani gripped the pitcher. She held a large glass with a cartoon image of the "Hamburgler" screen printed on it and dropped in a few rocks of ice.

The four of them took seats at the thick mahogany dinner table seated in the middle of the dining room. The cherry-colored table, measured 6 x 9 feet and its inlay contained crotched mahogany panels. It appeared to weigh as much as a car. If sold in the US, the table would fetch around $8,000 at the auction.

Rusty inspected the expansive penthouse. It was exquisite but dated. In the late 60s or early 70s, the decor was pioneering, avant garde even, but today it expressed banality.

"This is something," Rusty said.

"It reminds me of home," Blume said.

"What? How could it remind you of home? You're from Baton Rouge," Rusty asked.

"Have you seen the inside of the bars in the French Quarter? Some of those French Quarter bars look like this, except for the shaggy rug. They get the red color inspiration from France. Bordeaux? Get it?" Blume asked.

"I only remember one bar in Louisiana, and it was your friend Benny's bar. They painted it white." Rusty said.

"Oh, I remember Benny alright." Blume laughed as he turned on the TV. "Check this out." He flipped through the channels and all the programs were all in Arabic. Blume stopped on a channel where the program looked like a middle eastern version of 'Knight Rider.'

"Dani speaks Arabic," Blume said. "She can translate these shows."

"Wow, what a contrast," Rusty said. "I have never met an American who could speak Arabic."

"I am a civilian translator for the Navy, and I work in the Admin building with Fitz," Dani said. "All around, it's not a bad job. My boss makes me answer every time the phone rings, but I've met a lot of high end diplomats."

"Wow. I imagine everyone who comes on base must go through Admin."

Fitz elbowed Dani's arm. "Dani is smarter than us all. Plus, we've had our share of interesting visitors, huh?"

Rusty waited for Fitz to elaborate, but no details were given.

Instead, an awkward silence squeezed the room to the point of suffocation. After what seemed like minutes, Blume was next to speak. "So. What great ports have you visited?" he asked.

"Egypt was nice, and so was Israel. In Israel, I attended a Russian fashion show," Rusty said. "Also, we drank Tequila with a bunch of female Israeli troops. They were these attractive women in full desert fatigues, strapped with Uzi machine guns, drinking more liquor than we did."

Fitz leaned in, pressing her hands to her knees. She whispered in Dani's ear.

Rusty turned to Blume and said, "Once in Israel, I was drunk and asked an Israeli girl if she ever saw me on a battlefield, 'would she kill me?' She slammed a shot glass onto the table, looked me in the eye, and said, 'Absolutely.' Then she raised a toast and bought me two shots of Tequila. I *think* both shots were for me. But I couldn't understand her too well."

"Whoa, crazy," Dani said.

"Yeah. Everyone ended up dancing on the tables. These drunk Israeli girls were swinging their guns around, pointing them in the air, dancing, and drinking. The bar got trashed. It was epic. The bar owner was also the bartender. He was drunk and kept playing the same song on repeat as everyone started taking their clothes off."

Blume laughed, imagining the scene.

Rusty pointed to the couch. "Nice couch," he said, walking over to inspect the rich, plush fabric, pushing down on the firm cushions. The sofa was large and resembled a giant circular bean bag. The red leather couch could seat ten or more. Mirrors on the ceiling spanned the full length of the couch, and Rusty could only guess their purpose.

"It's called an Arabic Majlis floor couch. The landlord bought it from a hookah lounge in Saudi Arabia," Blume said.

"Where's the hookah?" Rusty asked as he sat down, extending his legs.

"I don't know. They smoke apple skins." Blume said. "There's a whole strip of shops downtown, lined with hookah bars. They sit in dark rooms and smoke apple skins."

Dani and Fitz walked out to the back patio. Fitz put her palm on Dani's shoulder and whispered something in her ear.

"Apple skins?"

"Yeah. I never tried them myself, but I guess the locals love it. So, what ship are you on?" Blume asked.

"The John Adams. It's a 'Spruance class destroyer,'" Rusty said, watching the girls as they conversed on the back patio.

"Golly. Y'all blow anything up yet?" Blume asked.

Rusty locked eyes with Blume and he felt the urge to share sea stories.

"Last week, the Gunner's Mates blew up a drone. A friend of mine named Ocean, shot it right out of the sky," he said.

Blume laughed. "No shit? I wish I coulda' seen that."

"Me too. They stuck me in Radar 2. So, I couldn't see anything," Rusty said.

The slider opened, and the girls came in. Fitz sat beside Rusty. Dani whispered into Blume's ear and seconds later, Blume said to Rusty: "Hey bro, give me a minute or two."

"I'll be here," Rusty said. He finished his tea and walked to the sink. After rinsing the glass, he put it in the sink.

Standing in the open kitchen, Rusty looked around the condo, as Dani pulled Blume into the master bedroom. Carpenters disguised the master bedroom door as a secret wooden panel — one of many wooden panels lining the length of the southern wall of the penthouse. Designed to remain hidden, as ostentatious as it was, it blended in with surrounding panels, and Rusty would have never known there were four additional rooms behind the wall.

Rusty was alone with Fitz. He felt perspiration run down his back as he pressed his clammy palms to the thighs of his pants, swallowing to clear his throat.

Fitz smiled at Rusty as she walked past him, heading into the kitchen. "What now, sailor?"

7

Fitz snagged a bottle of water from the refrigerator. She eased the bottle close to her lips and reached in her pockets to remove a pack of chewing gum, offering a stick to Rusty. He held his palm out, waving her off, refusing with a polite gesture. "No, thank you."

Several moments of standing in the kitchen, near the opened refrigerator door, were enough to cool Rusty, and he walked over to the couch to test the cushions, seeking a domesticated comfort he hadn't experienced in almost five months. Navy ships were not too keen on stocking their compartments with couches, and Rusty couldn't recall the last time he reclined on one.

Fitz shrugged and unwrapped the rejected piece of gum, sliding it over her waiting tongue while taking a seat beside Rusty on the couch. Trailing behind her was the intoxicating scent of her sweet smelling perfume.

"What do you think of his place?" she asked.

Sitting next to Fitz made Rusty shy and anxious. Being as nervous as he was, he scanned the room and petted the leather armrest to cull his polarized thoughts. "It's a piece of history," he said.

The alone time with Fitz gave him a new perspective. It was then he realized how attracted he was to Fitz, and he feared he no longer cared to spend so much time with his buddy Blume.

"It has charm," she said. Fitz drew circles on the leather couch with her middle finger.

Rusty interjected: "What made you join the Navy?" But before she could respond, Rusty offered his own reason without providing Fitz a chance to answer his question. "I joined for the travel. It's the cheapest way to travel, I suppose," Rusty said.

Fitz slid across the soft leather cushions, putting some distance between them. "What are you talking about?" she asked.

"I get paid to see the best places. Well, except here. I don't understand why anyone would want to visit here." Rusty said, rolling his eyes. His fingers caressed the label of the water bottle.

Fitz cocked her head and crossed her legs as she reached for her drink.

"I guess it's okay here. But there's not much here to like," he said.

Fitz turned to contemplate the fading sunlight that shone through the wide sliding glass door overlooking the balcony. Carbon filtered photons from the resplendent star charged the room with flaming orange as it retreated behind the horizon, stretching long shadows along the floor of the condo.

"That is so beautiful. Just look at that glow," Rusty said, reclining on the couch, resting his arms above his head. "I wonder if the architect designed this building with the sunset in mind? Maybe it's why they painted everything red."

Fitz looked to the window with a relaxed squint. Her eyelids looked closed as her face reflected the light, bathing her aureate skin with light. Her radiant complexion and auburn hair contrasted against the bright red background of the walls, making Rusty wonder if nature created the flaming sun for her, and her alone.

"I've seen a few neat places. This sunset is one of them," he said. "It's like a deep conversation."

"Totally," she said, processing his words, all the while looking through the window at the sun's last light. "You like deep conversation?"

Her once whiney voice had deepened and became more alluring. Rusty couldn't pinpoint the moment it transitioned, but it wasn't until now that he was aware of how mesmerized he was by her seductive powers of articulation.

Rusty swallowed to prime his throat, hoping to sound as eloquent as she. "Yes. I don't want to brag, but I can get deep. Also, I've been to the most beautiful places in the Atlantic. Let me think of a nice place." Rusty pinched his chin as he recounted his port visits in order — mentally tallying his long list of accolades and stored experiences. "I would say my favorite place was in Norway. In Norway, the air is so clean, and the mountains dip into water with shores so steep you can *feel* the water's depth. The troughs dive thousands of feet, just a couple hundred yards offshore. Of all the most beautiful places I've ever seen,

I would say my favorite place was Norway."

Rusty turned to Fitz, waving his hands to illustrate his story. "I wouldn't be able to describe it if I didn't see it myself. The tops of the mountains were snow-capped and I could feel the deep water troughs transition to the Mountain summits. With the right eyes, I could see everything." He drew an invisible 'V' in the air to explain what a trough was.

"Ah. Sounds nice," she said. "I wish I could've seen it." Fitz tightened her grip on the water bottle, making an irritating crunch.

"Well, you'd have to be stationed on a ship. Man, I loved it. The place was straight from a postcard. It was the most impressive setting on the planet. It had the best landscape I ever saw."

Rusty told Fitz how he toured every bar in town and how girls kept buying him and his friends drinks; how he spent the first afternoon on the German ship, drinking the best beer on earth, in the coolest galley; how he couldn't believe the German Navy allowed a beer dispenser to be placed onboard their ship. "It was one of the coolest things I ever saw," he said. Rusty looked around the room, avoiding eye contact.

Fitz sighed. "Do you always talk about yourself this much?"

Rusty felt the hot cascade of adrenaline. "Uh. What do you mean?" he asked, swallowing to ease the sudden dry glaze scratching his throat.

Rusty's mannerisms tied him to everything Fitz disliked. Having traded etiquette for moral high ground, she glared at Rusty with stern eyes. "You have done nothing but talk about yourself. I cannot recall ever having seen so many of the proverbial 'love me' buttons on any one individual. Not only that, but everything has to be 'the coolest, the best, or the most impressive' thing you ever saw. It's as if you're telling the world your experiences are superior to everyone else's, so everyone's life sucks by comparison." Her passion for her beliefs cast her in a new light; she radiated poise.

Thrill's perspiration welled on Rusty's brow. Her stunning criticisms paralyzed him even though her passionate expression for her beliefs cast her in a new light. No one ever challenged him in such a calculated manner.

Did she set me up? The 'valley girl simpleton' was not so simple, having pretended to be unsophisticated the entire day.

Without warning, Fitz had brandished her true intellect. Her glaring eyes exaggerated an expression he could not interpret. All in all, he was stimulated by the sudden intimacy the conversation brought, even if it embarrassed him.

With his moral power contested, Rusty retorted: "I'm not sure what you mean. I'm a selfless person. In fact, I am the most selfless person I know."

She laughed unkindly. "You actually believe your own bullshit. You aren't selfless," she said. "You haven't stopped talking about yourself this whole conversation. You preceded every statement with 'I this' or 'I that.' It all sounds very egocentric — as if you need the world to listen as you brag." Her words were beyond reproach.

Have I hogged the conversation? She is right.

Rusty's introspection gripped him with surprising shame. Her remarks were so full of merit, they left no room for debate.

"What do you enjoy doing?" he asked.

"Now you want to discuss me? I figured we would dive deeper into your totally perfect life." She was unrelenting.

Realigning himself, he sat up and straightened his shirt, soliciting composure. "I apologize. You're right, I monopolized the conversation. I did not intend to block you out. It's just.... well. Okay. I like you and wanted to impress you."

"If you want to impress me, impress me by being genuine. You can't impress people by bragging about how spectacular your life is. It's not cool to show a hungry person how much food you have, or a poor person how much wealth you've gained. It's insensitive."

"Well, I'm sorry. You asked to hear about my adventures."

"I never asked. You heard what you wanted to hear," she said.

Damn, she's right. She never asked. Why did I have to brag?

Rusty hung his head and stared at the shag rug between his feet. "The fact is, I dislike talking about myself. Or talking about things I have seen and done. I spend all my time onboard with competitive people and I believe I am so used to having to prove myself, I forget how to have a decent conversation. I assumed you wanted to hear about the ports I have visited because it's all I ever get asked about from strangers who learn I'm in the Navy," he said. "I suppose I'm conditioned and I rehearse my conversations. Replaying them over and over, because I get asked so many times."

"Now you're being genuine," she said. Her expression softened. "Maybe I'm being too hard on you. Or maybe I'm taking my frustrations out on you. People shouldn't be so judgmental. My apologies. You're only trying to make polite conversation, and I shouldn't be jumping your shit about it."

Rusty's defensive demeanor loosened. "No, you're right. I was gloating. But it wasn't to make me feel better. I wanted to share a small part of my history with you. Could you tell me a little about yourself? Like, what are your interests?"

She looked up from the couch. "Art," she said. Her stern expression shifted, inviting more questions.

"What kind of art? What medium?"

"Oil painting and sculpting," Fitz said. She stared into the silent television screen. Poor TV reception showed grainy commercials, advertising hygiene products with names neither she nor Rusty could pronounce.

"Have you found your style yet?" Rusty asked.

Fitz sat up. She set the bottle of water on the table and folded her hands in her lap. With a tilt of her head, she squinched her nose and said: "Not sure. I think it's impossible to know for sure."

"Well, what style or influences do you have?"

"Dada, and the early Surrealists, but I don't paint surrealism. I am more into Post Modern Expression and I dabble in Abstraction. I'm more of a dilettante than a serious professional."

"Why would you say that?"

Fitz looked away. "Well, because I am not a full-time artist, and I like to work in all different mediums. A professional artist has a consistent body of work. Bored with the same subjects and style, repeating over and over, I'm forced in many directions," she said.

Fitz knows more about art than she lets on. Most artists her age paint portraits of dogs and flowers and shit. She seems versed in the many art movements. And what happened to her valley-girl slang?

She continued: "Right now, my favorite artist is Gerhard Richter." Fitz stated. "I like his photographic paintings."

Intrigued, he'd never expected her to mention Richter. Rusty'd seen a Richter exhibit in New York years earlier. He had never heard of the German painter until he saw the one-man exhibit. The last thing in the world he wanted to do was brag to Fitz with news he'd seen the exhibit.

She added. "Occasionally, I do paint objective realism, but it's so disciplined it bores me to tears," Fitz said in an oratorical manner, orchestrating her hyperbole while setting the "drama dial" to max.

"To tears?" Rusty asked, laughing.

"To *absolute* tears." Fitz chuckled. "Besides, who needs a realistic painting when you can just take a photo? It might be nice to have a huge painting of a cityscape or something decorative or whatever. I wouldn't know. That's my opinion, anyway. 'Art snob' is my official title. But, I feel the hyper-realists of the seventies seemed to have explored all aspects of realistic art with thorough precision. What else is there to learn from copying reality? I mean it's nice to see the perfected techniques of realism, but I'd never want a five-foot-tall painting of a wine bottle to look at for years and years. It would be like looking at a huge photograph of commercial art. Yawn."

Hypnotized by her voice, Rusty laid back and looked at the mirrored ceiling.

"Do you like art?" she asked.

Afraid to answer her question and not wanting to talk about himself, he hesitated before offering a reply. "Yes, I'm very much into visual art."

"Do you have any favorites?"

No artist had ever asked Rusty about his art preferences. His likings leaned on the darker side, and he feared his preferences would scare her off. "Um, yeah, but you won't like them."

She placed her elbow on the back of the couch and rested her cheek on her balled fist. "Au, contraire," she said as her lips formed a radiant smile. "You presume to pre-qualify *my* tastes? You must tell me and don't lie. I'll know if you're lying."

"Francis Bacon and Lucian Freud," he said.

Lifting her head. "Ah... So, you like your art deep and disturbed. I see."

"I over-analyze too much. However, I feel those two are about as ground-breaking as it gets, especially in a scene where pop art is all the rage."

"Those are two very influential artists. Bacon is too dark for my taste, but I understand his work. He's honest, and he never filters his ideals. I'm impressed you know of those two artists. Perhaps one day you'll make an influential critic."

Her candor intrigued him. The shift in her vocabulary fascinated him even more so, almost as if she had morphed into a more refined version of herself. He expected the Yeoman to retreat in horror, but she remained unaffected by his art preferences, stoking Rusty's fascination with her even more. In a world of criticism, one person's taste in art was high on another person's list of judgments. If he were to cite the wrong artist, especially to an aspiring artist, things could spiral out of control in a hurry. No artist wants to hear about someone's preference for kitschy painters who produce cheesy art. She was not as timid as she could've been because he didn't scare her away.

"I know Bacon can be dark and he's not mainstream….. It's not like someone would find calendars with his art in them, hanging in a mall kiosk," Rusty said.

Fitz stiffened. She dropped her hand to her lap. "Is that how it's supposed to be? Art must be in mall calendars to be good?"

Fitz was downright intimidating, going straight for the kill at every turn. Again, her comment caught Rusty off guard as she probed him for weaknesses. The worst thing was he presented her with plenty of them.

"No, I made a judgment analysis. I suppose," he said. "I was just trying to be generous with my humor."

"Generosity is a facet of dominance." Fitz stared at Rusty with calculating eyes, waiting to gauge his reaction.

"Now you're toying with me."

"Am I? I thought you said you were deep. I'm just trying to keep the conversation on your advanced level," she said. Her grin was hard to read. It could have swayed from baleful entrapment to candid sincerity.

He brought his hands together and propped his elbows on his knees. "This isn't deep. You're picking everything I say apart and looking for my mistakes. I'm trying to make polite conversation and you're attacking me."

"Am I? For someone so set on self-preservation, you sure are giving me plenty of rope to hang you with." Fitz placed her dark red lips on the bottle of water and tilted her head back.

"I think so. If you want deep, let's take it up another level," he said, reclining and staring at the mirrored ceiling.

"Okay, let's." Fitz laid back onto the cushions, locking eyes with Rusty's reflection in the ceiling. They seemed to float on a sea of red. Her black-and-white striped shirt and his black button-down played well against the blood-colored backdrop of the couch cushions.

"How would you describe a Monet to a blind person?"

"You couldn't even describe a Monet to a person who wasn't blind."

Damn. She's pedantic as hell.

Dark tones of the conversation overrode Rusty's confidence, replacing it with trepidation, but he pressed on. A large part of his ego liked the challenge, being as stimulating as it was. In fact, it was the most stimulating conversation he'd had in years. "Can you think of a way to describe a Monet if you had to?"

"I guess you could always explain the texture by letting them touch something like a rough painting. And I'd have them taste blueberries for blue, and cherries for red."

"How would you describe green?"

"I would offer them a breath mint, and for purple, I'd let them eat a grape jelly bean," she said.

"I think a grape jelly bean would taste too tart," Rusty said, shaking his head and faking a sour face.

"Maybe you're right," she said. "Do you think it's a control thing?"

Rusty turned to his side and looked at Fitz as she continued to stare at his ceiling reflection. He studied her captivating profile. "What do you mean?" Rusty asked.

"Do you always try to control every conversation?"

"I didn't think I was controlling the conversation. It's just my way of cutting to the core, and weeding through the bullshit," he said.

"I see. It seemed you were trying to correct me, making you feel smarter by highlighting my perceived mistakes — censoring my opinions with yours — rejecting my ideas. The world knows grape jelly beans are tart, and I don't need you telling me 'as if' I'd never tasted a grape jelly bean."

Fitz rolled to her side, facing Rusty, watching his lips as he spoke.

"I wasn't trying to find fault in your comments. I know it may have sounded that way. I can see how it may have been presumptuous of me, but I was just rolling with the conversation." He turned his attention back to the ceiling. "I have this problem where I feel the need to fix things. When I see things that are out of balance with truth, they stand out to me, so I guess I'm always trying to right the wrongs of the world."

"Rusty. Have you ever considered the world doesn't need your fixing?"

He'd suspected Fitz possessed more understanding than she'd displayed. Now he was sure. She'd shut him down with a few simple words, and he was unaccustomed to being challenged; less so to being beaten. Dialectics was his thing, and he did not know how to feel about losing. But how could he disagree with her last inference? How could he disagree without appointing himself the pseudo-savior of humanity? — sanctimoniously hurling himself through life; writing the wrongs of everyone, while ignoring his own shortcomings; the epitome of hypocrisy. There was no way to reason his way around her question without highlighting his own egotism. The truth of it was, she was right. The world didn't need correcting. Even if it did, appointing himself the 'righter of wrongs' only highlighted his hubris, and Fitz was all too willing to point that out. Rusty always said he'd never force others to identify with his world views, but she'd unmasked the hypocrisy of his actions.

Fitz was a strong-willed person, and like Rusty, she would never burnish her opinions to impress others. He had to take it or he had to leave it. Fitz was not crazy and in fact, she was likely the most sane person Rusty'd encountered in a good long while…

A soft voice hung in the air, floating like soothing cellos, grounding Rusty, pulling him from the pensive place his thoughts slipped into. A warm palm rested on his arm. Her touch was soft. He turned to face her, mere inches away and close enough to feel her warm breath as she whispered.

"Hello? Are you still with me?" she asked with a voice as soft as a murmur.

Rusty looked at her, casting a reassuring smile. "Oh, I'm sorry. I was thinking about what you said. It made sense, and I wanted to process it all."

"We can talk about something else if you like," she said, rubbing his arm in reassurance.

"I'd like to see your art," he whispered back.

"Okay….. It's a date," she said.

Rusty's mood lightened with each passing syllable.

Being on a ship full of men dulled Rusty's mind. The feedback loop of casual conversations and uncontested philosophies softened his wit. Rusty was used to the logical, linear, thought process an all-male crew provided. His arguments repelled the mental rebuttals his shipmates challenged him with — the pedestrian arguments of cretins. But Fitz presented a larger hurdle. Her ideas were solid — a thick carapace, impervious to his dialectic gift of gab. In short, she was immune to his bullshit. She would not relent, nor would she succumb to Rusty's veiled attempts to impress her with pillow-talk. She made her position clear, while setting boundaries and negating his attempts at mental dominance.

And... Why the hell am I trying to challenge her intellect to begin with?

Rusty talked non-stop about his super-perfect adventures and his deep insightful concepts — always sitting around waiting to be heard, needing to be heard, needing others to validate his existence. He offered Fitz plenty of rope to hang himself alright — just an asshole among a distinguished list of other self-absorbed assholes to cycle through Fitz's life.

Finding his inane remarks in check, and realizing the universe controlled him and everyone else, the best he could mange was coming to terms with the insights she offered. In all his self-loathing introspection, one observation stood at the forefront of his observations. He liked Fitz. He grew fonder with each passing moment, and he feared the implications. Implications and complications often arose from attachments and affections.

Everything he had done that evening was an exercise in self-idolization. That was until a valley-girl simpleton who answered phones for a living shelved his grandiose notions of gender superiority.

He underestimated her and played the part of the condescending jerk. Wooing the small-town girl with his tales of glory, only to expose his warped ego. Providing her leverage to smite his pride in a most calculated manner.

She was not someone who argued just to argue — an outwitted troglodyte with whom everyone dismissed as stupid. No, she was an exquisite person who captivated Rusty, lured him in, and spent the past ten minutes relieving him of his surplus of amour propre.

Rusty was still zoned out, replaying the last few minutes in his mind, when Fitz broke his concentration. The softness of her voice enticed him from his self-loathing introspection.

"Do you want to go exploring with me?" she asked.

With a garnished smile, Rusty peered into her vibrant eyes. "That sounds fun. Where would you like to go?" he asked.

"We should let fate decide."

"I think that would be fun," he said. *Fate has a compass of its own.*

As they stood, Rusty found himself close enough to compare his height to hers. Fitz was taller than Rusty. It wasn't by much, but it was enough to notice. Insecurity masked as chivalry compelled Rusty to avert his eyes, forcing him to back up, while stepping aside to provide Fitz space to maneuver around the large plush cushions.

The two made their way down the darkened staircase as moonlight pierced the dusty windows, projecting frail beams across the steps and up the walls. Their shadows mixed with the long pale bands of light, silhouetting their dark shade across the ghostly lit hall — eerie shadows mixed with dark corners.

Exiting the staircase, a loud, booming voice echoed throughout the hard concrete structure, alarming the pair. Blume asked about Rusty's driving arrangements.

"Are you gonna take him back to base?" Blume shouted.

"Yes," Fitz said, stopping, quieting her step to respond.

"Rusty, when are you coming back?" Blume asked.

"I'm off Sunday at 'oh, seven hundred." Rusty stared at the darkened ground to better focus his hearing as he waited for Blume's reply.

"Okay, I'll see you Sunday."

Rusty looked up the shaft again. "Yes, I'll be here. Are you picking me up?" Rusty asked.

"Yeah, what time?" Blume asked.

"'Oh, seven-thirty," Rusty said.

"Okay. It was great seeing you again," Blume shouted. "I'm sorry we had little time to spend together, but I get it. You're in love." Blume shouted the last word for maximum effect, laughing. "Don't worry, we can catch up on Sunday."

"I'm not in love. What are you talking about?" Rusty said. He worried Fitz would notice him blushing.

Instead, Fitz lowered her head and laughed. "Bye Blume. Kiss Dani goodnight for me," Fitz said.

"I will. Hey Rusty, don't forget to shout my name out one time for me!" Blume said.

"Huh?" Rusty asked.

"You know what I mean."

"Good night Blume," Fitz said. She pulled Rusty's arm, urging him down the last few steps. "Come." She was the first to emerge into the darkened lobby. Electric light of Blume's condo was traded for the silver moonlight reflecting off of the desert sand, filling the lobby. It was bright enough to outline every shadow with precise detail. Outside, the lighter shade of sand played off the pitch black sky, making the landscape resemble the darkside of an alien planet.

The couple walked through the lobby, stepped into the brisk air, and climbed into the Jeep. Fitz pressed the clutch and turned the key, putting the jeep in first gear. Barking all four tires, the Jeep peeled out of the dilapidated parking lot. Chilly winds blew hard, howling past them as they hurried through Bahrain's dense night air.

"Where are we headed?" Rusty asked.

"To my place. You said you wanted to see my art."

"Well, that's capricious," Rusty said, surprised. He wanted to see her art, but he didn't think she meant right at that very moment.

"Well, you're the one who suggested it," Fitz said, and laughed.

"Don't threaten me with a good time."

Fitz winked at Rusty and put the Jeep into second gear as she merged onto the main two-lane highway. After ejecting the tape they were listening to on their way to Blume's place, Fitz reached into the console for a different cassette. She held the cassette close to her eyes, squinting to read the label, before inserting the tape into the dash's player, pushing it farther into the slot. Fitz leaned forward and pressed the large button with a big arrow. The bootlegged cassette played a tune Rusty knew well. It was an 80s new wave band from Liverpool.

"Do you like this song?" Fitz yelled, turning the radio up so loud the sound of the music overtook the wind.

Rusty nodded. Being as it was one of Rusty's new favorite songs, and because he knew the lyrics, he hummed along but not loud enough to be annoying. He'd seen the band play live in Chicago.

The two sailors didn't speak during the long trip to town. Fitz played her bootleg tapes, their sound quality being much better than Rusty'd expected, while Rusty tapped his fingers on his thighs, keeping pace with their beats, saying nothing for the entire duration of their return trip.

The Jeep ripped through town. Newer streets and bright lights gave Rusty a feeling of normalcy. They were back in civilization, or something close to it, and being around people relieved him.

There was no traffic at the late hour. The roar of Fitz's Jeep, amplified by the cool night air, disrupted the tranquil, sleepy town. Turning left, they pulled up to a retro-looking house. The single-floored dwelling reminded Rusty of the test houses used by the Army to observe the blast effects of atomic explosions. Painted a pastel baby aspirin blue and accented with white trim, the military built her home during the early 1960s. The sand-covered yard added to the overall test-case effect.

"Base housing," she said, rolling her eyes.

"I see. I'm sure it beats living in barracks. It looks cozy."

Fitz eased into the driveway and they both slid out of the Jeep. After a few steps, they paused outside her front door. She opened the unlocked door and flipped the light switch.

8

Rusty stepped into the foyer. The lighting was theatrical. He expected to see the dim glow of yellow incandescents, instead, a soft pure white light illuminated the room. The bulb cast synthetic sunlight onto an easel in the corner of her living room.

Stylized with a mid-century modern feel, the interior showed all the signs of being decorated by a professional designer. A long leather couch, minimalist wooden tables, and a walnut bookcase completed the look. It was stylish. Fitz imported an air of sophistication to an otherwise bleak governmental housing community, shaming the Navy's designers by comparison.

White walls emphasized the muted color palette of her home. The achromatic scheme of the room prevented contamination of the artist's color palette, and the sterile wall color was the calibrating equivalent of a musician's tuning fork, preventing ambient color reflections from tainting the artist's eye.

Fitz did not own a television. Her only entertainment was her books and music collection. She'd placed a modest record player and two large speakers on a repurposed bookshelf. She'd arranged two rows of records on the floor under the bookshelves.

"Would you like some music?" She asked, looking at him, trying to gauge his musical mood.

Rusty nodded.

Delicate fingers danced across the tops of the twelve-inch cardboard sleeves. Flipping through the row of vinyl albums like being in a record store, she paused on a specific cut. Having removed the record and placed it on the platter, she cued the needle and pressed play, filling the room with hip melodies of lounge jazz.

Her library was on a wall by her kitchen. She owned many books, two-hundred or more. What she lacked in quantity, she made up for in quality. It was an eclectic mix of contemporary non-fiction, genre fiction, literary fiction, and a notable amount of philosophy. Most of her books were timeless classics, not the hackneyed, decorative bound novels so often found in classic Victorian collections. Those uniformed books stacked in bulk collections with matching bindings, filled with dated constructs and outgrown theories science had long forgotten.

No, Fitz owned an extensive collection containing some of the most highly revered writings in all of literature. Critically acclaimed authors and their best work were mixed with other writers Rusty had never heard of.

There was an air conditioner perched in the opened window, but the brisk evening air negated the need for its artificial cooling.

A large ceiling fan rotated, stirring the stagnant air. She kept her windows open wide, allowing the gentle breeze to sweep through the room as curtains swayed in the steady flow of air currents. The dry air provided a pleasant contrast to the humid sea, which kept Rusty feeling oily for the past three months.

Raising her index finger, Fitz motioned him to follow her to an easel in the corner. Walking through the living room, he stopped under the bright spotlight. She'd laid her paints and dry pigments out, organizing them on her workstation — a vast assortment of powdered colors, from Cobalt Blues to Cadmium Oranges, and all colors in between, arranged in large glass jars like a colored spice cabinet. It was an alchemist's den used to transform crushed earth into pictorial works of art.

Exotic-haired brushes hung on a makeshift clothesline. Wooden clothes-pins gripped the brushes by their handles, dangling them with their bristles pointing down.

Fitz's voice broke the silence. "Hanging prevents the paint from seeping into the ferrules. Paint collects inside the ferrules and splays the bristles." Fitz displayed up-turned, fanned-out fingers, simulating frayed bristles. "Artist brushes are hard enough to come by, especially in Bahrain," she said.

A four-foot workbench ran alongside the easel. Her work stool was round and mobile. Hefty wheels facilitated easy rolling across hard terrazzo floors.

The focal point of the studio was the current painting placed on her easel. A black sheet covered the large painting. "It's a work in progress," she's said. Fitz stepped behind her painting, placing her back on the wall. She lifted the sheet and pulled it toward her, revealing her latest efforts.

Rusty stood with his hands on his hips as he took it all in. Fitz studied Rusty's expression as she watched from behind her canvas — waiting for subconscious tells which would remove any chance of him lying.

His expression was tinted by deep immersion — taking the proper time to understand what he was looking at.

It was a bunch of blobs of paint; the pattern did not look familiar. His first impression showed the painting seemed amateurish, like a poor Jackson Pollock ripoff.

He placed his interlaced hands on the top of his head and squinted without taking his eyes off her painting, struggling to find something positive to say. Anything positive would suffice. If he lied, she would know. Above all else, what she expected was sincerity.

Rusty was unaware of his perspiration until sweat rolled down his neck, causing him to flinch. He inspected the ceiling, expecting to see a dripping air conditioner register filled with condensation. When Rusty returned his attention to her canvas, he realized his initial assessment was way off. There was nothing wrong with the 'Matter.' It was his 'Mind' in need of recalibration.

Many times before, Fitz saw the same puzzled look reflected in other people's expressions. Her frustrated eyes rolled as she waited to hear his critique.

As Rusty focused on the painting. Hundreds of images came into focus. The abstract forms weaved in and out of the canvas. It was not a Pollack rip off and it was not representational of something objective, a mere photocopy of a noun or group of nouns. It was an amalgamation of subjectivity. A playground for a viewer's imagination.

After many moments of careful consideration, he formed his opinion, all the time knowing she'd studied his every expression. It was one of the best abstract paintings he'd ever seen.

It was a five-foot Rorschach inkblot, in monumental form. The painting was not symmetrical like a traditional inkblot; it was more like a surreal landscape. Her painting reminded him of an alien, shadowy landscape, where random forms replaced familiar objects rendered across the canvas. It was foreign, and not representational of anything found in life. Well, almost anything. Her work was as subjective as looking for faces on a cloudy afternoon.

She'd added minor tweaks of her own interpretation to some of the abstract forms. If an inkblot resembled a silhouette of a dog, she highlighted it, adding relief, rendering it to look more like a dog. If a shape resembled a fish, she painted fins, adding relief to the otherwise flat dimension of the inkblot.

All the refinements calibrated the viewer's gaze and did not dictate objective meanings. Fitz read the surface of subjectivity. Her paintings obeyed her many rules of light and perspective without forcing her agendas onto the viewer. It was original, as original as anything he had ever seen.

Rusty dissected the process. On an aesthetic level, the painting was in line with most art. It would present well in any gallery, especially the big ones in NY or Paris. Her work conformed to a proper balance of color, line, and value — it flowed and its technique was consistent.

With his evaluation complete, he found himself unable to plan his review. Rusty struggled to find the right words as he leaned in toward the painting. It was very dynamic. "I like the subjectivity of it. Did you see these objects and then render them, or did they happen by accident?" he asked.

Fitz perked. "A little of both. I start with automatic painting, then switch to traditional painting halfway through."

"Do you have more?"

"Yes, I tuck them away in my closet," she said.

Rusty turned his head to look for her closet. Not seeing it, he glanced back at the painting. His forehead furrowed with studying intensity.

"It's everything a painting should be. Academics aside, originality and innovation are what I am drawn to. It's incredible how the painting takes on an emergent quality. I've never seen a painting do this. It's one of the most original works I've ever seen in person. It is innovative, and I do not use the term 'innovative' very often."

Fitz walked behind him. She held her hands behind her back and smiled. "I'm glad you like it… Truth be told, you are the first person to understand my painting. I've shown it to people, and they don't get it. Thank you for taking the time to look and understand."

Rusty's measured voice interrupted the long silence. "Plato disliked art, believing it to be a cheap imitation of physical objects. But I've always seen Plato's narrow view of art as an erroneous understanding of an artisan's intent," he said.

Fitz walked to her canvas.

Rusty's gaze followed her. "Art is an actual object — a material extension of the mind. It is the artist's mind as it manifests into the physical world — the artist's mind as it sculpts matter in the most primal sense, manipulating matter into a piece of the artist's own essence. Art is a beautiful example of the mind-matter connection. In all its forms, art is the closest thing to free will there is."

"Well, then. You offered more than I expected, and I am so grateful for your insight. I think it makes sense, and I've never thought of art like that," Fitz said. "I'm convinced you'll be a fine critic one day."

They smiled at the moment before turning their attention to other things. Fitz covered the painting and strolled to Rusty, standing next to him, teasing her fingers through his bangs like a child with a new doll. The overhead flood light cast long shadows over her features and Rusty noticed just how symmetrical hers were.

The music stopped, and she walked to her record player to change the record. She grabbed the first record of the stack, hinting it might be a favorite. Her new selection had a primitive groove to it, and it was a musician Rusty'd never heard before. The relaxing music of a Hawaiian luau, or an exotic beach in the Southern Pacific. 'Girl from Ipanema' type of vibe. Fitz lowered the volume, making it more conducive to conversation.

"I like how you decorated your place. Where did you get the furnishings?" Rusty asked.

"I didn't. These are military issue. I bought the rug, the record player, books, and my art stuff," she said.

"Holy shit. I figured you designed this. It is *real* mid-century furnishings then?" he asked.

Fitz laughed. "Yeah. I guess it is. Should I take it with me and sell it back home?"

"I need to get you onboard my ship so you can decorate my bunk."

"I would totally decorate the shit out of your bunk," she said.

They both laughed at each other. "The 'shit' out of it?" Rusty asked.

"The. Shit." she said, laughing. Fitz twirled her hair. Her thick locks bounced as she tugged on them.

"Who are we listening to?" he asked.

"Martin Denny. I love his lounge music," she said.

Having never heard of Martin Denny, he found he liked the ambiance it provided. The mellow music was perfect for the evening setting.

Just then, a brisk gust swept through the room, and crisp air caressed Rusty's face.

Fitz watched the rotating record player. "I feel like making hot tea. Would you like some hot tea?" she asked.

"Yes, thank you."

Fitz filled a modest-sized kettle with water. It was the perfect pot for a single person, living alone. The cold water overflowed and ran across her hand. She slid the kettle onto the gas burner while igniting the stove's pilot. Blue flames erupted in a starburst pattern, cradling the bottom of the stainless pot.

"Do you like the Navy?" she asked. She removed a towel from a drawer and patted her hands dry.

"I expected more. I hoped for excitement, but I'm bored with the daily grind. All we do is simulate war drills, have meetings, and sweep the ship," Rusty said, thinking about the months leading up to his enlistment, recalling the excitement he felt as his first day of bootcamp approached, and how contrasted it was to his current situation onboard.

She turned to face him and smiled. "Oh, war drills, meetings, and cleaning. So it's like working in my office."

Rusty chortled. "I bet it is. Office politics and cleaning are universal Navy practices."

The pair sat on the couch, resuming the conversations but with deeper undertones.

"Do you believe in free will?" she asked.

"No. I feel everything is determined. The only reality anyone ever experiences is their unique present moment. The state of the physical world they find themselves in, determines their reality. Reality then determines their every thought and motivation, even if the person is not aware of it."

"Wow. Sounds like a real bummer."

"Not if you come to terms with it," Rusty said. "If you find peace knowing you are not in control, then it's comforting."

"And yet you feel you need to right the wrongs in the world."

"I agree with you. I am going to try much harder to just go with the flow of things. Also, you're right, it's not my place to fix the world," Rusty said. "A perfect example of determinism would be 'knowing I like you and there is nothing I can do about it.' In fact, I believe you are beautiful in all the ways a person can be."

Judging by her flushed expression, his admission surprised Fitz.

Rusty inched closer to Fitz. An unexpected intimacy steered their conversation, gripping them both by surprise as if the revelation had only just occurred; neither having recognized their mutual attraction until that very moment.

As Rusty leaned toward Fitz, she did not shy away.

With a hushed voice, Fitz said, "I'm unbalanced and have prescribed medication I'm not taking."

Rusty grinned. "I like that. I need theater in my life."

With eyes closed, their parted lips met.

A brief pause only fueled their fervor. Rusty backed off, lifting his eyes to meet hers. Her rosy, flushed cheeks contrasted with the lightness of her delicate complexion.

"Your lips are sweet."

"Oh, oops. Sorry, it's from my flavored lip balm," she said. "The desert chaps my lips."

"Don't apologize."

Engrossed in the moment, mundane thoughts slipped from his mind, taking with it all understandings but one. Her essence carried him away to another place. His hand caressed her cheek as they leaned onto the couch's backrest.

Breathing hard, Fitz paused. She pulled away with cautioned eyes. "I don't want to get hurt."

"I don't either," Rusty said.

"This relationship could get complicated," Fitz whispered.

"I'll deal with complicated later." Rusty pecked his lips up the side of her neck, stopping just below her earlobe.

Fitz shifted her hips, climbing across to straddle Rusty's lap.

"Your hands feel so nice." Her soft voice tingled his ear. She caressed his cheek and slid her delicate fingers down his chest. Her low-hung hair swayed, curtaining his face, blocking out the light, and amplifying their intimacy as her auburn tips tickled his shoulders.

She placed her hands over his, directing his touch — pulling him closer. Eager hands reached under one another's clothing, exploring and caressing.

It was then the kettle whistled and screamed, pausing the moment.

Fitz sat up with disheveled hair and a lazy smile. Rusty rested his palms on her hips and squeezed as she leaned back, pressing her hands to his chest. Pouting her bottom lip, she exhaled and blew her bangs away from her face, blowing at her hair in frustration. "Whew," she said, looking at the tiny annoying kettle. "Don't move."

Fitz dismounted Rusty's lap and rushed to the stove. Her pants were still unbuttoned and close to falling. Curvy hips swayed as she strolled into the kitchen.

As fate would have it, Rusty peeked at his watch and the hands read 11:30 p.m. "Oh shit! I have to be back on the boat in fifteen minutes! I have the Saturday morning mid-watch and I need to relieve the watch at twenty-three forty-five. Shit, shit, shit!"

With confidence, she turned off the burner. "I'll get you there," she said. Having already walked halfway to the door, Fitz buttoned her pants and fixed her bra before Rusty even got off the couch. She grabbed her keys and slipped her feet into shoes she had laid by the door.

Rusty stood and met Fitz at the door. She put her hand on his chest. "Relax. We're only five minutes from the base. I've cut it closer than this getting to work."

Minutes later, they arrived on base and passed through the gate with no delays, stopping at the end of the pier.

Rusty's panicked hands patted across his lap as he inventoried his pockets, looking for his wallet. Fitz leaned in. Her delicate hands caressed his arm, interrupting his search with her feminine touch.

"I need to find my wallet," he said.

"Just go with the flow. Either you have it, or you don't. Searching your pockets will do you no good now. Kiss me and you can frisk yourself on the quarterdeck." Something about the way she said it made Rusty laugh, and he paused his frantic search.

"When are you off duty?" she asked. Her warm voice tempted Rusty's "unauthorized absence." Fitz tried to conceal her disappointment with his sudden departure. There was unfinished business, and they both weighed the value of disciplinary action against satiating their desires. But in the end, logic prevailed.

"Sunday morning. There's no muster on Sunday," he said.

"Then I suppose I'll see you Sunday?"

"As long as Blume doesn't forget to pick me up. I'm bringing some friends. But I'm sure I'll see you there."

"Oh, he'll be here to get you. I'll make sure he doesn't get too drunk to be hung over," she said. "Even if I have to water his beer down."

"I had a great time tonight. Thank you so much for taking me to his house." Rusty returned to his search, finding his wallet in his back pocket.

"Well, I had fun too," she said.

She reached for him and put her hand behind his neck, pulling him closer, not letting go, demanding he stayed with her until the very last moment. The few minutes felt much longer, and Rusty could not recall having experienced such a passionate moment.

"I don't want to, but I need to run," he said. His gaze traced the contours of her face, bouncing from her lips to her eyes and back again. Wet light sparkled on her quivering lips, and the soft glow of her complexion reminded him of fine porcelain. Fine details of Fitz's essence lodged itself in Rusty's mind, and he knew this would be a moment he'd never forget.

"I know. See you Sunday," she said, releasing her grasp.

Rusty jumped from the Jeep and jogged to the Savannah. He waved to Fitz as he skirted across the gangplank, lagging more minutes than he liked, but confident he'd made it onboard with time to spare.

9

Later that evening, Rusty prepared to stand the Roving Patrol Watch. After changing into his dungarees, he climbed the ladder and exited Berthing through its hatch, headed to the Chow Hall.

Nighttime on a moored ship was most unusual. Liberty reduced the crew's compliment to a third, as everyone not on duty had left the ship to go ashore. While moored, the ship's interior was always lit by bright light, contradicting the dim ambiance while underway. During times at sea, most of the interior was illuminated by dark red bulbs when operating during night hours.

Onboard his ship, Rusty climbed another ladder well and walked down the port side passageway to the Mess Deck.

Mux huddled at a corner table in the mess hall, playing chess with a shipmate named Ocean.

Ocean was a Samoan from Hawaii. He was a hulk who stood six and a half feet tall, and weighed a metaphorical metric ton. Universal evolution purposed him with solid muscle, and with arms as big as an average person's thighs, he could lift a schoolhouse. Ocean spent most of his spare time in the ship's weight room, complaining to the supply officers in attendance that they needed to order more weights, as his max press exceeded what the gym offered.

The Gunner's Mate second class intimidated even the most senior of officers, commissioned or not; intimidation that stemmed from his habit of making himself comfortable in other people's intimate space while talking. Ocean's assertive mannerisms were unintentional and often misread, but Rusty wondered if Ocean was aware of the glitch he caused the chain of command.

Ocean stood, almost walking off to refill his orange bug juice, when

Rusty gripped his forearm. Using both hands, Rusty pulled Ocean back into his chair. "I need to tell you guys something. I found my buddy Blume, and he invited us to his house this Sunday. Do you want to go?"

"Sounds fun," Ocean said. "Will there be girls?"

"I don't know. Maybe. But even if there aren't, it sure beats hanging out in the Mess Hall with a bunch of nerds," Rusty said.

Mux locked eyes with a table full of Signalmen playing Blackjack. "He didn't mean you guys," Mux said.

The Junior Signalmen resumed their game without offering a response.

Rusty studied the chessboard. "You better castle or he's gonna catch your king." He pointed to Ocean's black rook and waited for Mux to see the move, pausing long enough for Mux to realize Ocean's intent. Although Rusty had caught Ocean's plan three moves ahead, he assessed his friend's strategy with precision.

"Thanks a lot," Ocean said.

"Sorry, I was just thinking out loud, I guess." Rusty smiled and shrugged at Ocean.

"Yeah. I'm in. How did you find your friend?" Mux asked.

"I met a girl. It's a long story, but I'll tell you later. I gotta relieve the watch."

"A girl?" Ocean asked. "Is she cute or is she just 'boat cute'?"

"Boat cute" was a derogatory term used by sailors to describe the beauty of "not so pretty females" after being around them for long months at sea. Rusty cringed. He disliked the demeaning term. Ocean meant nothing bad by it. It was just common slang — jargon used by everyone onboard.

"No. She is brilliant. You guys'll meet her Sunday," Rusty said, adjusting his gig line. He peered at his denim trousers and wiped his fingers across his scruffy chin. He failed to shave and farmed a considerable amount of stubble over the previous thirty-six hours.

"It will have to do, you 'un-sat' bastard," Mux said. "Maybe you can tell the OOD you have a 'no-shave chit.'"

"He would want to see it, and besides, I'm not worried," Rusty said.

"You ain't gotta 'be worried' to get your ass chewed out," Mux said, laughing. He held an outstretched palm and Ocean slapped it.

"Yeah, I just hope they don't notice," Rusty said. He waved at his friends and scurried from the Mess Hall.

Mux waved goodbye while Ocean studied his next chess move.

* * *

Topside, large spotlights flooded the ship, casting strong theatrical lighting over various parts of her gray hull and superstructure. The lights cast shadows along weather decks, projecting unusual shapes on the uneven corners of exterior bulkheads, rocket launchers, and gun turrets.

Petty Officer Harp stood on the quarterdeck, leaning across the rail near the Savannah, focused on lazy mullets swimming in random directions near the water's surface, gulping air like large depressed koi-fish trapped in hot, oxygen-starved ponds.

"I am ready to relieve you," Rusty declared.

Harp hesitated before turning to look at his relief. "Great," he said, spitting into the small school of mullet. The older Petty Officer dipped his chest to the top rail and pushed off, sending himself back a few paces.

The two walked away from the Savannah, seeking larger waters to inspect the firearm. They meandered to the port side weather deck, facing the open sea, both of them surveying the seas for small crafts or midnight swimmers. Moonlight cast its reflection on the water, tracing a sparkling path that connected the horizon to Rusty's ship.

"I much rather stand Roving Patrol than sit on the Minewatch," Rusty said.

"Why is that?"

"Because I can walk around and piss when I want to."

"Ah." Petty Officer Harp unsnapped the holster and removed a large pistol. He pointed the unloaded pistol at the open water and pulled the slide back to inspect its empty chamber. Satisfied it was unloaded, he turned it over to Rusty. "Yeah, but you can sleep on Mine Watch," he said, smirking.

Rusty received the gun and slid his fingers along its chilled metal surface, inspecting it. The Colt 1911 bore the subtle blackened surface-rust patina from carrying the pistol for untold years of duty, and it smelled of iron and rust. "You can sleep on the Rover Watch too. You just need to know where to hide."

After completing his inspection, Rusty released the slide lock mechanism and his attentive hands guided the slide into battery, softening its impact.

Harp bit his lower lip and sighed.

Rusty sensed Harp's impatience. "It's not good to let it slam. It might crack the slide," he said, returning the gun to Harp's eager hands.

Harp gripped the handle and re-housed the empty pistol into the duty holster on his belt. He unbuckled the heavy belt and swung it around his waist, catching both ends with a single gripping fist. Extending his balled fist, he handed the belt to Rusty.

Rusty adjusted the belt to his usual size, as marked by the sixth eyelet. He swung the belt around his waist and latched the buckle before repositioning the belt to hang lower on his right hip.

"I relieve you," Rusty said, saluting while standing at attention.

Harp returned the salute. "I stand relieved," he said before strolling down the weather deck and disappearing into the shadows. Seconds later, streaking light revealed his position as he opened the door near the forward fan room.

Rusty checked in with MM1 Loudon, who was the night's Officer Of the Deck. He acknowledged Rusty had assumed the Roving Patrol Watch and noted the event in his logbook, listing the time of the turnover.

While standing watch in port, it was customary for the OOD to dress in formal attire because it presented a good impression for visitors. The OOD was dressed in his summer whites, and Rusty noted how pristine the man's uniform looked. It was as if Loudon had access to a dry cleaning source the rest of the crew lacked.

With his outstretched arms and a yawn, Rusty walked to the log to ensure Loudon noted the correct time.

23:45, the last minutes of a Friday night.

Rusty closed the logbook and centered it on the pedestal. "Welp, I'm making my rounds."

"Very well," Loudon said. He sighed and rolled his eyes before walking over to re-open the book.

Rusty strolled below to do an initial check on the primary spaces. The ship tasked him with inspecting vital areas, ensuring his shipmates locked their doors. Every thirty minutes, he had to go check in with the OOD. If he were to report late, even by a minute, the ship would go into General Quarters. To miss a check in would cost Rusty his ass, pissing the crew off for days and resulting in a Captain's Mast. 'Shooting pool with the Skipper,' as they say.

The Roving Patrol 'walked his post in a military manner, keeping always on the alert and observing everything within sight or sound.' It was a general order and while moored in a foreign port, it was an order Rusty obeyed without question.

As he made the rounds, he grabbed at random doors and kicked at others. Heavy locks and firm handles, cold and worn, felt immovable — as rooted as the frame of a giant bulldozer. He checked every space with fervent enthusiasm, jiggling the locks, tugging at first. But with deepening ferocity, his compounded efforts escalated as he tried his damnedest to break in. Hardened steel prevented him from entry, as their barred doors would not budge. Soft hands were no match.

The Armory was a veritable bank vault, shut-off by heavy gauge mesh. Contents of the compartment were on display for all to see. Objects tempted any passers-by, but remained out of reach from any lawless miscreants or aspiring thieves. Various gun smithing tools, laid scattered along the workbench. A cornucopia of awls, punches, and files littered the cluttered workstation.

Farther forward, in the ship's Focsle was the VLS launcher's main entrance. Thick, white bars like prison cell doors prevented access to sixty-one Tomahawk Cruise Missiles. Each missile was capable of mass destruction, and stood poised for launch at a moment's notice. Some were nuclear, and some were loaded with fragmented explosives. Each rocket afforded enough explosives to take out a few city blocks, or even the entire city, if one factored the non-conventional rockets into the equation. Combined, the total arsenal could remove a country the size of Texas.

Rusty kicked the door with all his might, trying to infiltrate their "Top-Secret" nuclear compartment. But the door did not even vibrate. "Take that, you rat bastard!" he said. He kicked the door again, but the force of his leg against the immovable barrier sent him flying, and he slammed into the adjacent bulkhead. Rusty had fun trying to break into the highest security spot on the ship, but a glance at his watch told him it was time to check in.

He ran to the ladder and popped out on the quarterdeck, completing the trip in less than thirty seconds. MM1 Loudon paced with his hands behind his back, looking at his shiny dress shoes and how they contrasted with the dull gray deck. He caught the door fly open just as Rusty spun around to secure its latch. Rusty saluted, while announcing, "Roving patrol reports 'all secure.'"

Loudon snapped to attention and returned the salute. "All secure. Aye," he said, resuming his steady pacing.

Boredom inspired Rusty's 'about-face' and he took off on another round, switching his route to thwart any would-be pursuers. Denim pants swayed at their heavy bell-bottomed hems, all the while his gun clanked in its low-hung duty holster.

Hours went by before Petty Officer Connelly relieved Rusty without incident. After having stood a four-hour watch, Rusty meandered below to his rack, climbing in after only removing his boots. With his curtain open, he lay in his bunk, staring at the overhead, thinking of Fitz.

Sunday morning arrived, bringing excitement to the day. Rusty felt like a child whose parents planned a sunny day at the beach. He kicked Mux's locker, ensuring his friend was up and ready. No one wanted to be late meeting Blume.

On days faced with dread and unease, it was always better to lie in bed to skirt duty, hoping the day would pass with no one bothering him. But on days like this, Rusty demanded the full amount of life the day owed him.

"Mux, get up," Rusty yelled.

Mux pawed his curtain, sliding it back. "I'm reading a book," he said with a measured voice.

"Shit man, why didn't you wake me up earlier? Whatcha reading?" Rusty asked. His excitement outpaced Mux's, for sure.

"It's called 'The Dharma Bums.' I'm reading chapter four." Mux stuck the mass paperback through the curtain to show Rusty its cover. "My parents sent it to me in my last care-package."

"That was very nice of them. I might need to read it after you're finished." Rusty said, tilting his head to better make out the book's cover. "But we are running late. So, get up. We need to get ready. I'm gonna go wake Ocean." Rusty could not wait to leave the ship. He needed to experience the events awaiting him — a day ripened by the promise of uninterrupted leisure.

Mux climbed from his rack and placed his book on his unmade bed.

Rusty banged on Ocean's bunk. "Dude, wake up. We need to get ready. The boat leaves in fifteen minutes. You better not be waxing your dolphin."

The curtain slid back. Large knuckles wiped at closed eyes, and the large Samoan swung from his rack. As he dressed, he showcased various articles of clothing, like a teen trying on clothes for a big date. "Yo Rusty, do you think this will work?"

"I don't know. I am wearing jeans and bringing my shorts. Just in case we go swimming or something." Rusty threw his rolled articles of clothing into a heavy gauge cotton backpack. It was one he'd carried since eighth grade.

"Swimming in the desert?" Ocean asked.

"Shit man, beachfront property surrounds us." Rusty said. "There's a beach around this entire island."

Ocean opted to wear his shorts and pack light. He disliked the tight feel of backpacks and didn't want to wear hot jeans in 102-degree heat.

On their way to the quarterdeck, the three cut their way through the breakfast line. Sailors on duty eyed them with envy, but no one objected when Ocean reached over their heads to solicit a plate full of eggs.

A light menu was all they needed, as time nagged them to be somewhere else. Rusty rolled large muffins in napkins, stuffing them in his bag. The three friends stood over a dining room table, and everyone made egg sandwiches with toast and bacon, before eating the sandwiches as they climbed their way topside, eager to depart the ship.

Seabee's or SIMA piled long rows of restocked pallets at the end of the pier. The pallets awaited pick up, but being as it was a weekend, Rusty requisitioned them for immediate use as benches. Oxidized iron nails protruded from the warped, rotten wood. The three sailors plopped onto the benches, mindful of the tetanus-laden spikes, while awaiting their ride. Few things in life were as anxious as a sailor waiting for a ride under the Bahraini sun.

Off in the distance, the three men heard Blume's radio long before they saw his car. Blume screeched to a halt just outside the gated entrance — accompanied by loud punk rock and dust clouds, both of which enveloped his car, shrouding his Mercedes in a blanket of grunge.

Squinting through the grit, Rusty jumped into the front seat. "Hey Blume, this is Ocean and Mux."

"Climb in, fellas," Blume said, turning down the radio.

Blume studied the men in his rearview mirror as they slid across the large bench seating. Ocean rubbed his palm over the soft leather. The interior of Blume's sedan smelled like the inside of an aged Volkswagen Bug, reminding Rusty of his high school days, tooling around with his friend, searching for endless parties.

Leaving base, they began the long stretch through the open desert to Blume's condo. The vocals of Jello Biafra as he sang about a "Holiday in Cambodia" made the trip go much faster than the previous drive with Fitz.

It would seem German cars handled smoother when travelling vast distances over open highways, than Jeeps. The Mercedes acquired all the panache eighty-four years of auto engineering could refine.

The Autobahn is no place for a Jeep.

"How did you find this place?" Mux asked.

"Some guys on base told me about it. We rotate the lease based on seniority." Blume said, shouting over the opened windows. "Not only do we rotate the condo, but we all rotate the cars, too. I am the fifth person to drive this old car. Hell, I don't even know who it's registered to."

"It's pretty far outside of civilization, huh?" Ocean asked. He stared out of the backseat window, looking at the dipping cables of the slacked power lines. Closing one eye, he lined the black cable up with the top of the car's window, watching as the sagging line dipped and rose, bouncing in cadence with the passing of each wooden pole.

The German car handled the long stretch of highway with a smoothness that even a Cadillac owner would appreciate. Designed to commute vast distances the Mercedes did a fantastic job of shortening the desert's highways as well.

As the four squids pulled up to Blume's building, Rusty eyed several trucks parked near the structure, with one truck capturing his attention.

Fitz had backed her white Jeep near the front of the building. Someone parked a pair of black dune buggies beside it, nearer to the building. At first, Rusty assumed they were regular dune buggies. However, upon closer inspection, he noticed the dune buggies were far from regular.

Blume parked the car and exited the driver's seat. After slamming the door, he looked at Ocean who was eyeing the black buggies from the back seat of the Mercedes. "Are you two gonna get down or sit there all day bakin' in the heat?" Blume asked.

Hot rays of light warmed their shoulders as they squinted at the alien-looking buggies.

On the top of the buggy's solid black roll cages, mounted machine guns lay wrapped in black nylon slipcovers. Their black covers blended the guns with the black frames and roll bars.

Mux touched the frame of the buggy closest to him. "Shit, that's hot," he said. "Why would anyone paint these black, in the desert?"

"To keep pussies like you outta them," Ocean said. He put his hand on the roll bar and held it for a few seconds. Heat forced him to repel his palm — rubbing it to cleanse the lingering inflammation.

It was funny at first — casual and all. But the more the entourage stared at the buggies, the more they saw. It was almost like details materialized the harder they studied the buggy's designs.

Large springs wrapped around beefy shocks and huge four-wheel disc brakes shined in the sunlight. The wheels were fatter than normal, adorned with large, knobby tires, making the trucks look like stealthy Baja racers — designed by angry engineering ninjas.

Their owners parked them side-by-side, ready for action or to await inspection. The wheels were all in perfect alignment, hinting at the attention to detail when parking them.

"What are these?" Ocean asked.

"They're called DPV's," Blume said.

"What is a DPV?" Mux asked.

"It stands for 'Desert Patrol Vehicle.' They are fast attack vehicles. Don't touch."

Ocean pointed at the large, center-mounted machine gun. "Dude, that is a .50-caliber machine gun."

"They're a terrorist's worst fucking nightmare," Blume said. He motioned to the lobby entrance and waved for them to follow. "Come on."

Rusty stood beside the vehicles. His curious eyes remained fixed as the group headed to the lobby. The last thing Rusty saw before turning to follow was a rocket launcher. To be more precise, it was a FIM 92 Stinger rocket launcher, mounted between the passenger's seat and the frame. Rusty closed his mouth and hurried to catch up with the others.

Sunlight urged the entourage into the building, but it was darkness that forced them to pause in its main lobby, decontaminating from the sun's blinding radiation.

Ocean studied the elevator. "Does it work?" he asked.

"Yes, but I never take it. I wouldn't know how to get you out if it broke down," Blume rubbed his forehead, no doubt contemplating a familiar scenario he'd visualized countless times.

The large Gunner's Mate pressed the button, grabbing the attention of daring eyes fixated on the intrepid Hawaiian.

"Okay, but I warned you." Blume said.

The door opened, and everybody watched the Gunner's Mate step into the elevator.

"Vaya Con Dios, Brah," Mux said, waving with parade hands.

Ocean winked and pointed at Mux, just as the door slid closed with a metallic thud, cutting Ocean off from view. Ocean banged on the inside of the steel door. His muffled voice echoed from within the stainless box, telling everyone there's no fucking lights and he couldn't see the damn buttons.

Blume pressed the 'up' button, opening the door. "Hold your finger on the number five button, then push it and the door will close. It'll send you up to my floor," he said.

"I know how to work an elevator," Ocean said.

"Do you?" Mux asked. His eyes widened, and he pressed his lips, throwing the proverbial "dumb-ass" glance in Ocean's direction. Too preoccupied with the darkened control panel, Ocean failed to notice Mux's mockery. As instructed, his thumb pressed the number five button, prompting the elevator door closed again. After a few squeaks, the motor moaned as old cables pulled the heavy elevator up.

"Lets beat him to the top," Rusty said.

"Okay, maybe we can scare the piss outta him," Mux said.

The grown men raced like kids, and the rush to victory was too much to contain their laughter. Elbows jabbed, hands pulled, and feet snared as the group of miscreants fought their way up the stairway. Mux pulled Rusty's hand from the railing, sending him backwards a few steps.

"Shhhh. Don't yell or he'll hear us," Blume said, placing a finger over his puckered lips. He struggled to curb his fervor for winning, but the thrill of competition vented itself in giggles.

Rusty bumped into Mux. "Get off me, bitch," Mux said.

Rusty stopped snickering long enough to answer. "Dude. Please don't grab my ass."

Footsteps and laughter reverberated through the stairwell, and their loud sounds threatened to betray their stealthy intent. Regardless, the racing sailors beat the elevator to the top floor, where they waited for the doors to open — but nothing happened.

"Open the damn door!" Ocean yelled, banging from the inside of the sealed lift.

Blume yelled into the thin black seam of the stainless doors. "You're stuck! I warned you."

Ocean yelled again. "Open the…" The delayed opening of the doors silenced him in mid-sentence.

Everyone stared as Ocean emerged from the dark elevator. He loomed over Blume who stood a solid foot shorter than Ocean. "Did you know it would do that?"

Blume shrugged. "Do what? I never use it." He walked to his big red door and went inside the penthouse, yelling as he crossed the threshold. "Reveille-Reveille, douche-nozzles. Wake yer sorry asses up."

The funny thing was, most everyone was already up. A group of people laid on the floor, covered in a vast web of interlocked blankets, while others lay on the couch.

Everyone was busy in conversation, planning their day. It was still early morning and the oncoming day held potential, but the people under the blankets seemed in no hurry to get motivated.

Dani greeted Blume. She studied the group of clean-cut squids, fresh off the boat. "Hi Rusty, it's nice to see you again."

"Hey Dani, these are my friends Mux and Ocean." Rusty said.

Fitz was seated on the patio porch, along with another female friend of hers. Chairs overlooked the west end of the building, facing the pool deck. Fitz sat in an Adirondack chair, with her legs folded, tucking her knees to her chest. She'd perched her bare feet on the seat and her delicate arms waved at the empty air around her as she spoke to the woman at her left. Her friend wore dark clothing and her black lipstick complimented long strands of jet-black hair. Looking closer, Rusty studied her blue highlights as the sky reflected off stray strands floating in the wild breeze.

The Beatnik and the Goth.

Rusty gripped a drink from the fridge. The three sailors stuck together, clearing out a spot at the table. A stack of playing cards lay next to empty beer cans and wine bottles, daring Mux to grab the stack and start shuffling the deck.

Dani cooked eggs and bacon. "Would anyone like some breakfast?"

"No, thank you. We ate before we left the ship," Mux said.

"Tonight, we're playing poker. Do you guys want to play?" Blume asked.

Mux stopped shuffling and inspected the deck of cards, ensuring it was unmarked. "Yeah. I'd like to play," he said, placing the cards back on the table.

"I didn't bring any cash," Ocean said.

A blanket flew off, revealing one man who slept among the pile of people laying on the couch. Clad in skivvies, the unidentified man walked to the fridge and removed a bottle of water. His fingers scratched at his bare chest as he stared out of the tiny sink window. The man twisted the bottle top and took a drink of the crystal clear water, turning to stare at Ocean. "We don't play for money."

"Everyone meet Tody. He likes to deal the cards." Dani winked at Rusty. "I think he cheats," she said.

Tody smirked and winked at Dani. "You'll never prove it."

The large man was almost as big as Ocean and he wore a full beard — a full beard that incited curiosity and one that made him appear older. Rusty just knew he was a Spec-Ops guy of some sort. Maybe a 'Navy SEAL,' or a civilian contractor for the government.

Movement stirred under the large coverings as blanketed men and women rustled beneath the sheets, no doubt recuperating from their long night of hard drinking. One of the two bearded men perused the crowded kitchen. He assessed the situation and laid his head back down, unconcerned with any threats the newcomers might have posed.

It seemed like a small SEAL team spent the night on the couch of Blume's penthouse.

Later on, one by one, everyone sat up, replaying events of the night before, and making new plans for the day ahead.

Tody turned to Blume and Dani. "I have to take these fools to a meeting. I should be back later this afternoon. Do you need me to get anything while I'm gone?" he asked.

"I think we have enough hotdogs and burgers. Could you grab some ice?" Blume asked.

"Sure thing," Tody said. He finished his water and placed the empty plastic container in a separate bin from the regular trash.

Naked girls, bundled in a group, struggled hard to remain covered. Now and then, one girl would kick the blanket off, revealing glimpses of bare bodies and private parts. Giggling voices squeaked while the others yanked the blankets back, shouting at their friends for kicking the blankets off.

Blume walked to his bedroom. On his way, he addressed his friends in the kitchen, "I'm gonna take a shower. You guys make yourself at home."

On the patio, Fitz faced the sliding door — blinded by the silver-tinted glass — her reflection prevented her from seeing inside the condo. A comment made by Fitz's friend incited laughter, which was followed by an occasional glance at her reflection. Now and then, Fitz would tuck her shoulder-length hair behind her ear. Her shorter bangs hung down the sides, near her temples.

Rusty felt awkward not knowing how to approach her without seeming clingy. He opted to lie low. Passive.

Fitz appeared to be in a cheery mood. She wore dark blue Capri trousers and a white button down blouse. Her black, slip-on shoes lay on the concrete patio deck, beneath her chair.

With a tall stretch, she stood in order to straighten her blouse. Her hands reached for the long sliding door, and countering with all her weight, she flung the glass panel open. Air conditioning escaped the condo, mixing with the dry desert winds, sending her hair dancing in wild directions. She raked her hair to manage the frizz and scanned the room as she closed the patio door.

"Rusty," Fitz said. Her eager legs negotiated the obstacle course of naked people. She approached Rusty, kissing him on his cheek.

"Hi," Rusty said. He turned to his two shipmates. "These are my friends. This is Mux and this is Ocean."

"It's nice to meet you both," she said.

Mux and Ocean exchanged glances, and then they looked at Rusty with wide eyes.

"I'm from Hawaii and Mux is from Texas," Ocean said, not sure what else to say.

Fitz smiled. "Wow, that's great! Anyone want a beer?"

"Thanks, but it's too early for me." Rusty said.

"Well, let's make coffee then."

Tody tossed an empty water bottle in the bin and grabbed his beard, straightening it, before addressing the pile of naked people. "Let's head home."

The squad of men slid into their skivvies and sprang from beneath the cover of wool. Each man got dressed in their camouflaged desert fatigues, which lacked identifying markings.

Tody tightened his belt as he walked to the couch. With playful hands, he clapped a girl on her exposed rear. "See you later."

Still nude, the blonde girl jumped on Tody and her possessive arms grabbed him, pulling him to her entitled lips.

Embarrassment so often arrived without warning and Mux and Ocean diverted their gaze. What else were they to do when confronted with naked strangers?

"I'll be back before you know it," Tody whispered.

"Hurry," the blonde woman said.

Tody grabbed a duffle bag near the couch and followed the other men out. On his way through the kitchen, he stopped and kissed Dani and Fitz on their cheeks.

10

Fitz presented everyone with a bag of coffee beans. The flashy label depicted a stereotyped cartoon of a Hawaiian Hula Dancer, showcasing a bag of coffee. On the bag, large letters spelled "Kona." The exotic black-haired female modeled the bag most seductively, and the marketing depicted a more touristy vibe than any real authentic Hawaiian culture.

"It's Kona coffee," Fitz said, pouring measured scoops of beans into a grinder. "I love the smell of fresh-ground coffee beans."

Ocean's eyebrows raised. He sprang from the dinner table and walked to Fitz, inspecting the thick, soft paper bag. "Kona coffee is the best coffee on the planet! You can taste the lava from the volcanoes. May I have a cup?"

"How about I make an enormous pot and we can all have some?" Fitz placed the glass coffeepot under the faucet as water filled the empty container, ensuring everyone would receive generous portions.

"Hell yeah, thank you," Ocean said. "Lava is Earth's freshest dirt, and it makes the coffee taste so clean. It doesn't have all those weird after-tastes like regular coffee. Where'd you get it?"

Fitz shouted over the loud sound of the coffee grinder. She winced at the obnoxious sounds for fear of disturbing the girls, who had climbed back under the blankets. "My mom sends me care packages all the time. She travels to Hawaii once a month. While she's there, she picks it up for me."

"What are you guys, rich or something?" Ocean asked.

"No, she works for a design group in San Clemente. They fly her to Hawaii on business. So she buys five bags at a time and sends me one bag every week." Fitz said.

"I haven't gotten a care package in more than a year," Mux said. "The last thing I got was sardines, oysters, and crackers."

Tired of waiting, the goth woman opened the sliding door and entered the penthouse. Everyone eyed the dark-haired woman as she made her way over the blanket, stepping on anyone who placed themselves in her path.

"This is my friend Beyatte," Fitz said.

Beyatte waved at those seated around the large dining room table, indifferent to their stares. "Charmed."

She was an older girl, in her late twenties or early thirties. Someone later described her as "bitterly" single, but blasé was more accurate.

As Beyatte stood in front of the open fridge, smoke rose from a dangling cigarette pinched between dark-painted lips. She read the beverage selection like a fashion designer looking at the new fall line of dresses. "I think I'll have water," she said, turning around. She glared at two slack-jawed sailors, then she set her eyes on Rusty.

"Let me guess. You're Rusty," Beyatte said.

Mux and Ocean gawked at their friend.

"Hi, yes. It's nice to meet you," Rusty said, pointing to his shipmates. "This is Mux and Ocean."

Beyatte was an attractive woman. She wore dark eyeliner, heavily shadowed, and pulled her silky black hair into a tight ponytail, which added to her dominant demeanor.

Together, Fitz and Beyatte resembled two Bohemians — fashion models stepping off a sailboat onto a pier in Portofino, Italy.

Without warning, the master bedroom door flung open. Blume stood in the doorway, wearing sunglasses and shorts. "Did you guys bring your bathing suits?"

"Yeah, why?" Mux asked.

"He likes to go on the roof," Dani said.

"Come with me." Fitz grabbed her coffee and rushed to take Rusty's arm. With coffee in hand, the pair made their way to a door installed in the back corner of the kitchen. A utility door provided access to empty stairs leading through a tight maintenance staircase, where at the top of the stairs, another door led to the roof.

Before opening the door, Fitz paused at the top landing and threw on a pair of Ray-Bans. Shiny black lenses with shiny black frames complimented her auburn hair and black-and-white striped shirt.

The couple surfaced onto the roof, and Rusty squinted, struggling to survey the layout of the rooftop through the painful glare. White paint coated the entire deck. The roof was dirty, but dazzling. Amplified by the sun, white paint facilitated the tanning process from every angle.

Sunshades hung from the doorway to the far edges of the parapet, defining the perimeter of the roof. Large, black, triangular sails blocked a fair amount of light, providing oversized shade for anyone seeking refuge from the sun's savage power.

Lawn chairs and lounge chairs lay scattered on the deck. An eight-foot wide watering trough, used for hydrating cattle, was repurposed as a makeshift pool — with no obvious explanation on how the large tin tub found its way up onto the roof.

Behind the table, near the door, stood a shiny stainless grill with a long wooden plank reserved for food preparation. Blume, or someone else, converted the roof into their personal pool deck. It was an oasis on the rooftop, just as Blume declared. It wasn't formal, not like the penthouse, but it was cozy, considering the desolate nature of their location.

Arid winds picked up, blowing from the east. From the rooftop's vantage point, a panoramic scan of the desert revealed a big, blue sky in all directions. For 360 degrees, nothing but a single row of disappearing power lines, fading off to a hazy vanishing point and the ghostly hint of the city's skyline to the north. The city's subtle sliver line appeared faint, almost imperceptible from miles away.

Fitz removed a chair from under the table. Shade from the makeshift sail-gazebo mixed with the breeze, providing an extra cooling effect. Decorative ribbons, tied to a rope, swayed in the gentle wind. Glass wind chimes tingled as tin sails suspended on thin strings moved brass strikers from shard to shard, resulting in a dainty chorus of *tinks* and *clings*.

"I thought about you last night," Fitz said.

His wandering eyes turned toward Fitz, focusing on her lips. "I thought about you, too."

"What did you think about?" she asked. Absorbed in eager anticipation, she pressed nervous palms to her thighs.

"Aside from the moment we spent on your couch?" he asked. He felt his face blush, prompting him to look away.

"I talked about you so much last night. I think it irritated Dani," she said, grabbing Rusty's hand to inspect his open palm.

Rusty watched her hands. His gaze followed her arm to her eyes. "I couldn't stop thinking about your painting. It's great, and you should have no trouble getting a gallery showing somewhere. Hell, anywhere, if you chose to," he said.

Delicate fingers traced his lifeline backward to his love line. "I don't know if art exposure is what I want."

"I can understand your concern," he said. "But recognition for a new style of art is much bigger than your wants. Think of all the people you can influence and how you could contribute to art."

"Do you think it's original? So much so that it could be a new art style?" she asked, squinting her nose and cocking her head like a puppy listening to exotic whistles. She released his hand.

His hand retreated. "I wouldn't call it a new art movement. Maybe a new style, though. It'd still be Abstract, but an important sub-genre of Abstract art. I've seen nothing that compares to it. As far as I know, there's nothing in the Abstract movement, touching on what you're doing."

Comfortable silence filled the table, and several minutes passed until the rest of the group came topside. The intruders sat around the table, disturbing the intimacy of their conversation.

Rusty locked eyes with Blume. "Wow, this is something. Did you make this, or was it like this when you moved in?"

"A little of both." Blume said the grill and sails were his, but he didn't have any idea how the pool arrived.

The door slammed open, and three girls in skimpy bikinis emerged, wearing enormous hats and large sunglasses. They threw beach towels across the backs of colorful lounge chairs and strutted to check the pool's temperature before sitting — each girl dipping their toes in and commenting on how warm the water was.

The sunbathers held their ponytails clear of their shoulders, as they took turns rubbing tanning butter along one another's bodies — the glossy sheen of which mesmerized Ocean and Mux.

Fitz grinned and rolled her eyes at Rusty, who met her gaze, smiling.

Rusty asked Fitz how she ended up stationed in Bahrain. "I would have thought you could write your own ticket anywhere you wanted." He was aware the Navy offered orders, according to class GPA rankings — the best in the class got first pick and the selection order went down the list. "You seem like a smart person."

Her smile waned. Trading curiosity with regret and sensing his question was in poor form, Rusty belayed his last question. "I'm sorry. It's the last thing I should have asked."

"My boyfriend, well, ex-boyfriend, said he was going to pick orders to be stationed here. He talked me into picking orders so we could be together."

She folded her legs into a fetal position, pulling her thighs to her chest while pressing her chin to her knees. She watched her wiggling toes as they waved up and down. "I was a week ahead of him. So, I got my pick of orders. Bahrain was at the bottom of the list," she said. "Yes. My scores were high. I could've picked anywhere, but I skipped the best ones, Germany, Pearl Harbor, and even Japan. I chose Bahrain because the dumbass had such a low GPA. He knew he had the worst selection of duty packets and figured he stood a good chance of getting Bahrain. He said he wanted to be in the desert and we could share our time here together. So I picked Bahrain and then he picked Guam." She dropped one foot, pressing it to the deck. "I guess I wasn't so smart after all."

Rusty wanted to extend words of comfort, but offered only silence instead.

Laughter filled the dead space between their conversation as the bikini girls giggled and rubbed more oil across one another's tanned backs. Their laughter seemed to mock Fitz, contrasting the dark underpinnings of her backstory.

"What does it say about me, when I give up my dreams for someone else's?"

The question was rhetorical, and Rusty knew it. Even if he had the answer, it was un-welcomed. Instead of offering sagely advice, he listened, doing his best to withhold judgment.

The Yeoman and the Electronic Tech sat in shared contemplation. After a few moments, he looked at her. Her expression reflected the regret of having been duped by her ex-boyfriend. Fitz turned to face the wind and a reassuring smile crossed her lips, hinting that all seemed well once more. Her well-manicured fingers wiped a lonely tear from her cheek. "Oh, I'm sorry to be a bummer. Let's talk about other things."

Rusty turned away and stared into the vast landscape as her question resounded in both of their minds.

Morning turned to noon, and Ocean swapped Kona for beer. Ocean's buzz-fueled lecture taught Blume and Dani everything they ever needed to know before visiting Hawaii.

Ocean's ability to aggrandize his Hawaiian upbringing displayed no bounds. "Brah. I used to surf the North Shore with Keanu Reeves's little brother. I even taught him how ta paddle out in the huge break,"

Ocean said. "We always use longboards. That's how us Soul-Surfers ride. None-a-that short board Barney bullshit. We like to ride a wave, not carve it to shreds like those haole show boaters who think they have to prove shit to the locals."

Blume's expression flared, widening his eyes in sudden recollection. "I never knew he had a brother."

Ocean shrugged.

"You never met Keanu?" Rusty asked.

"He was always off making movies in California."

Everyone left the conversation at that. No one wanted to press the issue and ruin a fun afternoon nit-picking Ocean's past.

Blume handed Ocean a cold beer. "Hey. You're a Gunner's Mate? Were you the one who shot the drone out of the sky last week?" Blume asked.

"Yeah, how did you know?" Ocean asked.

"Rusty told me the Gunners' Mates blew the drone up by accident."

Ocean grinned. He took another sip of his beer. "It wasn't an accident. Our chief told us to blow it up," Ocean said.

"No shit?" Rusty asked.

"Yeah. Our Chief said to hit it if we could."

Beyatte sat beside Fitz. "This bright sun burns my fragile complexion," she said. Beyatte's dark-painted lips teased the straw of her mixed drink as she eyed Ocean with curiosity. She suspended the liquid in her straw, with suction provided by the amorous tip of her tongue. She pulled her tongue free. "Do you have a girlfriend back home in Hawaii?"

"What?" Ocean asked.

"You heard me. Is there a 'Mrs. Ocean?'"

"No."

The dark-dressed female slid a chair closer, patting the vacant seat. "Come."

Ocean approached and loomed over her. Her cocked head surveyed the length of his bare chest as she looked up at him. "Tell me about the black volcanic sands of Hawaii," she said. "I want to hear every tantalizing morsel."

Out of nowhere, a fat jet of water showered faux rain on the group. Blume aimed a charged hosepipe above their heads, saturating everyone on the roof like a chilled freshwater fountain.

Oiled girls screamed. Their body's reaction to the cold was obvious. It seemed their bikini's designers never intended the swimwear for actual swimming — the 'tan-through fabric' was far too thin for modesty, far too thin for concealment, and far too thin for frigid water.

The day progressed and everyone had a great time when hours later, the sound of an approaching truck drew the attention of everyone on the roof.

Blume walked to the edge of the roof and peered over the side. "It's Tody. He's driving his pickup."

Minutes later, Tody emerged onto the rooftop, holding two large bags of ice and a bottle of bourbon.

One girl hurdled her friends and ran to Tody, jumping into his arms. She wrapped her long legs around his waist as he cradled her, almost slipping through his grasp because she was so saturated with tanning oil. Seconds later, the smell of Coppertone inundated Tody's white t-shirt, embedding its overwhelming scent in everyone's nostrils.

"Where's Ronnie?" Blume asked.

"Business," Tody said without lifting his stare off his female friend. "He had to wait around for some technician nerds to show up and fix a satellite radio." Somehow Blume found humor in Tody's remark. "But, look what I found." Tody lifted the bottle of 'Old Taylor' bourbon.

"Man, where'd you get that?" Blume asked.

"A buddy of mine just got deployed and gave it to me because where he's going, he can't take it," Tody said.

"Wow. Where's he going?" Blume asked.

Tody climbed into the pool with the other girls, causing flooded water to form small puddles of clumped sand on the deck "I can't say, but I will tell you this: it's poor and full of militant assholes who like to shoot cheap Kalashnikovs at kids. He's going there with some guys to 'extend diplomacy' to the assholes."

Rusty couldn't believe what he heard, yet he suspected Tody was not the type to exaggerate a story to impress anyone.

Tody looked at Ocean, who was sitting at the table, having his back read by Beyatte. "What's your rating?" Tody asked.

"I'm a Gunner's Mate," Ocean said.

"No shit, I figured you to be some sort of Twidget or something. Blume here is a Twidget. No offense. I like Twidgets as much as anyone else… I heard you mention you're from Hawaii. What island?" Tody asked.

"Kauai. But I also lived on the main island for a few years."

Tody popped open a bud long-neck and took a drink. "I've kayaked around the north end of Kauai. Those cliffs are something to behold."

"Yes, they are. I used to take my friends Va'a and we would paddle twenty-five miles a day around that island."

"Shit. Twenty-five miles isn't far," Tody said.

"It is if you're the only one paddling in a canoe of four. My friends wanted to stop and look at the fish and shit. Sightseeing and whatever. I wanted to sprint around the island and maybe set a record or something."

Tody rolled his eyes. "Fuckin' Puddle Pirates. You should have thrown them in the ocean and forced those fuckers to chase you."

Ocean toasted his beer and chuckled in agreement. "Next time."

Sultry legs sat crossed under the table as Beyatte examined Ocean's tattoos. She slid long fingernails down the length of his back, tracing worn symbols of tribal designs. With his dark Samoan complexion, the faded blackness of the tattoos likened Ocean to a warrior descendant of a mighty ancient tribe.

Blume asked Mux about his hometown.

"My dad is a retired police officer in Dallas. Before he worked in homicide, he witnessed Kennedy's assassination and became obsessed with the events that day."

"Your dad saw Kennedy die? No shit," Tody asked.

"He's always maintained he knew who shot JFK. My dad was patrolling the sidewalk outside of the Texas Schoolbook Depository, and he heard every single shot. Oswald fired two shots at the motorcade, and one of Oswald's full metal jackets went through President Kennedy and struck Governor Connelly. But it was the third shot that struck Kennedy in the back of his head and exploded. According to my dad, the third shot came from the secret service in the second limo.

"It was all a big accident. The secret service discharged one of their hollow point bullets from an M-16 when their limo slammed on the brakes to avoid rear-ending Kennedy's limo. Pop always said, 'anyone who has ever hunted knows the wounding effects of a full metal jacket versus a hollow point.'"

Mux took another sip of beer. "It's all in the Zapruder film. Anyone can see it for themselves."

Dani asked Blume, "What is the Zapruder film?"

Blume shrugged.

Mux took a sip of his beer. "A man named Abraham Zapruder shot the Zapruder film. He filmed the only footage of the assassination. The news aired the film about fifteen years ago, but my dad has a copy on videotape."

"Shit. I guess your dad has spent a lot of time on the case," Blume said.

"He was in homicide and worked the case in his spare time. My dad worked it more like a hobby, but he had access to a shit-ton of evidence and stuff."

A girl sitting in the pool said, "Wow. Too long of a story to explain, but it sounds crazy."

Everyone else paused in silent reflection, as hard rock music played in the background.

Tody was the first to speak. "Your dad is right about everything."

No one asked Tody to elaborate, as his statement needed no elaboration. Everyone could imagine the weird scenes Tody witnessed in the theater of combat. Headshots from snipers were a common sight to Navy Seals.

In the desert, dusk transitioned slower than in a big city. There were no buildings to define hard edges on the shadow boundary. The flatness of the desert allowed light rays to pierce much deeper, as the sun retreated on the Earth's axis. Desert dusk was much more beautiful than Rusty realized. Windswept air grabbed the haze in just the right way, diffusing the light and giving the landscape a surreal quality.

Everyone except Rusty and Fitz was drunk. The hundred-dollar bottle of bourbon was long gone, consumed within thirty minutes of breaking its seal.

It seemed Blume liked to make mixed tapes and play them for guests. A diverse mix of Rock music filled the expansive rooftop as the sky turned darker. To the north, faint lights of the city cast an amber glow behind the horizon. To the South, blacker skies approached. Meanwhile, Journey and Steve Perry blared from the small speakers of the cassette boom-box.

Blume plugged in an extension cord and the strings of all-white Christmas lights lit the scene. Light strands zig-zagged along the large sails, casting golden light across everyone's faces. The tiny lights expressed a bedazzled feel to the overhead, that combined with the night sky, as stars filled in the rest of the backdrop.

Blume lit tiki torches secured in garden planters and placed them around the roof. Everyone watched as flames danced in the evening breeze. The torches were lit more for ambiance than any real practical purpose.

Fitz and Dani excused themselves and went downstairs. After a few minutes, Fitz returned wearing a loose-fit top and baggy shorts. She also wore a yellow polka dot bikini underneath her outerwear.

Blume grabbed two tables and placed them beside one another. Tody climbed out of the pool and drip-dried off. With two decks of cards in hand, he motioned for the girls to join him at the table.

"Yeah, this is strip poker," Dani said.

Ocean eyes coveted Beyatte, and her naughty smirk mirrored his sudden longing.

Just then, the sexy bikini girls donned knitted sweaters, enormous hats, gloves, shoes, and socks. Surprise gripped the sailors as they glanced down at themselves, inventorying the scant articles of clothes they wore. The irony of the bikini-clad girls who'd somehow transformed into large balls of bundled cotton wear was not lost on the two ill-prepared sailors. Somehow, the scant-clad girls became the most over-dressed people in the group.

Ocean wore a pair of swim shorts. "Who's brilliant idea was it to pack shorts, Rusty?" Ocean stared at Tody and Dani. "Hey, you guys aren't worried people will watch us?"

Mux still wore his usual civilian attire, having never swam in the pool. Wearing more clothing than Ocean, Mux pointed and said: "Brother, you're screwed."

Tody sat in the middle of the two tables. "There's no one around to see your naked junk. We are miles away from anyone. I just hope you boys washed yer filthy starfishes today."

Everyone took seats around the table — Beyatte sat next to Ocean. Mux sat between two of the bikini girls. The arrangement alternated boy-girl-boy-girl.

Fitz leaned and whispered into Rusty's ear. "I want to show you something." She extended her hand to Rusty. "Come with me."

Rusty took her offered hand. It became clear Fitz wanted to 'dip out' on the social gathering. The crazed group of louts was about to get naked, and Rusty didn't want to know anyone in that way. Besides, the forward nature of the game was too personal for the young courting couple.

Dani watched as the two defectors vacated the roof party. She saluted Fitz as they descended the rooftop exit before passing through the vacant penthouse. As they made their way through the kitchen, Fitz grabbed four bottles of water, a flashlight, two large blankets, and her keys.

"Where are we going?" Rusty asked.

Dexterous fingers tucked the keys into her tight pocket. "We are going to explore a tangent," she said.

"What?" Rusty asked.

"It's a surprise." Fitz shined the light on the stairs. They descended the illuminated steps and navigated through the lobby, emerging out into the open, brisk night air. All was dark, except for the light shining from the roof. The large full moon projected steady light in the cloudless sky. Ghostly silver radiated through the landscape, bathing the world in a faint glow.

Laughter and shouting emanated from the rooftop. They weren't sure who said it, but they both heard the distinct sound of a female voice yelling orders. Loud giggles and the drunk woman's voice were the last things the pair heard before starting the Jeep.

"Where are we going?" Rusty asked, rubbing his thighs to generate warmth.

"It's a place I like to go to be alone. You'll see." Fitz flipped a towel over the dash, blindfolding the cluster of instrument lights. She waited in darkness…

"What are you doing?" Rusty asked.

"Letting my eyes adjust."

"What for?"

"You'll see. Buckle up, Buttercup." With the dash lights obscured, the landscape lit in a blazing moon-tone silver, Fitz popped the clutch and the couple tore off — sand spraying from beneath all four wheels. The beat-up Jeep headed across the wasteland, into the shadowy night. With their eyes acclimated, the sandy floor was bright and easy to navigate.

Orange light from the penthouse roof disappeared from the rearview mirror. The Jeep crawled through the sand, and the two sailors rode with it. Ghosting through the desert at excessive speeds, they encountered many smooth bumps, but the Jeep drifted through the soft sand with ease. Occasionally, they encountered large dips, and with a series of *clanks* and *clinks*; the Jeep crashed over the troughs. Other times, they launched a few feet above the crest of a dune, feeling weightless for a few fun moments.

After about fifteen minutes, Fitz turned down the radio and stopped the Jeep. They both climbed out to look around.

"What are we looking for?" Rusty asked.

"I see it. Hop back in," she said.

300 feet later, the Jeep stopped, kicking disturbed dust in its broken wake. "Welp. Here we are," she said.

With time, it became clear where she'd brought them. She'd parked them on a leeward beach overlooking the Persian Gulf. The surf calmed and lazy ripples rolled onto the shore, breaking the stillness of the quiet beach.

Fitz reached into her Jeep to grab blankets. She fluffed and draped the blankets on the sandy shore. Purposed fingers unbuckled her belt, and she placed her hands on her hips, wedging long feminine fingers beneath her waistband to slide her shorts to her ankles. She stepped out of the pile and kicked the bundle on top of the blanket.

Purple polka dots speckled her bikini. Even in the faint light, something about the way soft shadows defined her exposed hips seemed sublime. Her body was still dense with the vigor of youth.

The Yeoman approached Rusty, working her step in all its seductiveness, enticing him with carnal desires. She tucked loose hair behind her ear and stared at Rusty's jeans.

"Are we swimming?" he asked.

"I am." Her eyes caressed Rusty up and down, instructing him to undress with her gaze.

"I need to change into my swimming shorts."

"So?"

Rusty walked to the far side of the Jeep to change.

Without announcing her intent, Fitz ran into the surf. The crunching sounds of her heels as they pounded the soft sand transitioned to the thudded-splashing of feet punching the water's surface. Her firm cheeks undulated in rhythm with the pacing of her step. Her cadence slowed by deepening water. With raised arms, her body tensed just before she dove into the sea, surfacing and bobbing in waist-deep surf. Her shadow floated on the sparkling surface.

"It's cold!" she yelled, looking at Rusty. Her glistening hands wiped sleek strands of wet hair from her eyes. Bobbing in the water to generate warmth, Fitz cocked her head, beckoning Rusty to join her. "Well?"

Rusty emerged from behind the truck. His bleached complexion reflected the moon and cast a radiant glow, highlighting his pale torso. Feeling exposed, he wrapped his arms around himself and approached the water's edge — feeling naked with anticipation and the wide-opened evening chill.

"If you dive in, it's much easier," she said.

"I'm not afraid, but it is cold and…" an interruption stopped Rusty before he could finish complaining.

"So?"

Rusty ran and dove into the chilled surf. Water washed over him and he found himself grateful for being acclimated to the Engineering Division's frozen showers.

Rusty surfaced a foot from Fitz, not on purpose, but by chance — close enough to reach out and touch her.

"There, much better now, isn't it?" she asked. Her tone was much softer, more nurturing, and more inviting.

"It's cold, but it's not unlike the showers I'm used to taking. But right now, there is nowhere I'd rather be than here freezing to death with you."

"How cheesy. Does that line work?"

Rusty laughed. He licked his fingers and wiped them on his shorts. "How bout we go back to my place and get outta these wet clothes?"

Fitz laughed. "That's better." She splashed Rusty before inching her way closer to him. He shivered as she maneuvered her body nearer. She wrapped him in a warm embrace, and the smoothness of her body pressed against his, sliding across his chest, radiating her immense heat in the waist-deep surf. He watched her in the faint light for a long time. Then they kissed in the dark, as surface ripples reflected lazy sparkles around them.

After their cool swim, the couple got out of the water. Rusty grabbed his shirt on his way to the Jeep.

Fitz beckoned Rusty to the rear. "Do you want to rinse off?" She removed a large can strapped to the rear bumper of the jeep. After unscrewing the cap, she held the container over Rusty's head. Freshwater flowed down his body, washing the salt onto the sandy floor. Rusty felt her eyes on his back as the water cascaded down his exposed skin. One at a time, he lifted his legs to allow the water to cleanse his draggled feet. Water fell onto the desert floor and its short-lived puddles seeped through its thirsty sand.

"Now you do me," she ordered.

Rusty held the can over Fitz as her hands slithered across the contours of her glossy body. Her fingers snagged the straps of her bathing suit, threatening to reveal private parts meant for concealment, before snapping tight to her skin.

Rusty reached for his towel and dried Fitz's back before drying his own body.

They lay beside each other on the outstretched blankets. Rusty flung the spare blanket, catching air, causing the large parasol to float to rest as they reclined to stargaze.

The breeze subsided, stilling the night, and seemed to slow time, quieting the atmosphere while amplifying all their other senses.

"Where do you want to be in the next ten years?" he asked.

"I want a cabin in the mountains, or somewhere I can spend my time doing productive things. What about you? Where would you like to be in ten years?" Fitz asked.

"I would like to teach philosophy at a major college. Somewhere snow falls in the winter."

With half-closed eyes, she curled into his embrace, whispering between breaths. "What about us? What are we doing?" she asked.

"I know what I want to do," he said, half-joking.

Fitz rubbed Rusty's chest. "It's self-destruction to commit like that. You'll be leaving soon, and we'll most likely never see each other again. Actions have consequences, ya know."

"You're right. As much as I want to, I don't want to hurt anyone's feelings. Let's enjoy the time we have and relax together." Rusty said.

He'd nursed notions that things could be 'worked out' with time, but logic shoved his romantic delusions aside. In the end, she was right beyond absolute certainty and there was little profit in trading one's long-term mental stability for short-term desires.

Fitz returned her head to his shoulder. Closing her eyes, she rubbed her index finger over his chin, then down his neck, before resting her palm on the center of his chest.

Chiaroscuro lighting highlighted her shoulder. "You are the best example of thirteen billion years of cosmic evolution," he said, whispering to himself.

"What did you say?"

Rusty cleared his throat. Although the words escaped his mouth, he never meant for his thoughts to be heard. "I guess I was thinking out loud. I said, 'you are the best example of thirteen billion years of cosmic evolution.' The universe is struggling for perfection, but with you, it doesn't have to anymore."

Fitz received countless compliments in her lifetime. But she knew that his was a genuine sentiment of adoration — the most sincere compliment she'd ever recalled receiving. The Yeoman quivered with excitement while restraining unbridled lust. With flushed cheeks, she rolled away, struggling against an overwhelming temptation and her stiffened body spoke the words her mouth couldn't find. She wanted to reciprocate his advances, but opted to stave her desires instead. Passive vibes of rejection resonated from her silent response to Rusty's compliments, but not unkindly. She took Rusty's hand and smiled to reassure them both that they were making the right choice to abstain.

Rusty rubbed her arm, letting her know he understood her unspoken fears. "We shouldn't make this awkward," he said in a wistful voice, a voice framed by a foreshadowing of their imminent separation.

Still, Fitz offered no response, leaving Rusty consumed with speculation.

11

The dial on Rusty's Montblanc watch read "5:34" when the couple returned to the condo. Fitz and Rusty parked at the front of the building. The lights were still lit on the roof, but silence replaced all the drunken banter.

With cautious steps, they ascended the stairs to the penthouse. Fitz opened the red door to find the dimmed room silent. People slept on the floor while others slept under blankets sprawled across the couch.

It took a few minutes, but after peeling the blankets back, he found Mux sleeping near two of the bikini-clad females.

"Get up and rally the troops. We have about ninety minutes until muster," Rusty whispered.

"Ah, man, okay. What time is it?" Mux asked. He squinted in the darkened room, focusing his eyes to better decipher his watch.

"It's late. Where's Ocean?" Rusty searched the room, trying to identify everyone and find his friend.

"Don't know. He was missing all night," Mux said. "Last I saw, Tody dealt him a shitty hand, and he lost his shorts, then Beyatte pulled his ass from the table and they left somewhere."

"Maybe he's with Beyatte in her truck," Fitz whispered.

The door to the master bedroom opened, and Blume entered the dimmed room. Dani followed, turning on the kitchen light, blasting the condo with a barrage of light and clanky noises as she removed ceramic mugs from the cabinets. She placed an empty glass pot under the coffee maker and soon the smell of French Vanilla floated through the room.

"So Rusty, did you guys have fun gallivanting around the middle of the desert at odd hours of the night?" Dani asked.

"It was fun. A Jeep is a perfect truck for this environment," he said.

Dani rolled her eyes. "I wasn't asking about the truck, silly goose."

Rusty and Fitz removed chairs from the table and sat down, waiting for Mux to put his boots on.

"I took Rusty to my beach spot," Fitz said.

"Wow, I'm jealous. You won't even take me," Dani said.

Fitz explained how she never went to the beach after dark, and how this evening was her first time.

"Well, I promise to never divulge your secret location," Rusty said, watching Mux search the blankets to find his other shoe.

"'Our' secret location," Fitz said. In a show of her playful jest, she winked at Rusty.

Rusty blushed. "You're right. It is 'our' secret spot." Rusty surveyed the room before pointing to the door. "I'm going to look for Ocean. Would you like to come?"

"We'll all go," Blume said. He grabbed a large black Cannon camera from his dresser and threw on an off-white robe.

Armed with flashlights, the five of them ran downstairs to the parking area. With stealthy feet, they approached the Toyota and peered inside the foggy glass windows. Steamy air inside the truck was too saturated to hold moisture and water collected on the surface of the truck's windows. Condensation made it hard to see past the layer of tiny droplets coating the fogged glass.

Dani cupped her hand over the glass to shield reflections of the rooftop's glare. She pressed her face to the window. Her eyes grew wide, and she turned to the others, covering her mouth to contain laughter. "They're still doing it" Dani whispered.

"As drunk as he is, it's more like workin' with rope," Mux said, shrugging as everyone turned to look at him. "What? Just sayin'. He's smashed beyond normal limits."

Blume readied his camera as Dani prepared to open the door. Their instinctive choreography hinted this was not the first time they'd ambushed unsuspecting lovers. Dani opened the door so hard it almost bounced closed.

Mux yelled from behind the group. "Hey! What are y'all doing?"

A series of flashes strobed as Blume snapped photographs in quick succession. Lightning-like flashes illuminated the couple in various provocative poses. Reloading as fast as he could, Blume snapped one photo after another.

Ocean jumped and banged his head on the low-hanging headliner.

He struggled as his fumbling hands lunged for the handle, attempting to close the door. Conflicted between covering up or grappling for the camera, Ocean slipped onto the floorboard. Beyatte giggled, exerting no effort toward self-concealment.

Everyone enjoyed a good laugh. After ten seconds, the voyeurs relented. Backing up, they allowed the couple time to regain their lost composure. Dani closed the door with a thud and she pecked on the glass with the knuckle of her index finger. "Don't take too much longer. It's late."

"Ocean, we need to head out soon, and you don't want to be late," Rusty yelled through the glass.

Minutes later, Ocean fell from the Toyota and picked himself up from the sandy floor.

"Dude. Where is your shirt?" Mux asked.

Ocean was too drunk to answer. He stared at Mux with vacant eyes. Almost looking through Mux's head, as if Mux's head were invisible.

"Shit. I think he lost his shirt somewhere between the roof and here. Should I go look for it?" Mux asked.

"No time. He'll just have to ride dirty," Rusty said.

Rusty accepted Fitz's offer to drive everyone back to their ship. Mux and Ocean climbed in the back as Fitz started her Jeep. She popped the clutch and sped down the long driveway to the main road. While looking in the rear-view mirror, Rusty watched as Blume and Dani waved from the condo's parking lot. Fitz honked as they turned onto the highway, headed north.

"Ocean's drunk," she said, shouting over the wind.

Rusty turned in his seat, straining to see his snoring shipmate in the backseat. Ocean slumped to the side, wearing only his shorts and nothing else.

"I sure hope the OOD is cool about this," Rusty said, turning back to look at the road ahead.

"He's screwed," Mux said, pushing on Ocean's shoulder in a half-assed attempt to keep his shipmate awake.

"I'm sure he'll be sober by the time we get back to your ship." Fitz adjusted her rear-view mirror to better see the events unfolding behind her. "Man. Ocean looks shit-faced."

The long drive home was silent, and being awake all evening began taking its toll. Exhausted, the droning of wind enticed early morning sleep, and Rusty feared Fitz would fall out behind the wheel.

Rusty stretched, yawned, and offered to drive.

"I'm fine," Fitz said.

"Well. Let me know if you want to take a quick nap." Rusty rummaged through some tapes she had in the glove box, looking for an appropriate track to complement the early morning commute.

"I'll be okay. If I sleep now, I'll never wake up," she said.

Rusty held up a cassette tape with no writing and inserted it into the player. After a few seconds, a mellow song started playing and seemed to be the perfect soundtrack for the long trip. It was an 80's track titled "Big Log."

They pulled up to the main gate, and the Petty Officer on watch waved the Jeep through. The base was deserted at 6:30 a.m., allowing Fitz to run the stop signs. She pulled the Jeep up to the pier, braking to a gentle halt.

"Well, this is my stop. Thank you for the ride. I had an incredible time tonight," Rusty said.

Mellow music underpinned Rusty's parting voice. But the obnoxious shouting of Mux disrupted the moment as he struggled to wake Ocean.

"What time do you get off today?" Fitz said, looking back at Rusty.

"'Oh four hundred,'" he said.

"Great, do you want me to pick you up at 'oh four thirty?'"

"'Oh four thirty?' Sure. I'll be right here," Rusty said. He leaned across the gap between seats, closing the distance between them, pressing his lips to hers.

"Get a room," Mux yelled, as he jumped over the side of the Jeep's rear quarter panel, landing hard on the concrete pier. With a violent shaking of the Jeep, Ocean stumbled out of the backseat and began his slalom stagger to the Savannah.

On account of being inebriated, both sailors decided jogging was preferable to walking in order to avoid tripping. Overcompensating by using inertia and momentum was an old trick they'd learned in London. To walk with caution would cause a person to fall backward or at the very least, side-step into a curb, landing in the harbor. Sprinting helped maintain a straight line by using a body's forward motion as a crutch. Running drunk was high on the list of a drunken sailor's survival handbook — as was the planting of one's right leg on the floor, when sleeping in horizontal positions, to avoid the "spins." But there wasn't enough time to ride their hangovers out in a darkened bunk, nothing to unburden their heavy bodies from the effects of alcohol and gravity. They needed to be fit for duty in less than thirty minutes.

Mux boarded the Savannah before Ocean even made it to the gangway. The Hawaiian threw his hands in the air, gesturing to the car and back at the ship, as if directing invisible traffic to park on the Savannah's Quarterdeck. With no shoes, no shirt, and wearing only his shorts, the skimpy-dressed sailor attempted to board the Savannah. The OOD stopped Ocean to inspect his condition. He circled the Gunner's Mate, judging the sailor from all sides — from head to toe.

For a moment, Rusty feared the OOD was about to make a fatal mistake and touch Ocean. Both men resembled roosters poised to fight, and Rusty knew Ocean could smite the Officer Of the Deck with a single backhanded slap. Ocean dominated and towered the OOD, making the short watchmen appear adolescent by comparison.

"Dude, Ocean's so screwed," Rusty said.

"Nah, they have to let him onboard," Fitz said. She watched with a subtle grin, almost enjoying the drama unfolding.

"I'm just gonna pretend I don't know them," Rusty said. His concern was genuine, and he knew it would soon be his turn to cross the watchman's quarterdeck.

After a long minute of inspecting Ocean, the OOD shook his head and waved him aboard, allowing the soused man to stagger from sight.

"Well, this is it. I hope to see you after work."

"I'll be here," she said.

Rusty smiled before climbing from the jeep and swaggering his way to the Savanah. He crossed the gangway and saluted the stern and the OOD. After being granted permission to board, he waved peace signs over his head like Nixon and disappeared into the Savannah's midship superstructure.

Many places provided stealth for Rusty's resting retreats.

First option. He could visit the Flight Tower on official business and hope no one bothered to check up on him. It was a bold prospect where sleep was concerned. But too much activity in the hangar and the bright lights of the conning window were a distraction. Besides, there was no valid reason he could explain being in the tower if Palmer were to bust him.

Second option. Tacan provided the "unlikely" factor, as it was more of a closet than an actual space. It was also a risky move — reserving the "unlikely" factor for the most desperate occasions when the crew's full complement filled the ship.

Third option. The most obvious place was his own berthing rack — often used on those rare occasions when the high command permitted them to sleep.

Last option. Rusty most appreciated Radar 2. He spent many hours 'skating' in the radar room. Rusty would grip blankets from the hangar and stow himself away in his small, unremarkable space, with little scrutiny being paid to it. In fact, Palmer had never busted him in Radar 2 and it was there he went after being dismissed from the morning's meeting.

Rusty and Mux were the only members of the Combat Systems Division to show up. After having showered, gotten dressed, and entered the Shop, the pair waited for five minutes before departing the space and seeking refuge to sleep. Mux headed for Radio, and Rusty retired to Radar 2.

Meanwhile, throughout the day, voices echoed from the ship's loudspeakers, announcing the comings and goings of important personnel, announcing the commencement of routine operations, and announcing requests for certain persons to report to certain places — the usual ramblings of any ship moored to a pier.

Laying in the darkened space of Radar 2, Rusty recalled events of the prior evening. Recollections bounced through his mind and each time, he felt their effects less intensely, but the memories solidified themselves forever in his mental vault. He recalled the events in Beyatte's Four-Runner, and how casual she was about the intrusion; fond memories of Fitz's graceful sprint into the water, and the enticing way she pulled him from the poker game; Dani as she made coffee, along with the way she teased him about spending time with her best friend.

Soon, he skipped from thought to thought and brainstormed in random patterns. Hypnagogic hallucinations of imagined sensations preceded sleep, or the "Tiny Death," as Rusty called it. The subtle word games he played to fall asleep occupied his mind and before long, dreams filled his head with the familiar pattern of incoherent associations. Soon after, he wouldn't call it anything, as he slipped farther from consciousness.

Peaceful rest, that was, until a loud interruption woke him with official sounding undertones. The Officer Of the Deck passed an announcement on the 1MC and the recognition of his own name startled Rusty from sleep. It was as though the OOD knew Rusty was sleeping during working hours and wanted to reprimand him for the entire crew to hear. But reprimanding Rusty was impossible because no one knew Rusty was napping but Rusty.

"Petty Officer Russell, your presence is requested on the Midship Quarterdeck." *Sh-click*

The OOD blared again, for the second, or third, time — Rusty could not be sure of how many announcements he might have missed. The OOD emphasized his words to convey urgency — stretching and contracting syllables like an evening news reporter.

Hands on Rusty's Montblanc wristwatch read 4:53 a.m. He was late meeting Fitz. Tardiness was a sign of disrespect, and he felt the regret of dissing her.

12

The door to Radar 2 swung open, and Rusty stepped into the hall. He fidgeted with his wrinkled uniform, ran his palms over his hair, and straightened his gig line before dashing to the midship watch post.

"What's up?" he asked with labored breaths. His hands pressed to his hips, attempting to act casual, concealing self-abasing guilt at having slept all day, all while his shipmates performed their assigned duties with steadfast dedication.

Petty Officer Timmens was the standing Officer Of the Deck. "You have a visitor," he said, having never taken his gaze off the visitor. Instead, he pointed to the western side of the Quarterdeck with longing stares. As Fitz turned to face Rusty, he noticed sunlight penetrated her dress, exposing her nude figure to anyone standing in her shade. She was braless, and Rusty feared someone would reprimand her for violating the Navy's dress codes.

"Hi," Fitz said, oblivious to the watchman's stares.

Rusty extended his hand, she accepted it. He pressed his lips against the top of her hand. Like a pair of ballroom dancers, he steered her to the opposite side of the Quarterdeck, positioning her shadow side against the vacant water, shielding her from intruding eyes.

"I am sorry I'm late meeting you."

"I don't mind. It gives me a chance to see your ship."

She looked radiant in her strapless white sundress. The low-cut dress went to her mid-calf and was bedecked in purple paisleys. It billowed in the playful breeze and the windward side conformed to the contours of her shapely body, outlining her youthful and firmed figure.

She'd styled her hair in a braided, messy bun. Brown leather

Birkenstocks isolated her well-groomed feet from the ship's harsh non-skid texture.

"I want to see where you work. Hell, I'm dying to see it," she said. Rusty had forgotten Fitz was an enlisted person in the Navy, and he suspected she had never been on a ship before. The hypocrisy of military recruiters convincing females to enlist in the Navy, then prohibiting females from serving on a combat ship was ridiculous.

"Yes, ma'am, I would be delighted to be your escort. Where would you like to go first?"

"Captain's discretion."

"Well, we can start from the basement and work our way up," he said.

"Okay."

Fitz held Rusty's hand as they walked to the rear of the ship. Rusty escorted her down the ocean side of the port deck to avoid exposing her. Upon reaching the fantail, Rusty slid down the ladder by gripping hands on both rails. He floated down with feet skipping the ladder's rungs. His heavy boots landed on the deck with a stomping thud, drawing attention from the sailors loitering on the fantail. Their eyes looked at Rusty's feet, before running their gaze to the top of the ladder, resting on Fitz and her flowing sundress.

Rusty turned back to Fitz, coaching her as she made her way down the steep ladder. Dexterity carried her down the angled ladder and she paused near the bottom, jumping off the third rung into Rusty's waiting arms. A girlish squeal chirped from between her excited lips.

"This is the fantail," he said.

Fitz walked to the side of the ship and peered over the rail. "Is this where you like to stand and look at the ocean?"

"Sometimes."

She leaned back onto the deck before twirling around, resting her back on the rail to stare at Rusty. "I expected it to be higher off the water."

"It's around fifteen feet to the waterline. Imagine the view when you're facing a forty-foot wave." Rusty paused long enough for Fitz to stare again at the open water — imagining a forty-foot wave rushing at her, blocking half of the sky with it — connecting the ocean and clouds with a towering horizon line, the feeling of being swamped by a wall of water.

"This is where I stand when we enter and leave the ports. My division assigned me to perform line duty, so I have to handle the mooring lines on the fantail. It's not so bad, unless I'm hungover."

Rusty pointed to the base of the tall masts and upward to the vast array of antennas. "On the weather decks, up there. That's where I go to look out at the Ocean. Sometimes, I like to be alone and I go to the top of the pilothouse to watch as waves crash across the ship's bow… Do you see my antenna?"

Fitz's eyes looked at Rusty's arm, tracing his arm to his pointy finger, following its trajectory to the two giant masts guarding the ship. "The big one?" she asked. She squinted at the array of sensory clusters and spotted the curved, basket-looking antenna, which was stationary and secured, aimed forward.

"Yes, that's the Forty antenna."

"You'll have to show me your radar," she said.

"I will, but it will have to wait until last." Rusty took Fitz's outstretched hand. "Come on. I want to show you something."

Rusty escorted Fitz to the Pilothouse. Along their way, he pointed to the open Mess Hall where a dozen sailors sat at tables, playing chess or poker. Rusty's lady-friend interrupted their trash-talking because the sight of a female onboard a warship was a novelty, especially in a foreign port. She was immune to the crew's leering eyes. Instead, she displayed a genuine interest in the ship's architecture, ignoring the stares of its gawking crew.

They stopped in front of the ship's store, which was almost always closed and only opened a few hours a week. Dispersing officers seldom posted the schedule of the store's capricious operating hours. So any chance of buying items from the ship's store was based on timing and luck — like children snagging a passing ice cream truck. If word spread that the store was open, sailors would run down, hoping to make it inside before the clerk closed up. In all the years onboard, Rusty had only been inside the ship's store a handful of times. In fact, he'd touched more nuclear missiles in the VLS, than candy in the ship's store.

Fitz placed her hands against the window and looked at the cartons of cigarettes and sugary candy which lined the short cabinets. Fitz's eyes widened. "That is a lot of gedunk," she said.

Rusty said: "The only thing worse than trying to buy candy from there is booking a seat with the ship's barber. Everything is always closed. I don't even know why they exist."

With a crew exceeding 300 sailors, the Navy figured it would be a great idea to allocate one person to groom the entire crew. His name was Petty Officer Tucos. Everyone called him 'Too-close, Tucos' because he only knew how to trim hair to within the closest of margins. Rusty hypothesized that 'Too-close' buzzed closer than normal, to lower the amount of cuts he had to perform in a month. The crew judged 'Too-close' as a moron, but Rusty understood him for what he was, a genius acting the fool.

Rusty escorted Fitz the long way around the ship to show her the VLS entrance and the two entrances to the Gas-Turbine engine rooms. She pressed her face close to the tiny window, peering into the large engine space at the naked engines. One could find the same turbines on the wings of DC-10s, but the ones powering the ship lacked the smooth outer housings of the familiar commercial jet engines.

"Those engines look scary," she said.

"I imagine they are scary. Scary to fix. They provide twenty thousand horsepower each and there are four of them."

"Eighty thousand horsepower? That's all?" Fitz asked.

The two laughed as Fitz looked back into the tiny window.

"I have much more to show you. Ready?"

"Lead the way, Captain."

They made their way up the ladders and snaked through the halls until reaching the port side bridge wing, where Fitz then entered the Pilothouse. The uncluttered space welcomed her to explore the bridge. Her curious eyes inspected the layout while Rusty guarded the door. The Yeoman, having never been on a Navy ship, perused the sophisticated navigation, communication, and observation controls as her gaze zig-zagged around the room, trying to capture everything in at once.

A thirty-foot window spanned the length of the bridge. Composed of half-inch thick glass, the window provided an unobstructed view of the ocean, while providing crewmen with safety against the sea's harsh elements.

Fitz's gaze followed her dainty fingertips as she slid them over the window's housing bolts. Not minding her step, she bumped her thigh on the Captain's Seat. She turned, pulled her hand back, and studied the chair with inquisitive eyes.

"Can I sit in it?" she asked.

Rusty waved his inviting hand toward the seat. "I couldn't stop you if I tried."

She placed her foot on the step of the tall barber's chair and climbed up. Her dress billowed as she performed a small pirouette to back her ass into the seat. She planted her bottom on the brown leather cushion and tucked her dress between her pinched knees, taking to her new position as though assuming command.

Phone receivers littered the bulkhead and ran along the overhead console, which was mounted above the Skipper's seat. Fitz teased at grabbing the phone that read "Executive Officer." Rusty closed his eyes and shook his head from side to side.

With pouted lips, she lifted her chin and peered across the dash, scanning the bow of the ship. While looking through the glass, her attention pulled back, focused on the foreground. A coffee mug, placed in a cup holder near the window, read "Commanding Officer."

"This is where all the fun happens," she said. She rubbed her hands across both armrests.

"It's where the Duke sits almost every day," Rusty said, walking away to inspect a nearby radar indicator. He leaned and buried his face in its rubber blinder, staring at the display's blank screen, scanning the interior of the black rubber cone for light leaks.

He looked up just in time to watch Fitz grab the Duke's coffee mug, raising it to eye level. With careful precision, she pressed it to her mouth, stamping its white porcelain with her puckered lips. After painting the mug, she returned the cup back to its original position having been vandalized with dark red, kissed-lips, on its rim.

He laughed and shrugged the incident off for fear of appearing square. "Would you like to see more?" he asked. Rusty offered his hand to escort her down from the Duke's command chair.

She jumped instead, causing Rusty's eyelids to squint and his eyebrows to raise for fear of being gouged by erratic fingernails. Her long legs wrapped around his waist as he caught her, cradling her with his sturdy arms.

For a moment, Fitz's firm thighs gripped him, and he feared she would crush his hips. "Is that the steering wheel?" she asked, relaxing and dropping her legs.

"It is." Rusty approached the large center console positioned in the center of the bridge. The thin console stood five feet tall and five feet wide. He offered his hand for her to join him at the helm.

Fixed to the back side of the console was a large stainless steering wheel. The polished wheel shined as bright as chrome, and Fitz's compressed reflection grinned back at her as she turned it from side to side. Rusty reached around her waist and placed his hands near hers. They steered, course-correcting with a fantasized turning of rudders at the ship's rear, never knowing if the massive fins did indeed twist.

Fitz stared at the bow through the wide glass window, feeling the imagined weight of a 529-foot-long steel destroyer, bobbing and heaving the crew according to her whim. The perspective of her mammoth bow, combined with the width of the pilothouse, bestowed them with the ship's titanic sense of scale.

"I would love to drive this ship," she said. "Have you driven her?"

"I did a few times. A buddy of mine would let me steer during his pee breaks."

"Wow. Well maybe someday females can drive a destroyer," Fitz said.

"Maybe," he leaned in and whispered in her ear. "I want to show you my personal space."

She replied in a soft voice. "You lead the way."

Her hands caressed the back of his neck as she pulled him closer. With closed eyes, their lips met and for a moment, her kiss crushed all other plans or thoughts Rusty had, annihilating his itinerary and awareness of the external world with it.

After the enchanted moment, Rusty urged Fitz to follow him. As the two left the Pilothouse, she turned once more to inspect the Duke's coffee mug, ensuring her puckered lips were visible to anyone who walked through the Bridge.

Rusty bypassed Radar 2 and proceeded to the helicopter hangar where Airmen performed preventative maintenance on the helo. Their attention shifted, accommodating Fitz's welcomed visit.

A large Seahawk helicopter sat ready, strapped to the deck with thick chains, like a grounded dragonfly with bent-back wings, bonded into submission. Airmen folded the fan blades back for compact storage, all the while large tie-downs secured the propellers in place, giving it a wind-swept look.

There was nothing Rusty could say to dissuade Fitz. She walked to the helicopter and ran her hands along its sleek gray fuselage. Fitz withdrew her hand and inspected her fingers, rubbing them together. "Weird. I expected it to be dirty," she said.

Rusty shrugged.

One of the Airman, an Aviation Electronics Technician, approached and opened the door to the cockpit. "Would you like to look inside?"

Fitz nodded. She leaned in and looked at the flight console, rubbing the smooth pilot seat, petting the cushion with her palm.

The Airman turned his back. She gripped the moment and climbed into the cockpit. She put her hands on the center stick and glared at Rusty. "Get in," she demanded.

Rusty waved her off. "No, thank you. You go ahead. I'll catch the next one."

Being careful not to disturb anything, she did her best piloting impression of the large airship. Her hands gripped the control stick, and she placed her Birkenstocks on its large foot pedals, mindful not to depress the pedals because of the imagined fear of breaking something expensive. "Have you ever flown in this helicopter?" she asked.

"I've never flown in any helicopter."

"It would be fun," she said.

"You're right. It looks like fun when I watch them take off and land," Rusty said.

"You get to watch them take off?" she asked.

"Yes. I'll show you." Rusty pointed to the small ladder in the hangar's corner.

The curious Yeoman climbed out of the helicopter and looked at the helo mechanic. "Thank you."

The Petty Officer smiled. "You're welcome, Miss."

"Look here," Rusty said. He pointed to an unassuming ladder hidden in a cluttered corner of the hangar. The ladder was between a bunch of coats on one side, and fire-extinguishers on the other. A cluttered juxtaposition of mechanical objects camouflaged the ladder, nearly hiding it in plain sight.

"Up there is where I spend my time during Flight Quarters," he said, motioning for her to climb.

The small compartment was cozy, and they spent a substantial amount of time in the tiny tower. Rusty explained the flight quarter procedures while Fitz listened. He stood behind her while she sat in his chair, peeking through the tiny window.

Designers and ship planners engineered the flight tower to oversee helo operations, situating the tower at the highest point of the helo hangar just twenty feet from the readied Seahawk. Planners positioned the tower close enough to the helicopter's blades to rouse excitement when the airship launched, but far enough away to safe-guard Rusty from any unwanted decapitations.

Rusty found Flight Quarters to be more interesting than being holed up, tucked away inside Radar 2 during General Quarters. During Flight Quarters, he saw everything displayed in his window — the rear five-inch cannon mount, the Seahawk helicopter, and the Sea

Sparrow surface-to-air missile launcher. All were visible to Rusty's tiny private skybox. He sat in the only seat with a view of all the weaponry on the back half of the ship's rear. Although he'd never seen a rocket launch in person, he knew someday he'd experience a Sea Sparrow launch from his vantage point. Witnessing the massive rocket launch would be a high point in Rusty's enlistment.

The purpose of Rusty's job, during Flight Quarters, was to relay the status of the helicopter to the Pilothouse because the Pilothouse could not see the flight deck from its 180-degree vantage point.

Rusty told Fitz about his time spent at Flight Quarters. "When we entered the Persian Gulf, we were at Flight Quarters and General Quarters for eight solid hours. Can you believe that shit? I was up here and had to listen to Lieutenant Pratt as he snored the entire time. That was the only time it sucked to be here — listening to him snore for eight hours was agonizing."

"I bet. You should have smacked him with a pillow. No one would have known, as it was your word against his. Besides, how could he tell on you for hitting him while he slept? Seems he would have gotten into worse trouble for sleeping than you would for hitting him with a bag of soft feathers. Besides, if you were fast enough, he might not even think it was you. Just smack him and turn around to look out the window, like you didn't know what he was talking about — smack that bitch and then deny *everything*!"

Rusty wondered why he never thought of that.

The sun crept closer to the horizon and from their view, nature cloaked the sky in the dark purple hue. Inside the flight tower, it grew darker still, almost as black as night. Yellow-tinged light from the hangar blasted through the ladder hatch on the deck.

"Where's your radar?"

"Follow me."

Rusty was first to descend the ladder. Reaching the bottom, he held his arms out to catch Fitz if she slipped on the stair's rungs.

They looked around the hangar for Airmen, but it seemed everyone left for the day, no doubt seeking recreation on the Mess Deck or hoping to catch a movie in their Berthing compartments.

Before leaving the Hangar, Rusty went to the far corner beside the Airman's tool chests. Eight folded 'Woobies', painted Forrest Camo, lay stacked in the corner. He grabbed a large hand full and met Fitz near the door.

"These Woobies will be nice to sit on. I don't have seats in Radar 2."

"What's a Woobie?" Fitz asked, looking down at the bundle tucked between Rusty's arm.

"Poncho liner. They're the blankets used by the Marines and Army when they are deployed. I like to think of Woobies as 'tactical comforters.' I grab as many as I can when I can."

Walking out of the Hangar, they stopped at the second door on the right, fifteen feet from the entrance. The tiny metal label, positioned in the center of the hefty watertight door, read "Radar 2."

Rusty keyed in the cypher lock combination. Fitz's eyes followed his fingers while he typed the code "2434." After a few clicks of the locking mechanism, he opened the door and stepped back, allowing her first unhindered access to the space.

She walked in and Rusty followed, closing the door behind them.

Shivering hands ran the length of her goose-fleshed arms as Fitz embraced herself to keep warm.

"Are you cold? Shit. Sure you are."

"Like a naturalist, skinny dipping during a Chicago winter," Fitz said. Judging by her stunned expression, he forgot to warn her of the chilled nature of the radar space — an oversight on Rusty's part.

"Hang on." He dropped the stack of Woobies and grabbed his favorite utility coat, placing it around her exposed shoulders. The thick jacket was too large for her thin frame, but it muted her chill to manageable levels.

"Thank you," she said, looking at the radar cabinets. "You know how all this electronic stuff works?"

"Yes, I do, and I know how to fix it all, too."

"Wow, I bet it can get confusing," she said.

"It can," Rusty recalled his first week of school. The curriculum was Basic Electronics and Introduction to Direct Current. For two weeks, schematic symbols of resistors and capacitors plagued Rusty with nightmares of being chased by the rotten things. Logic shifted his mind in ways he was not comfortable with — shifting his thought patterns from the right to left hemispheres. The mental shift teetered on physical pain in all the ways that headaches hurt.

"I imagine electronics like a game of 'Mousetrap,'" he said. "Electrical current is much like ball bearings that travel through a bunch of obstacles. The obstacles alter the bearings — manipulating and forcing them to do different things."

Rusty pointed to two large cabinets on the right wall of the room. "These are the receiver cabinets. They take signals from the antenna and they signal this unit, the video converter. The signal then gets sent to the repeaters, in Combat, and on the Bridge."

Rusty tried to keep it interesting because electronics could get convoluted — even for a nerd like him. He opened one of the two transmitter units, displaying the slender modules that made up the transmitter's amplifiers. "This is where the transmitters amplify the RF — that's 'Radio Frequency' — and the transmitters send two hundred and forty thousand watts of RF up to the antenna." He had bored her to the point of yawns.

She interrupted his lecture, brushing against his back with her chest as she reached around his body. Her hands slid down his chest, rubbing across abs sculpted from countless Navy sit-ups, feeling for his buckle. Fitz's fingers clutched at his belt from around his waist.

A person's hands are windows to their intent.

Fitz spun Rusty around to face her. She shifted her gazed to his waistline and continued unbuckling the shiny stainless utility buckle, dragging the belt through one loop, then another, and another.

Rusty swallowed to lubricate his drying throat, and his breathing deepened. "What are you doing?" he asked, looking at the top of her down-turned head. His voice squeaked.

Fitz lifted her head and locked eyes with Rusty, refusing to answer his question. Greedy fingers gripped the straps of his freed belt — stroking them, slapping them, wringing them through her clenched palm, as she strutted to Radar 2's heavy door.

She forced the long handle down, tightening the latch as hard as it would go — cutting off the world. Then she ran the belt through the center hinge and around the door's handle, closing and cinching the door with her improvised tie-down strap — locking the crew out, and isolating Rusty from the safety his shipmates offered. No one could get through the door without sixty minutes and a plasma cutter.

The kicking of her feet sent her sandals skidding across the deck, casting them into a darkened corner of the room. She removed his coat and let it fall near their feet. Hiking her dress, she caressed peach-fuzzed thighs as her hands slid up and under, searching for the laced band of her panties. She thrust her fingers between her waist and her intimates, sliding her undergarments down to her ankles, far enough to step out, before kicking them aside.

The spontaneity of her pleasure-seeking gesture showed premeditation, a rehearsal of sorts. Her prior indecisions grew into a heightened state of sexual greed.

"Let's get sticky," she said with a voracious smile, which only deepened her sultry expression. Fitz pinched her bottom lip between her teeth and looked up from Rusty's crotch, daring him to undress with just the suggestion of her leering eyes.

Although he was no virgin, no one had ever propositioned Rusty to 'get sticky' before. He choked, attempting to clear his throat. "What?" His voice deepened from an overloaded mix of adrenaline and testosterone. His face flushed with heat.

"You heard me. I want to 'inappropriate you.' Long and hard," she said.

She placed her hands on his broad shoulders, whispering. "I want you to think of me every time you are in this room," she said, lifting her dress and letting it fall. Overcome with frenzied lust, she drew him closer with possessive hands and parted lips, dominating the moment with her kiss.

After having been denied erotic yearnings for so long, Rusty's exhilaration was absolute. Because of the sailor's involuntary abstinence, staving his libido for months on end, his excitement at her sudden effeminate aggression was indescribable. For a moment, he froze, not knowing how to react. She was stunning.

His eager eyes glimmered, casting a caressing gaze along her bare body — counting the subtle freckles sprinkled across her exposed skin — coveting her in all ways possible.

There comes a time when two connected bodies aren't close enough, and all the touching and caressing in the world could never be enough to tame libidinous desires. More than anything, Rusty knew what he wanted and Fitz made it clear she welcomed it.

Still embraced, he turned off the clinical-looking overhead lights, allowing the soft glow of radar dials to guide their wanton way. In the darkened room, they committed themselves. Consequences be damned.

13

The couple laid on the deck, cushioned, insulated, and sandwiched between the soft Woobies. It was a cozy arrangement with the two of them balled together in the darkened room.

Sweating under the blanket's warmth, Fitz flipped the Woobie, exposing her bare chest. Her fingers lifted sweat small droplets from her neck, and she rubbed her fingertips in circles, attempting to air-dry them in the chilly space. The arid air pulled moisture from her skin like evaporating alcohol.

She turned and curled in Rusty's arms. Her dry fingers found their way to the tiny patch of Rusty's chest hair, and she swirled them through its curly fuzz.

"What are you thinking about?" she asked.

"I'm just thinking of all the versions of me in parallel worlds who would sell their souls for the time I just had."

Fitz squeezed Rusty's hand. "Parallel worlds?"

"Yes, parallel worlds. Have you ever heard of Max Planck?"

"No." She sat upright and crossed her legs, grabbing Rusty's coat to cover her shoulders.

Rusty felt under the blanket to hold Fitz's hand. "How many times could you divide a number in half to reach zero?"

"I'm not sure."

"In theory, you could divide any number in half an infinite number of times and you'd never reach zero," Rusty said. He sat up, crossed his legs, and covered his lap, facing Fitz in the dim light.

"Okay."

"Well, according to Max Planck, the universe is pixilated and the smallest unit of measure is trillions of times smaller than the atom.

Space and time are made of these pixels."

"Wow. That's crazy."

"It gets weirder. Planck also came up with the smallest unit of time. How many times could you divide a second to reach a 'true instant' or the 'present moment?'"

"I guess you could divide a second in half an infinite number of times, too."

"And you'd be right. It makes sense, in theory. You could divide a second forever and never define the present moment. Well, Max Planck came up with fundamental constants, formulas, to bookmark the basement of reality. His theories work and the upshot is, life is a 3-D movie that has a frame rate of ten to the forty-fourth second. That sounds fast, and it is fast. But reality is not seamless. Reality is digital, not analog."

"That's neat. What does this have to do with parallel worlds?" Fitz asked.

"Every ten to the forty-fourth second, the universe makes a choice. Reality splits into alternate dimensions. Each dimension is as real as the one you and I are in now. Realities branch into separate planes of existence, trillions of times a second. The universe is infinite, so it can hold infinite varieties of each of us, and every other potential reality — over limitless dimensions."

"You've spent a lot of time thinking about this," Fitz said.

Both of them laughed. Fitz rolled over and pressed her back into Rusty's chest as he draped his arm around her.

Rusty rubbed Fitz's exposed shoulder. "Yeah. I *wish* they were mine. Brilliant men have devoted their entire lives developing these theories."

They laid in the dark and after some time passed, Fitz closed her eyes. Soon afterward, her breaths deepened to tiny snores. Snores so faint, they reminded Rusty of a kitten's.

Light from the Forty defined the soft curves of her smooth skin. The contours of her exposed shoulder captivated him like nothing else could. It was hard to admit, but Rusty made a critical error. Up to this point, he'd structured his spartan lifestyle to avoid stapled attachments, and as a nomad-sailor, he had no business getting involved with Fitz. It would be a valid question to know if 'involved' was even the right word to define his feelings for her. In a few short days, fate would separate them, and Rusty was ill-equipped to deal with its fallout. Soon those damn consequences would need to be addressed. But not tonight.

He pulled her tighter to conserve their warmth. "It's time for me to escort you off the ship," he whispered in her ear.

With half-opened eyes, she stretched, and her arms bumped into a radar cabinet. "What time is it?"

"Almost nine."

She grabbed her dress from under the pile of Rusty's dungarees they'd been using as a pillow. She unfurled the dress to slip it over her head. The soft fabric flowed like a silk tapestry. Her caressing hands slid down the curves of her full-figured hips, removing creases and wrinkles from her dress.

Rusty dressed beside her. He left the Woobies on the deck and put his coat around Fitz's shoulders. It was cold and with her light dress; it seemed to be the only proper thing to do until they got topside where Fitz could warm herself in Bahrain's heat.

Rusty smiled as he removed his belt from the handle and opened the door. He ran his belt through his pant's loops, securing the buckle before offering his hand to Fitz.

Using the shortest route, he escorted her to the quarterdeck, and the pair emerged behind the OOD. The air was chilled, and Rusty made the call to let her wear his favorite coat until she felt like returning it.

The new watchmen seemed puzzled. His mouth slacked as he checked Fitz out. "Petty Officer Russell. I didn't know you had a visitor."

"She's in the logbook." Rusty pointed to the green hardback.

The OOD approached the book and ran his finger down the page, stopping on the only space that did not have a time logged under the departure column. "Petty Officer Fitzgerald?" he asked.

"Yes," she said. Fitz saluted the stern and then the OOD. "Request permission to go ashore."

"Permission granted." The watchman returned the salute, then entered the departure time in the log.

Rusty and Fitz walked along the pier holding hands until they arrived back at Fitz's jeep.

"I don't have to be anywhere until 'oh, seven hundred tomorrow. Do you want to do something?" Rusty asked.

A grin formed across Fitz's mouth. "Of course I would, but what do we do? This is Bahrain, and it's almost nine on a Monday night."

"Well, I don't know what to do. I've never been to Bahrain before,"

Rusty said.

Fitz snapped her fingers. "I know. I've wanted to do this for a long time," she said.

"What is it?"

"You'll see."

"Okay. I'll go change out of my uniform and meet you back here in ten minutes." Rusty kissed Fitz and ran to change.

With Rusty sitting beside her, Fitz sped her Jeep through the main gate. The screaming of her revved engine drew the attention of merchants who occupied display tables lined along the major thoroughfare outside the gated entrance. Men and women, dressed in robes, with wrapped shemaghs and turbans around their heads, looked up from their wares and watched as the Jeep raced past their market.

Long rows of merchants resembled gypsies from old Mesopotamia. Soft ambient light from fire torches and lamps illuminated long rows of tables with an ancient ambiance. Tables of jewelry and textiles hung in the open air. A cornucopia of painted scarves and robes littered the roadside, filling the cracks of the bleak landscape with a rainbow of colored mortar so rich Rusty could almost taste the sweetness of their vibrant colors.

Each merchant displayed their own assortment of cassette tapes, placed in neat rows on their tables. Music bandits squatted behind tables of contraband, along with dozens of other entrepreneurs who profited from cheap imitations of pirated western culture.

A waving hand drew Fitz's attention as one merchant stood out from the dozens of others.

Fitz waved back. "Those are bootlegged cassettes. You can buy all the American music you want for a dollar a tape. I have tons of them." She reached behind her seat and presented Rusty with a shoebox of tapes from the back floorboard. He wrestled the flimsy box and placed it in his lap.

Pirates recorded all the music onto blanks from original album copies. Some audio outlaw wrote the name of the artists and album titles over the brands of the various cassettes. Using homemade printed labels, words like 'Memorex, TDK, and Maxell' were replaced with the best names in contemporary 80's music.

"The tapes sound great, too. Not like you'd expect," she said. She explained the contents were an eclectic mix of the most solid jams — dozens of tapes, enough to satisfy any respectable collection.

"You can get any cologne or perfume, too. They sell knockoffs of the most expensive and famous perfume brand names. I like to buy those just because they are cheaper than the $100 bottles you buy in the designer stores ," she said.

Fitz steered with her knee while opening a small bottle from her center console. She put the bottle to her wrist and turned it upside down. "Here smell. I think I paid three dollars for this one."

Rusty leaned in and held her wrist to his nose. Jasmine scented perfume. "Wow, it smells great. What perfume is this?"

"Shit if I know, I just like the smell. It smells great, but it doesn't last long. After about an hour, you can't smell it anymore. Something about the way expensive whale piss lasts longer, and I think the merchant made these perfumes with cheap imitation oils instead. But I don't know." Fitz explained how the shopkeepers also sold Drakkar Noir and Calvin Klein colognes.

Rusty grabbed the handle on the dash. "The scent only lasts an hour? I bet it's perfect for strippers and married men." He improvised his joke, but no one had ever voiced truer words. "I would like to stop and look at some tapes, if we ever get a chance," Rusty said.

"We will, but the place we are going holds the promise of fonder memories," she said.

"How could anyone argue with that? Where are we going?" Rusty asked, tilting his head and loosening his neck.

Fitz's grin was almost conniving. "We are going on a tangent," she said.

The Yeoman pulled the Jeep into a passing gas station. She jumped out and walked to the back to fill the tank with gas. Rusty joined her.

Bright lights drew the attention of every flying bug in sight. They congregated overhead, and Rusty wondered how bugs survived in such harsh extremes as the arid desert.

The pumps appeared the same as the gas pumps in the U.S., but the Arabic pumps had 'Petrol' written where it should have said "Unleaded." And the pumps tallied the amount of gas in Bahraini Dinar. 1,460 BD a gallon.

After filling the tank with 30,000 dinar worth of gas, Fitz reached into her Jeep and grabbed thirty dollars in cash from her console. "Do you want anything from inside?"

"No thanks. But I would like to come in and see the store."

Two men in turbans stood outside the entrance. They opened the door for Fitz as she approached the curb. "Thank you," she said, avoiding eye contact with the men. Eyes were the window to the soul, and it was apparent Fitz was choosy with whom she shared hers.

Inside, the small store was very crowded. Fitz bought two gallons of drinking water, pretzels, gum, and a road map. All the items made Rusty curious, but the last item left him concerned. He saw many such evolutions and knew full well what her intent signaled.

She's conducting a 'Supply Replenishment' for a long trip into some deep, backcountry excursion.

Items on the shelf looked very similar to junk-food items found in United States convenience stores, except in Bahraini stores. Someone wrote the labels in languages Rusty could not understand. Aside from water, even halfway around the world, there was nothing healthy to be found in quickie-marts.

At the crowded check-out line, Rusty removed his wallet and offered to pay for everything. "Let me get this," he said, holding a fresh hundred-dollar bill. "How much is it?"

"I think it's like twenty-eight dollars total."

"Well, let me pay for this." Rusty wanted to pay for everything. He insisted.

Still donning Rusty's jacket, Fitz put her cash back into the coat's pocket. As all eyes watched, she stared at Rusty's outstretched hand and reached for the money. "Okay, but for the last time, I'm still not going to have sex with you!" she shouted, blurting loud enough for the entire store to hear. Rusty laughed with embarrassment. While watching Fitz exit the store, the clerk giggled and offered Rusty's change.

Rusty surveyed everyone's expression, shrugged, and accepted his change. He slid the exotic arabic coins into his pockets, intending to keep them as souvenirs. As he exited the store, he smiled large enough for Fitz to notice from across the parking lot.

The night cooled, and the air grew cooler still, persuading the Yeoman to install the top on her Jeep. Fitz wrestled the folds and corners with practiced hands. She knew every snag, bend, and burr, lining up each snap with a watchmaker's precision. She even side-stepped her protruding trailer hitch without taking her eyes off the Jeep's black vinyl top.

"Would you like me to help you 'batten the hatches'?" Rusty asked as he dawdled near the gas pump.

"Nah. Thanks, but I can do it faster by myself."

Rusty peeked into the backseat and spied a thick green sweater. At any time, Fitz could have swapped jackets for her own sweater, and returned Rusty's favorite coat, but she didn't. Then the thought occurred to him he might never get his coat back, and he was okay with the notion.

Across the street, a prolific and ubiquitous fast-food restaurant begged the couple's patronage. The familiar double golden arches of a McDonald's fast-food restaurant, with its red and yellow sign, was a peculiar sight. Rusty was eager to compare menus of the Arabic McDonalds to the ones he'd visited on countless occasions back home.

They pulled into the drive-thru. At first glance, the menu seemed the same, but on closer inspection, instead of the usual names, the meals were "Mega J, Spicy J, Triple J, and Roast Beef Mushroom."

Suspicious of his own experience with the ship's mess hall, he skipped the Roast Beef Meal and ordered a Mega J. Fitz summoned heat from the Spicy J combo.

They waited as the car ahead of them exercised due diligence. Fast-food aficionados choked the steady pace of the quick moving drive-thru. The occupants of the van inventoried their complete order, right down to the straw count. A delay would not have been so bad, except a party of six filled the van and each person strived to have everything just right. It seemed the driver returned more bags than he received.

Fitz and Rusty watched the car. Neither offered anything in commentary because they were too entertained to be perturbed.

Gassed with a full tank and stocked with provisions, Fitz headed south on a major highway, out of town and toward the vacant night landscape. Aside from occasional headlights, darkness cloaked the desert, detaching the couple from civilization.

Cool wind blew Fitz's hair in all directions, forcing her to roll up the window, amplifying the mellow, psychedelic music playing in the background. After lowering the volume to a level more suited for conversation, Fitz unwrapped her chicken sandwich. Talking between bites, she said, "I was thinking about what you meant when we were in Radar 2. You mentioned alternate realities and stuff. How do you think that affects freedom of choice and freewill?" she asked.

Rusty peered through the window with a musing stare — electric light from the dials having obscured most of everything outside his window. With the absence of distracting objects, his focused thoughts constructed a more concise explanation.

"I'll try not to scare you, but I don't believe in freewill," Rusty said.

"Why not?"

Rusty grabbed his burger and removed it from the bag. He held his burger and waved it in the air as he spoke. "Everything we know is based on the physical world and events of the physical world can be predicted and therefore so can your thoughts and actions."

Fitz glanced at Rusty between taking bites of her chicken sandwich and monitoring the highway.

Too chatty to eat his burger, Rusty placed it back in the bag and just nibbled on his fries. "Well, in a determined universe, or a world of cause and effect, the physical world influences every thought you have — thus the name, 'cause and effect.'"

Rusty added, "The mind is not independent of the physical world, but is an emergent property of the physical world and is controlled by empirical reality."

Fitz pressed the gas pedal closer to the floor, speeding beyond the set limit of one hundred kilometers per hour. Without taking her eyes off the road, she asked Rusty to look at the map. "Can you tell me if you see a spot that says 'Askar'?"

He wrestled with the map's folds while clicking on the overhead light to study the island's rendered layout. "What road are we on?" Using his index finger to draw invisible lines, he retraced the route from known locations as he studied the map.

"I need to know if we already passed 'King Hamad Highway?'" Fitz pointed a thumb over her shoulder.

Rusty asked her if she knew two thumbs up meant "fuck you."

"Yeah, I do it all the time to assholes at work," Fitz said, slowing down. A large sign read, "King Hamad Highway." She turned onto it and proceeded along the route.

Rusty stared at the radio lights. "So in a determined world, freewill does not exist. We only think it does, but in reality, our brains decide microseconds before we are aware the mind made the decision. Terms like 'reflexes, inspiration, and intuition' all have deterministic undertones. If you wanna know how reality determines thought, stick your finger over a flame and try imagining daisies. Or, try not eating when you are starving, and abstaining from drugs if you're an addicted user. The physical world motivates all thoughts and actions regardless of how minute those thoughts are."

"I suppose you are right, but it's sad to think we are not in control of our lives. There has to be more to it than that," Fitz said.

There was a long pause of silence as Fitz and Rusty both

contemplated what they would say and who would speak next.

Rusty threw his fries into the bag and rolled it up, saving it for later. "Levels of determinism may vary, but from the highest to the lowest levels of choice, everything we think and feel is determined by external influences — even if we are unaware of those influences. It is arguable, but if consciousness originated from external sources, like Dualists claim, then everyone would know everything there is to know. Our physical brains and physical experiences wouldn't limit our minds' understanding. Every person and animal would know all there is to know. If consciousness was external to our brains, why would it be governed by a brain's design, or lack thereof? Everything we know and feel is based on memories, so much so that those experiences define our very essence."

"Well, I think we still determine our own future, even if we can't see it," Fitz said. "I mean, what is the point of all this, if we are just here for a pre-determined ride? There's got to be some agency in my awareness that allows me to decide my own fate."

"You might be right."

They drove another ten minutes before Fitz pulled to the shoulder to look at the map. She squinted, straining to read the maps tiny print. After a moment of study, she crumpled the oversized chart onto her lap and looked past Rusty, scrutinizing the desert which spread into the darkness outside his window. In order to see past the console's glare, she turned off the dash lights to better study the desert's topography.

"But aren't external truths hidden? Isn't finding external truths the goal of scientific discovery?" she asked, turning on the lights and bringing her attention back to the map.

"Fair enough, but those universal truths are determined by the laws of the universe, and truths influence our reality. Determinism is inescapable."

"Shit," she said, laughing as she traced her fingers over the map. "I think you're right. Reality is inescapable."

"What? Are we lost?" Rusty asked. He stared at the darkness ahead, retracing their route in his mind, in the event they needed to backtrack their way home.

"No. We're not lost, but if we follow the highway, it's like twenty miles longer. If we cut across the desert, it's only one mile." Pointing to her three o'clock position, she extended her hand in front of Rusty's face and pointed straight to the passenger's side window.

Rusty watched her hand, turning his head to look in the direction she pointed — nothing outside but blackness in all directions — and nothing to hint at the condition of the terrain.

"That's where we are heading. It's only a mile west of us. In that direction," she said.

Rusty stared into the blackness. "So either twenty miles of pavement or one mile across whatever the hell is out there?" he asked, tapping the glass with the tip of his thumb.

Fitz grinned. It was the same grin she showed while explaining dead bodies and severed limbs in Blume's staircase. "Screw it." She threw the map into Rusty's lap, turned her wheel to the right, and headed off-road.

Rusty attempted to fold the map while watching the path ahead. It was a jostled affair. Bouncy as hell, but more fun than he'd expected. A small part of him worried about the suspension, but the Jeep seemed to handle the uneven terrain like a champ.

"Sorry about this." She pushed the accelerator. The desert on that part of the island was much rougher than the stretch near Blume's house. "You might need new fillings before this is over."

As they made their way across small ditches and embankments, Rusty couldn't help but recognize he was on a real adventure. Once in a while, they caught air. Growing tired of the heavy bouncing, Fitz sped up, and the Jeep planed out, skimming the small sand drifts like a fast boat over a light chop. The faster they went, the smoother the ride.

A few minutes later, they approached a wall of sand. The nine-foot embankment was the last hurdle toward reaching the highway. Fitz put her Jeep in first gear and ascended the steep incline.

"We won't flip," she said.

"I didn't think we would."

"I wasn't talking to you."

The Jeep climbed to the top of the tall slope and rolled onto the highway's plateau. Idling perpendicular to the two-lane road, she stopped before the tires reached the asphalt, sending dust floating in front of the bright fog lamps.

Scanning left and right, no headlights shone in either direction. They were alone in the middle of nowhere, and Rusty didn't even know where the final destination was supposed to be.

"Well, we have a choice to make, right or left?" she said.

Rusty knew this meant south or north. He picked north and pointed his thumb out of his window. "Right."

"Right turn, Aye," she said. She pulled the wheel and headed north on the two-lane highway. The smooth pavement felt like silk.

Fitz squinted for something on the side of the highway. "It should be here."

They both searched for lights, signs, or any structures of interest.

Minutes later, he keyed in on what Fitz had searched for. Fifty yards ahead, the sign read "Tree of Life."

"Do you see it?" he asked.

"Aye shipmate. There she blows!"

Alone in the middle of Bahrain, with not a single man-made light in sight, they exited the Jeep and walked toward the ill-defined shadow. By the light of the full moon, Rusty read the hands on his watch — 11:30.

Fitz turned off the lights.

"Shouldn't we leave them on?" Rusty asked.

"As if the world doesn't have enough light pollution as it is?"

"I think you make an excellent point," Rusty said. It didn't take long for his eyes to adjust to the tree's silhouette, and the sight of its towering branches emerged from the darkness, blocking most of the western sky. Bright moonlight tossed a silver hue over everything, and with the help of a billion stars, it defined the outline of the gargantuan-sized tree.

Aside from the flat parking lot and a few small wooden posts designed to direct foot traffic, they were removed from human influences — just Rusty, Fitz, and "The Tree of Life."

"What kind of tree is this?" he asked.

"I don't know."

Located to the couple's left was a small pole topped with a plaque, and in the faint light, Rusty leaned closer to read the bold letters printed on it. "Prosopis Cineraria. The Tree of Life is over four hundred years old. Many believe this tree is standing in what was once the 'Garden of Eden.' There are no known sources of water to sustain it. It is thought to be fed from a mystical source," he said.

Plaque makers drew Arabic symbols above the English translation. Rusty's inability to read the symbols demanded a higher appreciation for Dani's linguistic abilities. Arabic was harder to read than calculus written in Roman Numerals.

It was a large tree, with no other vegetation in sight and no obvious water source for irrigation, at least none Rusty could see. He kicked the arid sand. Even in the darkness, the dry dust cloud was visible, maintaining its shape as it skimmed low over the desert floor, floating off into oblivion.

"How could this tree survive in the middle of nowhere?" Rusty asked.

"It's a mystery." Fitz laced her smile with serenity. "It's not supposed to be solved." She snaked her arm under his and clenched him tight. "Or maybe it's a miracle."

The word resonated in his mind, and he couldn't shake it.

They circled the tree and stopped every few feet. A single main branch split in half and its outer branches rested on the desert floor. The branches were so heavy the tree grew like a giant shrub. It was twice as wide as it was tall — a wedge as tornado chasers would say.

"Thank you, Erica." Rusty pulled her closer. Uncoiling his arm, he wrapped it around her, embracing her as they both admired the tree's beatific stillness.

Soon after, they dawdled the tree's perimeter. The whole time, Rusty kept cadence with her footsteps. After a few laps around the majestic plant, they meandered to the Jeep to sit and marvel in shared contemplation.

"Garden Of Eden," he said. "What a most auspicious occasion."

"I heard about this place from Beyatte. She's been here a few times on dates," Fitz said.

"What is the story with Beyatte? She seems… bitter."

"She's a Yeoman in my building. We're great friends. She's from New York and enlisted to get away from an abusive ex-boyfriend. He was a wife-beater. From the horror stories she's shared, she's lucky to be alive. Bastard even stabbed her with a steak knife."

Rusty offered no verbal response. Instead, he peeked out the opened door, staring at the ground and shaking his head, disturbed by the new insight.

Enlisting in the Navy is a brilliant way to shake a stalker.

"What's it like being at sea?" she asked.

Rusty blinked, shook his head, and searched for Fitz's eyes in the darkness. "It depends on the ocean. Some oceans are rough, cold, and stormy. At other times, they're glassy, hot, and calm. On clear nights, I like to go topside near the aft mast to sit alone and stare into space. I'm the only one who's ever outside at night. Three-hundred and sixty guys, and none of them stargaze. It's unbelievable. They like to sit inside and play cards or watch re-runs of movies on TV. It's a synthetic life for most, I suppose."

He wiped his mouth with the backside of his hand. Thoughts of dehydration worried him. He'd remembered reading about people dehydrating in the desert, all the while possessing gallons of water. It was alleged they weren't aware of the vast quantities of sweat they'd lost in the arid atmosphere, as their bodies remained dry throughout the dehydration process. Growing up in the humid swamps of the south, he knew a person could calculate heat exhaustion based on how drenched a man's shirt became. Not so in the thirsty climate of a desert.

"Can I have a bottle of water?" he asked.

"Oh, yeah." Fitz grabbed a bottle from the cooler and handed it to Rusty. She grabbed another bottle of water for herself. As she drank, water escaped both corners of her mouth and ran onto her chest, dampening her shirt and soaking her cleavage. Her head dropped, allowing her eyes to inspect her drenched chest. Rusty's fingers met her chin, begging her to look in his direction. Light glistened on her wet lips as he leaned in to kiss her in the Garden of Eden.

The vagabond structured his whole life around the avoidance of attachments. Relationships and emotional baggage were obstacles to navigate, like pothole-ridden freeways. The sign always read "Danger!"

His new outlook troubled him, for he felt a powerful urge to share moments, all his moments, with Fitz. The experiences he'd shared on previous occasions with his friends did little to compete with the compulsions he felt around her. But Rusty was less inclined to divulge his experiences than he was to sponge the experiences she offered. And as someone once said, "the unshared life was a life wasted," and one might think Rusty outgrew his immature, negative opinions of cohabitation.

Everything was determined. Trying to structure his reality, or structuring anything at all, for that matter, was as inane as shingling a roof with paper. Fate hurled Rusty and 4.8 billion other people through an endless vacuum, and the determined universe had plans for everyone. Reality was a never ending game of pool. One atom hits another and on and on until the hologram of the multiverse forms complex patterns according to physics.

Given a long enough timeframe the world, and even the universe, would cease to exist. The fundamental constants of the true multiverse comprised the infinite somethings, the infinite nothings, and the infinite changing of matter in space and time. Eventually, even the hologram of a single universe would dissolve into nothing — only to be reborn, cycling over and over for eternity.

As crazy as it sounded, the circle of birth, life, and death was not a fundamental constant. It seemed consciousness was an emergent phenomenon — a miracle. And love was the most perplexing paradox of them all.

14

The next afternoon, Rusty accompanied Fitz to their private beach.

"We should be fine. We'll have enough time before it gets too late. I brought some of my blankets in case we decide to stay after dark."

"You thought of everything." Rusty perused her tapes, searching through titles for suitable music.

"I try." The wind blew Fitz's auburn hair in wild directions, but squinting and Ray-Bans kept her bangs out of her eyes. "I hope we get there with plenty of time to swim."

Rusty glanced at the afternoon sun, thinking of important times when *hope* failed him. He popped open a can of Sprite — recalling how it'd been years since he last drank soda.

"*Hope* is control," Rusty said.

"What? Do you believe that?" she asked.

"Have you ever heard of the 'Carrot and the Stick'?" Rusty asked. "Right now, *hope* is driving you to speed to the beach before the sun sets. *Hope* motivates every action in life."

"I think you are so focused on the details that you can't see the entire picture."

"What is the entire picture?" he asked.

Fitz held out her hand and eyed Rusty's can of lime soda. Rusty's eyes followed her arm to her hand and placed the can in her outstretched fingers.

She downed the entire drink and wiped her mouth. "It's easy to suppose your mind is an emergent product of an 'atomically arranged' brain. Every experience you have ever had, since birth, has sculpted your mind, via imprinted memories," she said, down-shifting to navigate a large dune that drifted onto the road. "You speak with such certainty when you say nature made the universe of fields and you claim matter pops in and out of these fields."

"Yes. Matter does pop in and out of energy fields." Rusty said, opening another can of lime soda.

Fitz waved her empty can in the air to emphasize her point. "Great. Fair enough. So if there are only 'somethings' and 'nothing' then by default, the universe is infinite, because only 'somethings' exist and things that don't exist cannot contain things that do. The 'somethings' are made of these energy fields and the matter which springs from the fields."

Rusty crushed his can and tossed it in the cooler. "Yes. Spacetime is made of energy fields, and matter is another state of those fields. Physicists refer to this as 'coherence and de-coherence.' As far as the infinite universe, I would have to agree with you. Our universe is one of an infinite number of universes in the multiverse. Limitless numbers of bubbles form, burst, and collapse like bubbles and currents found in a boundless ocean."

Both he and Fitz remained silent as they replayed the conversation over and over in their minds.

Arriving at the beach, the sun was still high in the sky.

Fitz removed a cooler, blanket, and a large white and blue striped umbrella.

After a brief swim in the isolated stretch of surf, they both laid on a blanket, shielded from the sun. Fitz removed her bikini top to take advantage of the seclusion and laid in the cooled shade beside Rusty. Shade and her light complexion made her look purple when compared to the bright beige sand.

Rusty reached for her hand, taking it in his. "Can you believe my ship leaves in two days? This port visit went by so fast."

"I know. It sucks," she said. "But for now, you are here. So I intend to make the best of the time we have."

The entire port call had been a momentous encounter, and their current predicament was Rusty's fault for walking into Fitz's life. He could walk away before investing more emotion into a dead-end relationship. He could tell her how much he enjoyed her company and end everything there and then — treat it like an addiction.

But it was too late. He was powerless to quit. Only the fear of 'Captain's Mast' and a dishonorable discharge could compel Rusty to board the ship when called and leave her behind for good.

"Let's not talk about this now," Fitz said.

Palmer and his family came to Rusty's mind, and he realized how much stronger Palmer was. Rusty had never experienced a departure of such significance. How would he handle it? Once again, the universe compelled his actions, choosing life's path for him.

Fitz turned to Rusty, and they looked into each other's eyes, saying nothing. The limited time hardened his resolve to make their last days happy, for fond memories were more valuable than sad ones. And as enamored as he was, he sought to capture every enchanted moment she could give.

The couple arrived at Fitz's house in the late afternoon. Sunbeams fell across his face as Rusty sat on the couch. Fitz stood over him. Wrapping her arms around his head, she pressed his ear to her chest so she could better comb her fingers through his short hair.

After a few minutes, she extended her hand, beckoning Rusty to take it. They swayed into her bedroom and her clenched fist relaxed its grip. The young Yeoman walked to the window, and in a calculated motion, she unhooked the cord suspending her mini-blinds. With a subtle tug, she let the heavy blind fall shut with a loud *clank*.

Keenly aware of being watched, she turned and grinned. "I want to forget about 'goodbyes' for the time being. You should too. I want to enjoy you while I have you wrapped in my web," she said with a greedy grin.

"You'll be the death of me, you know," he said.

"Don't say that."

Rusty lowered his gaze. "I'm still trying to understand who's caught in a web. You or me?"

In a hushed voice. "For whatever do you mean?" Fitz asked. She walked past Rusty, running her hand across his chest as she made her way to the bed.

"I think you know what I mean."

Fitz sat at the foot of her mattress. "Come," she said as she spread her legs and pointed to the floor between her feet. "We have to see where the story goes." Fitz's glaring eyes commanded Rusty's obedience. "Now strip," she said.

Rusty complied, assuming he knew what she wanted. He slipped his shirt over his head, dropping the bundle on the floor at her feet. Topless and with messy hair, he looked at Fitz, who remained still on the bed. "Like that?" he asked.

"Oh yeah. I like that," she said, her eager eyes running the length of his chest. She reached for his belt, pulling him closer. Her fingers slid into his waistline, lowering his beach shorts, and exposing his clean white skivvies. The whiteness of his underwear made his tan look much darker than it was.

Rusty bent down, and they kissed, falling onto the bed. Resting on his knee, he leaned over, supporting himself, while she clung to him, weighing him down with her clingy, embracing arms.

Her hair, redolent with the scent of fresh jasmine, laid across her pillow wavy and wild like dancing flames. Fitz ran her palm over Rusty's chest while her entitled fingers inched their way past his navel, stopping at his underwear's waistband.

Rusty pulled away, standing beside the bed.

"What's wrong?" Fitz asked, resting her weight on a bracing elbow, as her gaze traced his bare chest.

"There is something I have been 'dying' to do, and I am tired of waiting."

The sting of rejection vexed Fitz. "Your timing is flawless." She sighed and blew stay strands of hair from her eyes. "What do you want to do?"

"I want to take a bath."

Fitz's eyes widened. "Let's."

Squeaky knobs and splashing sounds lured Rusty into the bathroom. A huge white tub rested in the middle of the large white room. It was an older tub, an oversized freestanding clawfoot — porcelain coated cast iron. Small chiclet tiles on the floor were tone-on-tone white, alternating between shiny and flat-sheened.

Fitz bombed the bath with mild fragrances and exotic soaps. The high-water mark threatened to breach the rim of the tub with clumps of flooding bubbles. Hot water flowed, and the air became saturated with condensation, causing steam to fog the mirror. She had converted the room into a candle-lit spa.

At last, she found the opportunity to finish stripping Rusty. Her slender fingers slid his skivvies down to his ankles. After tossing the balled underwear into her hamper, she went into the living room to put a record on the turntable. The soothing sounds of Vangelis complimented the relaxing mood.

Inch by inch, Rusty slipped into the steamy bath, submerging his body up to his neck. After a few deep breaths, he acclimated to the hot water as Fitz ran a soft sea sponge over his bare chest.

The Yeoman squeezed the wet sponge. Suds cascaded over his head, forcing dirt into the bubble-filled tub. "I can't believe you haven't bathed in such a long time." Her gaze caressed his naked body as she bathed him. Massaging, more so than cleaning, she continued to rub him down. "I would go crazy if I couldn't get a bath. I take baths at least once a week," she said. She pointed to the sink and all the soaps on display, along with a shrine of candles.

After she cleansed Rusty, Fitz cycled fresh water into the tub.

"Make room," she said. Before Rusty could even see her do it, she lifted her loose-fitting dress over her head, removed her panties, and climbed between Rusty's legs. Through the candlelight, the pair resembled naked lovers on a bobsled as Fitz reclined against Rusty's chest.

An occasional giggle made her stomach tighten, and her back muscles flexed against him. Using the sponge, she squeezed water over her forehead. She presented Rusty with a hand full of small, foamy bubbles. "Atoms in your brain are like the arrangement of these bubbles. If given all the time in the universe, would it be safe to assume these bubbles would find themselves in this exact arrangement again and again? Forever?"

"I guess so. I would think they would have to if given an infinite amount of time."

Fitz dunked her hand, washing away the bubbles. For a long moment, there was silence as they relaxed in the warm water. Not long after, Fitz broke Rusty's concentration with a tangential idea of her own. "I have a capital idea," Fitz said.

"What's that?"

"I think we should make matching necklaces."

"Do you know how?"

"As a child, I was very precocious, and I loved to play with clay. Sculpture is another one of my many proficiencies. We can sculpt clay and cast it in silver," she said.

"What do we do first?" he asked, rubbing the sponge over her shoulders.

"First, we sculpt."

Fitz stood to leave the tub. She turned and faced Rusty, who remained seated. Looking at her figure, he touched her knees and slid water-logged palms along the outside of her shiny-smooth thighs, resting his hands on her hips. His gaze followed her sleek contours with carnal longing.

Her firm body defied gravity with youthful contempt — toned with newness, unburdened by life's wear. Smooth, tight skin glistened beneath cascading bubbles as reflections highlighted her soft, feminine curves.

Fitz ran her fingernails through Rusty's wet hair. It was futile to contest her amatory advances. As innocent as it was, the flirtatiousness of her pose was unmistakable, and even if he chose otherwise, Rusty was no longer captain of his desires. With sultry seduction, she'd hijacked his freewill, while displaying her own erotic demands.

The necklace would have to wait. And wait, it did. For they were obligated for hours... and even after, they were obligated much longer — well into the night.

The couple laid in the darkened bedroom, drinking iced tea, and watching the ceiling fan.

"Have you ever heard of 'Schrödinger's Cat?'" Rusty asked

"No."

"Well. It is the name of a famous thought experiment by a physicist named Erwin Schrödinger. The thought experiment is based on interpretations of the double-slit experiment. I won't bore you with the details, but the double-slit experiment shows that elementary particles behave like waves or particles, depending on how we observe them.

"To help put the 'double-slit' experiment into context, Schrödinger devised a thought experiment called Schrödinger's Cat. In the experiment, physicists place a cat in a box with a trap. After some time, the cat has a fifty-fifty chance of being alive or dead. No one knows if the trap went off and killed the cat or not. So, technically speaking, the cat exists in both states, until an observer opens the box to measure the cat's condition," Rusty said. "The cat is both dead and alive until someone measures or observes the cat's condition.

"The point I'm making is, there is a term for the cat's condition. We consider the cat to be in a state called 'superposition'. Things in superposition exist in all probable states at the same time. According to quantum physics. With varying degrees of interaction, just measuring quantum states breaks coherence and matter emerges from energy fields to assume a defined point in space-time — just like the cat or a coin toss. Until you raise your hand, the coin is both heads and tails.

"The future holds *everything* in superposition, just like the cat in the box. We travel through space, breaking superposition with each passing moment. The past is a sorted, categorized, and labeled version of the future. Sentient minds break the wave potential of future events and sort them into organized paths we call experience. We spend our lives playing a universal lottery, or bingo, waiting to see what numbers reality gives us, based on probabilistic chance, trillions of times a second."

Fitz asked, "Do you think the future holds every scenario, and the past is a realized version of a single scenario — or a choice made by *fate?*"

Rusty scratched his chin. "Yes. I would think you are correct, but *fate* might be a loose term for 'determined.' Human minds slice their way through the ocean of reality, breaking superpositions ten to forty-fourth times a second. The past derives the effects from causes. Meanwhile, the future converts causes into effects. And, until events happen, everything in the universe is in superposition."

Fitz put her hand on Rusty's arm.

Rusty searched for her eyes in the darkened room. "We are forever surfing the present moment, trying to get ahead of the future, while looking back at our past, and the whole time we convince ourselves memories are real, when they are as illusionary as hallucinations," he said, pausing for a minute. "I struggle to understand why I can't remember my past lives."

Fitz bit her bottom lip as she considered Rusty's question. "Who says you don't remember your past lives? What's saying every thought you have, and every memory you have, are not the same ones you have always had, living on infinite repeat?"

"What do you mean?" Rusty asked, sitting up to grab his drink. Ice clanked in the glass as he took a small sip. "I wish I had a cigarette. I don't crave them often, but once in a while, I do."

Fitz leaned over to her nightstand and opened a drawer. She pulled out a black-colored box of Djarum Clove cigarettes.

"Do you smoke?"

"No, these are Beyatte's."

This answer confused Rusty more than any other answer could, but he chose not to ask Fitz why she kept Beyatte's cloves in her nightstand. After all, it was none of his business.

Fitz handed the pack and a lighter to Rusty. "From what you told me, events of the future are unknown, because your mind has not broken through the moments of superposition yet. Once your mind breaks through superposition, reality categorizes your experiences, filing your experiences into the correct paths of your distinct past reality — forming appropriate memories based on who you are. Memories make you. They do not belong to you. You belong to them," Fitz said.

"It is something to consider." Rusty fumbled, feeling for the box's lid.

"Could you imagine having memories that aren't yours — like having memories of space flight, in a world where men still rode horses to capture castles? It would seem death protects you from going insane," she said.

"Maybe." Rusty removed a black cigarette and lit it. The snapping and crackling of burning clove leaves resounded in the silent room. The sweet-smelling smoke of burnt cloves lingered in the air above them. Rusty licked his lips, savoring their candied taste, while he examined the clove's glowing ember.

"So you mean everything I remember has happened over and over? I remember the events because those events determine which version of myself I am living? And not the other way around. The events make me, I don't make the events?" he asked.

"You could say that."

Rusty watched the spinning ceiling fan, stunned by her revelation. "If every other version of Rusty never met you, but I did, then I would be in suspended animation until the universe made you and I again. I would be oblivious to the time spent waiting to be reborn. Also, the universe would have to make these, exact, same conditions for me to exist again."

"Maybe. Let's face facts. This version of you could never exist without this version of me." Fitz laughed and extended her hand, making a scissoring gesture with her two fingers. Rusty handed her the clove, and she held it to her lips, squinting as she inhaled.

The billowed smoke mingled with the fan's blades. Fitz licked her lips and said, "you are breaking 'superposition' in Planck Time over countless eons, and the universe is subjugating you to the precise path you belong in — not the other way around. Your life is pre-determined by every event since the Big Bang, and every memory accounts for the moments you've had. Your past has everything to do with the conscious state you find yourself in now.

"Every sentient mind is always living in a present moment," Fitz added. "Even people who died in the past are living in present moments in their own lives. Right now, trillions of alternate versions of

General Custer are getting shot by arrows, on infinite repeat. And people in the future are living their respective present moments, flying in spaceships to their families living on Mars. Anyone who is not experiencing a present moment does not exist in any dimension. Everyone lives in the 'now' and nowhere else, regardless of where their relative time relates to you and me. We do not travel through time. Time travels through us. We filter time like air and it changes us physically."

Fitz held the pinched clove between her lips.

It surprised Rusty that he'd missed such an obvious inference. "You're right. How could a person experience the memories of this life in a different universe? It would drive them insane as reality would not synch with memories of their prior experiences of a different life. Someone might end up remembering a cat in a universe where cats do not exist. It's not sane holding old memories from infinite lifetimes, rendering a person unable to experience life in *any* universe. Imagine having an unlimited number of memories of every life you've ever lived," he said. "Your mind would be too full to function."

"The universe knows what it's doing," she said. "Don't argue with its perfection and don't fear it, either." Fitz exhaled a long cloud of smoke. "'Now' is all that is real, and the physical world is moving through time while your consciousness remains fixed; only clicking on and off from life in the present moment to death in oblivion. Your consciousness is forever repeating the cycle of awareness and oblivion. It's as though you're only alive when the universe flips your switch. The periods you're switched off do not exist, or at least they do not exist for you. A zillion eons mean nothing when you're dead."

Fitz licked her lips, savoring the diminishing flavor before requesting the clove for one last taste. "Just remember, the universe knows full well what it's doing. Nature perfected the universe throughout its infinite evolution. 'Truth' wants to reveal itself to all sentient beings. We just need to look outside ourselves to gain the correct perspective."

She offered the clove back to Rusty, but he waved her off.

"Want some more to drink?" she asked, slipping out from beneath the blanket to put her robe on. As she waltzed into the kitchen, she flipped the switch. Fresh light spilled into the bedroom, highlighting Fitz's silhouette in the doorway as her shadow fell across Rusty's blanket.

Laying in bed, he put his hands behind his head, trying to assimilate her theories.

15

Fitz tasked Rusty with making art, putting his stored experience to the test, while evaluating his sense of "taste." Did Rusty have good taste, or was his mind full of kitschy ideas based on a sheltered existence? If Rusty replayed enough memories in the correct sequence, juxtaposing them in random order, it would be possible for him to conceive an acceptable idea for an art piece for her necklace. Possible, but unlikely without a refined eye for art. Still, he was never one to shy away from a challenge.

Once kneaded, sculpting clay became malleable. After the misshaped lump spent a few seconds between an artisan's fingers, the sienna red-colored clay softened like chewed bubble gum. If left undisturbed, sculpting clay firmed to a hard consistency — remaining stiff until kneaded again — repeat and repeat.

Fitz transformed her dining room table into an artist's surgical station. Like a gloomy poker table, centered floodlights beamed intense light onto the table's flat surface, which was filled with modeling clay and an assortment of sculpting knives. Wooden utensils took various appearances — some tools resembled tiny oars, and others seemed more specialized. There were pointed, pick-like tools, used to form nuanced details in the refinement stage of sculpting, small wooden rakes for creating tooth for additional layers of clay, and Sgraffito tools used for smoothing and burnishing the clay's oily surface.

Rusty combed through all the images stored in his mind, weighing the level of difficulty of each of his recalled images with his refined sense of taste. It would be easy to make a square or circle, but Rusty wanted to find an image that held significance. In order to have meaning, the shape must hold sentimental value for Fitz. Rusty had to presume to know her preferences and what she liked.

On the opposite side of the table, and with her idea already conceived, Fitz was well on her way to completing the "realization phase." Her fingers sculpted away at the rudimentary shape.

"Our minds are molding matter," Rusty said.

Without pausing her work. "What?" she asked.

"We are conceptualizing an image in our mind and manipulating the matter to the shape of that image. The atoms of this piece of clay are being pushed around by the atoms in our hands, and the atoms in these wooden tools. We are moving these atoms around as a projection of our thoughts — thoughts which come from different atoms, inside out brains."

Fitz looked up from her sculpture. Their eyes met in the bright overhead spotlight. Long shadows stretched down their faces, making them look hollow, skeleton-like. She leaned in and her wavy copper hair blocked the light, obscuring more of her expression. "How is your sculpture coming?"

After working his fingers for ten minutes, Rusty's clay morphed into a familiar object. He scratched his nose with the knuckle of his index finger, keeping clay oils off his face. "I'm close. I have a few more things to do before I feel it's finished."

In the time it took them to sculpt the forms, the re-workable clay had stiffened. Fitz peeled the wax paper from the back of her creation and held it in her hand. It was a cat. "Schrödinger's cat is alive," she announced.

"Wow! It looks so rad," he said. "I can't wait to see it cast in metal." After judging the caliber of his sculpting ability, a deluge of insecurity dampened his excitement. But he forged on.

Five minutes later, Rusty finished his design and raised his big reveal. Still stuck to the wax paper, he presented her with a tiny tree. "I know it's tawdry, but I wanted to make you something to remember the Tree of Life."

Fitz was drawn to the design and walked around for a closer look.

The tree was sloppy and unskilled. In fact, it did not look like a tree at all. It resembled a flat hunk of chewed bubble gum with a stem protruding from its base, like a sienna-colored piece of flat broccoli. But what it lacked in technical merit, the sentimental value it provided offset its shortcomings.

She pressed her hand to her chest. "Thank you."

"I'm glad you like it. I was afraid I might disappoint you."

Fitz looked at Rusty through teary lenses. "No one has ever made me anything like this before."

"Your sincere smile is worth my humiliation. I suck at art," Rusty joked. "What do we do now?"

Without taking her eyes off the small tree, Fitz said, "now we need to make our molds."

"Let's do it," he said.

She met Rusty's gaze. "I have a shed out back."

Fitz kicked open the utility door leading behind her house. Her backyard resembled an industrial storage yard, more so than any green, salad-like yards found in middle suburbia. Sand substituted the nutrient-rich soil reserved for lush green lawns, while dry-stemmed weeds replaced manicured shrubbery.

In the corner, back against a short metal fence, stood an unassuming twenty by ten-foot aluminum shed. Constant sandblasting painted its aluminum exterior the same grey and beige hue as the desert floor, leaving the 'decades old, wind-swept, shed' indistinguishable from the desert. Lit by an intense amber-colored streetlight and a lingering haze, the night scene took on a dusty-noir-ambiance.

Fitz walked to the shed. Rusty followed, negotiating the loose sand while holding their fragile pieces of sculpture in both hands — like a parishioner holding an invisible bible.

A well-worn bolt secured the shed's door, sheltering the shed's interior from the elements. Fitz wedged her heel into the sand and pressed her toes against the door's base, releasing tension on the long bolt. With the latch slacked, she pinched the hex-shaped head between her dainty fingers and lifted the three-inch bolt from its slot. Removing her foot, she allowed the door to swing open. She swept the door aside with her heel, walked into the dark shed, and pulled a chain.

With a *chink,* the low-wattage incandescent light lit up, revealing a swinging chain and a vast assortment of tools, most of which Rusty could not identify. Some tools he could: torches; chisels for sculpting soapstone; a potter's wheel, with an unfinished vase resting in the center of the platter; two large kilns for firing sculpture; a tall crucible for melting small quantities of steel. The crucible sat cold in a corner. Thick gloves, used for handling hot metal, hung on the wall beside large tongs.

With crazed eyes, Fitz grabbed a large torch and held it up. "This will do. First, we make a mold, then we make the cast," she said. "We will use molding sand."

Mindful of Rusty's limited knowledge, she instructed Rusty on the fine art of metal-casting. Her instructions, as detailed and explicit as they were, were easy enough to understand.

Fitz opened a drawer to grip a single stainless steel sheet pan, placing it on the worktable. She removed a couple of three-inch metal squares which resembled drink coasters, and centered them on the tray. "We'll pack it in the molding sand. But first, put the sculptures on these squares," she said, reaching into the drawer and pulling out a pair of metal cuffs.

Rusty peeled the clay pieces from the wax paper. He positioned them in the center of the square metal coasters, centering them. Using a large spoon and what appeared to be brown sugar, he scooped the ultra-fine sand and packed it into the metal cuffs, burying the clay sculptures to make impressions.

"Thats half. Now we need to repeat it for the back of the piece. Then we sandwich the casts in the vise."

She flipped the entire assembly, repeating the process. Once finished, she added a small dowel in the mold, making a hole where the metal was to be poured.

"Okay, now that we have the molds, we cast the metal," she said and pointed to a pair of lockable tongs on the wall. "You'll need to grip the crucible. Put the torch to it, and when the metal melts, pour the liquid silver into the tiny hole. Got it?" she asked.

Rusty nodded. "Easy enough, but where is the metal?"

Fitz's frenzied sneer grew larger and larger in anticipation. The jilted sailor reached into her pocket. Pinched between her two fingers was a bracelet.

"The douche-nozzle gave this to me before he boarded a plane for Guam," she said. "It's annoying and clunky."

Jewelers polished the thick silver chain to a brilliant shine, but over the years, it tarnished — symbolic of Fitz and her ex-lover's relationship.

Someone designed it for a man's wrist, because the large chain was too brutish for a woman. Being as no reputable jeweler would recommend it for the delicate wrist of a female, it seemed apparent the douche-nozzle purchased the tacky chain secondhand.

Fitz aspired to make necklaces as mementos of their shared time, but the process was also a cleansing ritual for her. She wanted to kill all connections to her ex.

"Grab those bolt cutters and cut it in half." She pointed at the wall and a pair of hanging cutters, commanding Rusty to follow her instructions.

Rusty hammered a two-inch nail into the wooden bench. With a loud *bang* of the hammer, dust flew from the wooden bench and floated in the dim light. He looped one end of the bracelet onto the nail and Fitz grabbed the other. She pulled tight as Rusty placed the chain in the mouth of the heavy bolt cutters. Together, they cut the link and the soft metal snapped like warmed pewter.

Fervent eyes inspected the severed chain in the dim light. "Now let's melt this and pour yours first," she said.

Fitz pushed a pair of tinted safety goggles to Rusty. "Wear these, the metal might pop and I don't want you to blind those handsome gray eyes of yours," she said, placing a pair over her own.

Rusty donned the dark-lensed goggles and slid one hand into a thick, flame-retardant glove. The heavy glove was far denser than an ordinary oven mitt. Using his other hand, he gripped the torch and held it ready, pointing it in a safe direction.

Bending down, Fitz turned a knob on the oversized propane tank, allowing the gas to flow. A moderate *hiss* let her know the hose held gas, prompting her to spark the torch.

A soft thud announced the ignition. She tossed the striker on the workbench and turned the propane's control knob, narrowing the long flame — concentrating and streamlining the broad flame to a focused jet, heating the surrounding space.

Flames reflected in her goggles. The Yeoman's desire to melt the silver, and purge the past, boiled into border-lined delirium. Her teeth clenched. Her brow furrowed.

Talking louder than the sound of the torch, Fitz ordered more commands. "Preheat the crucible. Hold the flame over the center and move it in circles to disperse the heat. When I put this in, aim for the center, but circulate across the entire piece of silver," she said.

After a few minutes, the cup, resembling a large lead shot glass, glowed a subtle shade of orange. Exercising due diligence and gripping the chain in metal tongs, she lowered the silver, bunching it into a tight ball.

"What is the crucible made of?" Rusty asked.

"Graphite. Keep the flame on it and move it around so it heats evenly."

Rusty did as he was told. It took a long time to build up enough heat, but once it reached the melting point, the crucible radiated intense white light, hinting the silver was close to liquifying.

Sweat dripped from their faces and rolled down their necks. Fitz stared, mesmerized by the fiery flame. Its brightness reflected in the glossy lenses of their eye protection.

"How hot do you think it is?" he asked.

"I don't know, but when it melts, the bitch will be one thousand, seven hundred and sixty-eight degrees!"

Rusty licked beads of sweat off his lip, waiting for Fitz's instruction. "How hot does the torch get?"

"About three thousand and five hundred degrees. It's not the heat. Most torches get hot enough to melt silver, but it's the size of the flame that counts. The bigger the flame, the faster the melt. This is plenty of flame for this small amount of silver," she said, instructing him to mind his work by looking at the blazing crucible. "I cranked the gas just to be sure."

"Makes sense," Rusty said. The scientist in him was determined to watch the silver melt.

Without having changed much of its original color, and without warning, the silver transitioned from a solid to a liquid. The liquid silver resembled orange mercury rolling around a shot glass made of molten magma.

Fitz pinched a bag of white powder and threw the dust into the molten silver.

When Fitz pointed to the molds, Rusty inched the crucible to the vise. He handed the torch to Fitz, who aimed it away. With the utmost precision, he poured the molten silver into the tiny hole in the brown sugar sand. The tiny hole swallowed more metal than he thought it would. The mold filled, and Rusty jerked, raising the cup to stop the flow.

Fitz sweated and grinned with euphoria. "Whoa there, don't splash it. I don't know what I would do if you got some in those pretty little eyes of yours."

Fitz elbowed Rusty. An enormous grin formed on her mouth, and she winked. "We can let it cool. It might take a while until we can touch it. That sand holds a lot of heat. Now we repeat the same process with the other mold."

After pouring the silver into the second charm, Fitz held a rectangular-shaped mold and instructed Rusty to pour the remaining silver into it.

"I think that's about a half ounce of silver leftover. Wanna get some coffee while it all cools?"

"Have any Bud in a can?"

As the two emerged from the shed, they stumbled into the chilly night air. Steam billowed from their sweat-covered bodies, dissolving into the dry air in all directions.

"That was fun." Rusty said. "I think I need another bath."

Fitz removed her gloves. "I love working with torches and fire. It's so primal."

Bright light blinded their eyes as they entered the kitchen. Fitz walked to the dimmer switch and lowered the dial, setting the light to a more appropriate level.

She reached into the fridge and grabbed two bottles of 'Old Milwaukee' by their necks. She held the bottles between her fingers as she extended her arm, offering them for Rusty to open.

"Where did you get all that stuff?" Rusty asked. He stood near Fitz with bottles in each hand.

"There's an opener screwed to the wall beside the pantry."

Rusty approached a beaver bottle opener. Its teeth were large and its mouth was wide open. Rusty placed the bottle in the beaver's mouth and pressed down.

"I got the torch from the same person who sold me the Jeep. He couldn't take it with him. It was too big." Fitz took a sip of her beer. "The kiln belongs to an artist friend I know. She lives on base and comes to visit and we do pottery. I don't use it much, but sometimes we get together and make cups and bowls."

"Oh nice. Can I see some?"

Fitz pointed at the coffee mug on the counter.

He walked to the counter and lifted the mug, looking at its sheen against the light. The round cup, tapered at the bottom, held tiny ridges running around its rim. Her fingers made the ridges used to shape it.

Rusty's thumbs caressed the cup's lip. "Wow."

"It's just a cup," she said, blushing.

"I know, but it's neat to see a cup that was made by someone I know," he said. "I think it's wonderful."

"Thank you. I'm glad you like it," she said. They finished their beer, and each drank a few more. After spending the next hour laughing and telling stories, Rusty asked about the molds. Judging by the look in Fitz's eyes, she must have forgotten about them.

The molds, freed from the vise, opened like shucked oysters. She grabbed the cooled silver stem left from the dowel hole. The charm resembled a piece of silver, shaped like a tiny broccoli lollypop.

She held the charm by the stem. "We need to cut this."

Using a Dremel, Rusty severed both stems, cutting them close to the charms.

Resting in the dark corner of the shed was an old bench grinder. "Now we sand and polish," she said.

Rusty held the charms to the fast-spinning polishing wheel. Careful not to bite into the details, he polished the pieces to a brilliant, chrome-like shine — freeing the fettled edges of snaggy burrs.

Fitz inspected the trinkets. She instructed Rusty to use the drill press to make eyelets for the chain. With a flip of the switch, the drill bit ate into the soft metal, and a silver pigtail emerged from the hole.

After rummaging through her jewelry box, Fitz withdrew two chains and removed the necklaces. "White gold," she said. "You take the bigger one and I'll take the thinner one."

The bibelots were works of art, sparkling with the same excitement as they felt holding them.

Rusty tried his on first. It was perfect. His cat was long and lanky, like a stretched Siamese in a seated position. Much taller than wide.

She ran her fingers across the tree, feeling for burrs that weren't there. "It means a lot to me."

Together, they walked to the bathroom mirror and stood beside one another, looking at their creations. After a brief inspection, Fitz ran her fingers along the chain, stopping at the tree pendant. Pinching the charm, her loving fingers tempered its surface with sentimental value, and her arms welcomed Rusty's embrace.

In two hours, Rusty and Fitz would have to head to the base, reporting for duty. This day would be their last together.

16

After getting off work, Fitz prepared a large candlelight dinner, and the couple sat facing one another at the small dinner table. The steak was softer than the ones Rusty'd received on his ship. In fact, it was the best steak he'd eaten in years.

"This is great," Rusty said, holding up a small cube of beef skewered on his fork.

"Thank you."

Silence accompanied an awkward feeling bordering on melancholy. Minutes passed before Rusty spoke, breaking the tension. "I'm leaving in twelve hours. Can you believe how fast the past two weeks have flown by?" His words were a poignant reminder of their imminent separation.

Fitz stared at her plate. "I know."

"I can write," he said. He realized how contrived his words sounded.

The Yeoman managed a forced smile. "Writing would be nice. And who knows? Maybe in a year, we can meet in Hawaii," she said.

Fitz slid her hand across the table and Rusty met her halfway. "I know I had a great time. I want to always remain friends."

"Of course, we'll remain friends. I wouldn't have it any other way. I might make an influential art critic, but I think I would make a better art agent."

"Who knows? One day we can team up and you can sell my paintings." Fitz said.

"I would totally sell the shit outta your paintings."

Rusty stood and walked around the table to stand near Fitz. Fitz dropped her fork and stood to hold him. They moved to the sofa and held each other until the sun set and night darkened the room.

Hours later…

It took Rusty five minutes to pack his bag and set it beside the front door. The couple reclined on the couch in the darkened room, watching the slow churn of the ceiling fan while listening to the wind and cars outside.

They wasted little energy engaged in idle conversation. For conversation sped the passing of time, and they wanted to stretch their shared moments as long as possible.

Fitz and Rusty walked to the bedroom. They spent their last moments staring at the stars through the open window, wrapped in one another's embrace. Soon after, Fitz fell asleep. But Rusty could not.

Shadows of the swirling fan blades shrank and stretched on the ceiling as they spun in the streetlight shining through the window.

So much of Rusty dwelled on the past two weeks that the port visit defined his every thought. Memories occupied his thoughts, classifying him and leaving little room for anything else. But thoughts were continuous things. Thoughts flowed from one atomic state to the next. That much Rusty knew. Nature replaced atoms in his body a billion times a second, filling the voids with new atoms, and consciousness thought rolled with those changes — seeming continuous, analog, and uninterrupted.

Rusty buried his eyes in the pit of his elbow, isolating the world from his contemplation. The harder he tried to sleep, the more his head exploded with ideas. He constructed new images of visualized realism. His mind raced from thought to thought. His…

A gentle hand pressed against Rusty's leg, pulling him back to the awakened world. Fitz rolled over and lowered her voice to whisper in Rusty's ear. Her warm breath caressed his cheek. "Can't sleep?"

"How did you know?"

"Your leg is twitching."

Rusty stopped kicking his foot. The stillness provided an uncomfortable sensation. "I'm sorry."

Within a few minutes, Fitz's light snoring resumed.

At 6:00 a.m., it was still dark. In the following hour, it would be dawn, and with it the coming of day. Time spent with Fitz was fun, and the last two weeks left Rusty with many fond memories, but the moment had come to part ways. There was no sense in making a big deal of it because all the melodrama in the world would solve nothing.

He drawled as he pulled his arm from under Fitz's head, leaving her to sleep. Gentle hands laid her head to rest on the pillow as he rolled out of bed.

Silent steps led him to her nightstand, where he removed a folded envelope from his back pocket. Holding it in his hands, his thumbs caressed the wrinkled paper. On its cover read, "Erica Fitzgerald." He propped the envelope against the unlit lamp and glanced back to see if she was awake, before exiting her room for the last time.

Rusty paused at the front door and gave a last look at her bedroom, hoping he would never forget how her home looked, wanting to remember every subtle detail. His fingers felt for his necklace. Satisfied it was around his neck, he rubbed the charm through his shirt and opened the door.

Outside, the bracing morning air jolted him, heightening his senses the way cold air always did. He struggled with the first step — then the second — then the third. As hard as each step was, he trudged on until after a dozen steps, his hesitancy resolved, and he quickened his pace to a brisk walk.

Looking at store windows along the route, he watched his reflection as he strolled past them toward the pier, almost walking into a display of oranges piled near the curb. The annoyed fruit vendor glared at Rusty. Other shopkeepers busied themselves by laying out a kaleidoscopic array of colored textiles and cheesy souvenirs, planning for the daily procession of tourists.

At 6:45 am, Rusty approached the Quarterdeck of the Savannah and the Adams. "Request permission to come aboard," he said.

"Permission Granted." The OOD waved him onboard.

Rusty sauntered from berthing and emerged topside in his dress whites, prepared to 'man the rails.'As he wandered the fantail, he watched as his shipmates performed line handling duties — tossing slacked mooring lines to the tugs. Rusty walked over and pulled on the thick lines, releasing the Adams from the Savannah. The line crew snaked the lines through a small hatch, stowing the lines in a large storage room below deck. Tug masters ordered deckhands to toss tug lines to the Adams, ready to pull the massive destroyer toward the open waters of the gulf.

Rusty turned from the rail facing the Savannah. He stood at parade rest, watching the morning water chop as lazy ripples rolled against the hull of their sister ship. His gaze crept from the water's surface, over the decks of the Savannah, before settling on the gate shack at the front of the pier.

Less than a hundred yards out, he spotted Fitz running down the pier. His hands relaxed, and he felt the weight of the deck officer's stare as he broke Parade Rest.

Fitz stopped aft of the Savannah's fantail, looking at Rusty. Hell, everyone looked at Rusty as he tried to ignore her. But his body was at odds with his intent, and his posture stiffened.

What are the odds of jumping ship and swimming to her without drowning?

Fitz stood near the stern of the Savannah, having chased Rusty from her house to the pier in a desperate attempt at closure. Her long, flowing sundress swayed in the gentle breeze, and she remained motionless as Rusty's ship drifted farther out to sea. Rusty knew her well enough to know the compulsion she felt for resolution was stronger than her fear of humiliation at having been exposed in such a vulnerable way — exposing her emotional weakness to the crew present on both ships.

Eventually, Fitz grew smaller and smaller. The ship drifted... Two hundred yards from the pier, three hundred, and then four. Loud horns blared from the tugboats, ordering the Adam's line handlers to release their heavy, saltwater-soaked lines. The loud honk, drawn out over seconds, mocked Rusty's dwindling window of decision. Like a timer for a demented game show, the intrusive sound signaled the finality of his escape window, the deadline for accepting his own dare. Or were the horns urging him to action?

Rusty remained steadfast to the port side rail, alone, not wanting to break sight of Fitz. The line safety officer motioned to yell at Rusty, but knew the sailor would not answer the order to grab the rope, he would not comply, and would not budge from the rail. In fact, he would do nothing to break contact with Fitz's line of sight. With each passing moment, he felt their relationship dissolve regardless of how much he sought to prevent it.

Gas turbines revved, and their pitch increased. The ship's engines whined higher and louder. Her whistle-hum rose, making her scream like a distant jet airliner launching on a short runway.

A large wake formed at the stern of the ship. The massive, nine-foot wall of whitewash trailed the stern as the ship moved forward. Vibrations flowed through the deck as her screws pitched, propelling the ship forward at an ever-increasing speed. The world moved past Rusty — the world, the air, and the sea. They were underway, at last.

Hot wind pressed Rusty's left ear, soft at first, then harder, more persuasive. He stepped forward and gripped the rail, and for a moment..... for a moment.... A heavy clarity invaded his thoughts.

I could jump and swim for it. It's not too late.

Crew members inched closer, their stealthy arms at the ready. Everyone seemed poised for action. Some sought to restrain Rusty. While others waited with morbid curiosity, hoping to see Rusty jump.

Moments passed, and for a time, the activity of the fantail froze. All hands watched the drama unfold.

The ocean grew expansive, and the shoreline grew thin. One minute later, he could barely see Fitz's copper hair. Minutes passed before the Savannah's signature slipped from view and Fitz along with it.

By the time Rusty figured he'd jump, the opportunity was gone — passing him by at thirty-five knots.

A damn tragedy indeed.

Had he jumped, propellers would have shredded his body and his lifeless corpse would end up surfing the wake all the way to Egypt.

Fate had taken it upon itself to decide for him, leaving him to stare at the thin strip of featureless coastline. Rusty realized his destiny, and the reckoning was over, having exchanged whatever possibilities he may have had with Fitz for the concrete reality of where his duty carried him.

A hand rested on his shoulder. Rusty turned to find Mux standing next to him. "You two will meet again. I know it. Come on man, let's go get some green eggs," Mux said. "I'm buying."

Rusty looked at the hand resting on his shoulder. His gaze traced the arm to Mux's smiling lips. "Sure. Let me go change first," Rusty said.

In berthing, a "not so hungry" Rusty cleaned out his seabag. He dropped the heavy bag on the deck and fished for the items one by one. As he reached toward the bottom, he felt a hard object wrapped in a t-shirt that smelled of jasmine. The object was cold and heavy. He unwrapped the feminine white cotton undershirt for a more thorough inspection. It was Fitz's coffee mug. She'd stowed it in his bag while he packed, unbeknownst to him.

The cup ushered harsh realizations. Rusty never let Fitz say goodbye. Instead, he robbed her of the chance. It was a selfish move on his part. What if she had something she needed to say? He wanted to go back and change things, but knew he couldn't, for the arrow of time only goes one way.

Besieged with remorse, he placed the cup on Palmer's rack, put both hands on his head, and began pacing the isle.

I'm an asshole.

His compunction was overwhelming.

Would Fitz ever forgive me? I doubted it. And why should she?

With a forced appetite, Rusty walked to chow and waited his turn in the short line, accompanied by his best friend Mux.

Dazed, he stood in the passageway, contemplating what happened and how things went so badly, so quickly. Rusty knew Mux was speaking, but could not understand what was being said. But not because he ignored Mux. No, he did not ignore his friend. In fact, he struggled to listen, but he could not process the words coming from Mux's mouth. Rusty was fogged up, blacked out.

He swallowed his breakfast, but the omelet might as well have been a stale pickle. He would never finish his meal.

His shipmate's faces mocked him. Or was he deceived by his skewed perception of the morning's events? He'd always tried immunizing his emotions, compartmentalizing them to protect himself from attachments. But alas, it was too late for Rusty. Having already been exposed, the illness had laid dormant the entire time Rusty was in Bahrain. The wayward sailor had caught the bug when he first met Fitz. She was contagious. Her radiated energy had dosed Rusty, and he withered from the fallout. Rusty was sick with love.

The ship steamed on. In a few short weeks, they would make for their home port in Mayport, Florida. Fitz and Rusty would, in the most literal sense, be a world apart.

Rusty abandoned Mux and left the galley to go topside. The weather decks were his place of solitude. He went to the signalman shack, perched above the Pilothouse, to ponder the turning of events.

A strong headwind blew in his face, irritating his squinting eyes. Through watery lenses, he looked over his right shoulder at the thin strip of beach as the pitching motions of the shop's prow carved its way through the ocean's wake. It was Fitz's private beach on the eastern coast of Bahrain, and it reserved a place in Rusty's thoughts. Knowing he'd never see Fitz again was the worst thought of his life.

Even the most abhorrent universe is incapable of conceiving such bitter cruelty.

Sometime later, the Fight Quarter's alarm blasted Rusty awake, evicting him from the comfort of his warm rack. The announcement reverberated through the ship's interior and repeated its distorted dynamics through the low-fidelity loudspeakers of the 1MC for everyone to hear.

***Ding-Ding.* "Flight Quarters, Flight Quarters. Man your Flight Quarters stations. The smoking lamp is out on the fantail. Now Flight Quarters."** *Sh-click.*

Although there were many flight crewmen attached to the helicopter squadron, Rusty was the only enlisted person assigned to flight duty who was part of the ship's regular crew. Because of this, Rusty always felt the crew passed the call to Flight Quarters just for him.

Berthing was dark. Rusty studied black hands contrasting with the white face of his German-made wrist-watch, displaying a reading of 9:41. He didn't know how long he'd slept. But he surmised he'd been asleep for a while. He cursed and stumbled, contesting the rocking motions of the ship while trying to slip into his denim bell-bottomed jeans.

Mornings always suck.

He slid his cold feet into shiny black boots before staggering from berthing — flummoxed. Unsteady legs carried Rusty to his Flight Quarter station, and he was still half asleep when he climbed the final ladder near the hangar. As he reached the top of the steps, a thought crossed his mind... *How did I miss the morning's muster?*

Rusty snaked his way through the ladders and various passageways, headed upstairs through the superstructure, prepared to burst on-scene in the bright helo hangar. He stopped just before opening the door, squinting his eyes in preparation to meet the incandescent blaze of blinding sunbeams.

At first, Rusty assumed the hangar's large sliding doors were still closed. Except for the faint glow of red electric lighting, the hangar was nowhere as bright as he expected. No natural daylight. This catalyzed Rusty's immediate confusion, a disorientation only sleep and sensory-deprived individuals could know. Rubbing his eyes, the bewildered sailor glanced at the time again. He then leered at the open doors and beyond, off into the chilled night sky.

Crap. It's 9:49 p.m., not morning. Have I been asleep all day?

Sleep deprivation, and no natural light inside the ship, exhibited profound effects on Rusty's waking cycles. Time dilated in the Berthing compartment because of the extended absence of natural light. With no sunlight, sleep cycles and circadian rhythms were being torqued on all crewmen who worked the night shift. There were only five windows on the ship, and this meant a sailor could have spent weeks below decks without knowing if it was day or night. It's why the military used twenty-four-hour military time. Booger's mom knew the score better than Rusty did.

Airmen readied the Seahawk. Donned in their flight uniforms, the aircrew wheeled the large helicopter out onto the flight deck and prepared to unchain the enormous wheels of its landing gear.

Rusty stopped near the bottom of the ladder, struggling to remember his afternoon and recall earlier events to put his mind in its proper orientation. He climbed the ladder into the tower, searching his thoughts for clues to make sense of the time lost. He peered outside the rear window to observe the status of the helicopter from his tiny window.

Rusty gathered his headgear and reported in. He pressed the button on his microphone to speak to the Pilothouse, announcing his state of readiness. "Pilothouse. Flight tower. Manned and ready."

The pilothouse acknowledged Rusty as the ship-wide speaker system blared "amber deck."

Another long night began.

A week later, during the morning muster, Mr. Kistner walked into the Shop. The smell of ironed polyester and aftershave trailed him as he entered.

"Attention on deck!" Palmer said, rousing everyone to stand up straight and tuck their arms to their sides.

Mr. Kistner stopped in the center of the space to address the division. "As you were. I'm here to tell you we are to escort the USS Dallas through the Suez Canal and onward to Greece. In one week, we pull into Corfu for a five-day port visit."

The Shop erupted in thunderous applause, forcing Mr. Kistner to wave his clipboard. "Alright, settle down. It may change, but as of now, orders scheduled us for liberty in Greece. On a side note, Petty Officer Washington, have those parts come in yet?"

"No, Sir. Supply says they should be here within two days," Mux answered.

"Stay on it and let me know. Does anyone have anything for me? No? Okay." Mr. Kistner turned to leave.

"Attention of Deck!" Jones shouted.

"Carry on."

After the meeting, Rusty walked outside the forward fan-room door to stand on the starboard side weather deck. In the distance, clouds shaded the ocean, casting random black patches across its surface.

The sun projected the ship's silhouette as she skimmed the water, outlining the rotating shadow of the Forty's radar antenna in the sea's wake. The spinning silhouette conformed to the contours of the small three-foot surface chop.

Moshing waves struggled to break through the ocean's surface, churning, heaving themselves skyward, only to be pulled back by Earth's gravity.

Without warning, a gigantic shadow darted outward from the ship to the horizon, causing Rusty to flinch. Moving at unbelievable speeds, the shadow of a jet plane emerged, separating from the ship's shadow. Without making a sound, the jet moved at such a high velocity; it was a football field away before Rusty looked up from the water to see the ass end of an F-14 Tomcat. Two orange flames glared from her round afterburners as the jet traveled at speeds far exceeding its sound.

One second later, a loud, thunderous shock wave blasted Rusty in the back of his head. The Tomcat was two football fields past the ship before her blast wave reached the Adams. Her shock wave hit with a loud crack, which sounded like a lightning strike from thirty feet away — followed by the sound of long rolling thunder, the smell of jet exhaust, and hot air which trailed her flaming engines. The after-effects flooded the ship like spray from a crop duster.

Bitch just buzzed the ship!

The Tomcat flew so low, its shock waves recoiled along the water's surface.

Did it fly between the masts?

Rusty experienced supersonic flight and felt the sound barrier as it hit him in the back of his head. He was *inside* a sonic boom. Meanwhile, the entire crew heard the sound barrier as it smacked the ship.

After making a twelve-mile loop around the ship, the cocky pilot pulled the jet up and rocketed into a blanket of clouds, only to emerge miles away just seconds later. The jet flew at incredible speeds, flying faster than sound from one edge of the sky to the other.

Her pilot performed maneuvers over the ocean, buzzing the ship twice more, before slipping from sight — over the horizon. The occasional roar of screaming afterburners echoed through the sky, bouncing sounds off of clouds, all the while she remained undetectable — out of visual range. But now and then, the tiny speck of a jet would peek between the clouds, only to disappear again.

Rusty glanced down the side of the ship. A handful of crew members emerged, looking for the jet.

"What was it?" they asked. Disappointed, the horde of spectators scoured the ocean, hoping to catch sight of the fast-moving jet.

"Tomcat. I think it was from the Dallas. He was supersonic too," Rusty shouted above the ocean's wind noise.

Rusty ran upstairs to the Shop and busted through the door at a frantic pace. "Dudeman, did you guys hear the jet?"

"Yeah. What type was it?" Bones asked.

"Tomcat. It buzzed the ship."

"Wow, sucks we missed it," Bones said.

Senior Chief emerged from behind the bookshelf. "The Dallas is about a hundred miles north of us," he said. He knew the flagship carriers' position, as the rumor mill stocked Chief's Mess with better information than it did the low-ranked enlisted's Mess Hall.

The USS Dallas was an older carrier from the 70s. She was the flagship of the armada of which Rusty's destroyer was assigned to protect. Although she was an older carrier, hardened from tours in Korea and Vietnam, she'd experienced a lot of combat — much more than Rusty's ship. Rumor had it the Dallas was so old, the crew still slept in hammocks. Although Rusty knew this was only true of the older battleships.

On the way to the Persian Gulf, the Adams followed the Dallas through the Suez Canal, trailing a distance of a half-mile or so. Her massive flight deck spanned the width of the canal, and her wake swept the shoreline, just about wiping out the small docks and all the tiny boats tied to them. The Dallas was a massive marvel of human engineering.

17

The next morning, over two weeks had passed since departing Bahrain. Rusty had spent most of his free time on unproductive attempts at writing a letter to Fitz. But every letter seemed contrived and full of melodrama. With each endeavor, the letters got harder to write, and Rusty wondered if it would ever be possible to write a normal letter at all without sounding clingy and emotional.

Standing on the starboard side of the fantail, Rusty was in mid-contemplation when he glanced at the ocean's horizon. Through the haze, a small dot of a ship steamed in the far distance. The vessel seemed bigger than any of the civilian ships Rusty'd seen on previous occasions.

Rusty shrugged it off and turned his attention back to the water. The Persian water was black, and the sea assumed a cold and lackluster look.

To his right, aft of his ship's wake, the large dot drew closer — bearing down on the Adam's position — closing the gap on her right flank.

He left the fantail and ran upstairs to the '01' level to gain a higher vantage point. It was unusual to see a ship, especially a civilian ship, coming toward a Navy destroyer, and he intended to have a front-row seat. Most of the time, merchant ships kept a safe distance. And yet, the unknown ship still sailed closer.

Everyone onboard knew what a destroyer looked like. Destroyers and frigates steamed alongside the Adams. But the encroaching ship appeared much different from any of the frigates or tender ships. It looked much larger. Instead of the nondescript dot, it morphed into a large rectangle of a ship — resolving into a familiar outline, allowing

Rusty to identify the interloper's signature.

An aircraft carrier! She must be the Dallas.

The Adams continued to steam at full speed, forty knots, but the Dallas closed the distance, sailing at a slightly sharper degree while pulling alongside Rusty's ship. Or was the Adams pulling alongside the carrier? Just like Einstein said, "it's all relative."

Like Blume's building, the ship seemed small until it got to within a mile. As the carrier closed in, her perspective seemed off, not appearing to grow larger, as one might have expected. Her color resolved and her details became more pronounced, but her size remained small.

She was much bigger anchored in Israel.

She drew closer and, with little warning, she had swelled at an unnatural pace, seeming to inflate like a giant carrier-shaped balloon. A balloon that grew, and grew, and grew more than larger; it grew massive. She exploded in size as she closed the last few hundred yards — fast approaching at full speed.

That bastard's gonna ram us!

No one but Rusty could imagine the unnerving feeling of being run over by an aircraft carrier. Feeling exposed, he backed up five feet, banging the back of his head into the Sea Sparrow rocket launcher. He ignored the pain, having never taken his eyes off the titanic vessel.

Just as she came within shouting distance, the gigantic ship turned at the last possible moment and assumed a parallel heading to the Adams. The Dallas came in at almost forty-five knots and pulled up right beside Rusty's ship — slowing to match the destroyer's speed.

The mobile airport dwarfed Rusty's large ship. A veritable floating football stadium pulled up to within fifty yards of his ship, covering the small destroyer with her behemoth shadow. It was Rusty's first encounter with a real-life "bird farm."

A huge whitewash of water, fifteen to twenty feet tall, pulled the carrier from her bow. Rusty stretched, looking upward for the flight deck of the floating airport. Her main level stood at a higher elevation than the top of the superstructure of his own destroyer.

The mighty carrier sliced through the ocean, sounding like Niagara Falls. Loud rushing water, the crashing of never-ending waves, resounded through the air, blocking out all other ambient sounds between both ships — much louder and more violent than the small swash of Rusty's destroyer.

Frozen with curiosity, Rusty glanced forward and aft on his

starboard weather decks, hoping to see his shipmates beside him. Again, not a soul topside. Rusty stood alone to witness the spectacular moment.

You must be shittin' me.

The loudspeaker of the carrier rang orders for ready conditions. **"Flight Quarters, Flight Quarters. Man, all Flight Quarter stations. The smoking lamp is out aft of frames one and two. Set condition one-Alpha. Now Flight Quarters."** *Sh-click.*

Distant voices echoed across the water, reverberating between the two ships.

It was a colossal mass of metal. Her hull, gray and dull, was so large, Rusty could not see the front and back of the ship in his peripheral. Boatswain's Mates painted her conning tower with various designs of ribbons and medals, displaying the ship's many achievements. The adorned ribbons showed the trials, struggles, and qualifications, proving she'd been through so much in life.

A loud *roar* broke the steady drone of the plowed waves. It was deafening. The jet engine was loud enough to spur Rusty's fear response.

"Wow!" he said out loud. He'd heard afterburners, many times, during his long port visits in Mayport. But this was not Mayport, where the runway was half a mile away. This was much more intimate, less than a football field away.

An A6 Intruder took off and flew across the nose of Rusty's ship. The magnificent jet had a rounded nose and a long tail fin. It was a silver jet with a blue and white star painted above the word "NAVY." Skilled painters illustrated emblems and crests on the tail fin — a skull and crossbones superimposed over a black and gold shield.

Rusty watched the Intruder fly away as long condensation streamers trailed her graceful wingtips. Wiggling trails of condensed vapor displayed expanding air pressure as the wings generated lift.

Another loud *roar* made Rusty look back at the carrier. A Tomcat took off chasing the Intruder. Someone painted a galloping silver stallion on its black tail fin.

A third jet followed the F-14 Tomcat. All three jets launched from the Dallas, and Rusty was close enough to smell their exhaust.

Men wearing red, green, and yellow vests moved about, busying themselves with flight operations. Their uniforms matched their colored helmets. As they scurried around the flight deck, a few of them noticed Rusty.

Instead of waving, the men carried on with their jobs. Many times as they'd performed in front of crowds, and being onstage so often made them numb to being watched. The flight crew was uninterested in showing off and paid little attention to the Adams.

The carrier remained on a parallel course alongside the Adams, and the two ships steamed through the Persian waters for almost half an hour. Without warning, the carrier leaned toward the Adams, as the massive ship pulled away. The gap between the two ships increased. Once the Helmsmen established their new directions, she righted herself, taking a diagonal heading and sailing away from the destroyer. It was only a few degrees, but it was enough to break away at a quick pace.

She increased the distance as fast as she'd approached. The hulk of a ship pulled away and ahead of Rusty's ship. The carrier was faster than Rusty's destroyer — much faster.

She shrank as she reached the horizon, drifting far out to the open ocean. The aircraft carrier shaped balloon deflated and the sound of her waterfall swash fell silent. Minutes later, the floating city of 5,000 sailors was a tiny dot tracing the horizon, before slipping over it, out of sight.

Mundane sounds returned to Rusty's ship, heightening the carrier's absence, and the ocean was still, once again.

Inside Transmitters, Rusty found Mux prepping to work on a radio transceiver. He secured the cabinet open with a strap and held a grounding probe in both hands, ready to discharge a sizable, fully loaded capacitor.

"Did you see the Dallas? She was outside doing flight quarters," Rusty asked.

"Yeah, I was on the third deck," Mux said. "Where were you?"

"First deck. Shit. Why didn't I think to climb higher?" Rusty asked.

"Don't know. But we had a pretty good view of the jets lining up," Mux replied.

In a far corner of the transmitters room, Radiomen piled flammable burn bags behind a couple of high-powered transmitters, leaning them on hot cabinets. Rusty shook his head and rolled his eyes. "Those are gonna catch fire."

"I'm saying, but they won't take 'em out of here," Mux said, too preoccupied with his work to offer Rusty his full attention.

"You look busy. Get to work and we'll meet up later. Ocean wants to play chess. You in?" Rusty asked.

"You know it. I'll see you guys in the mess hall in about an hour," Mux said.

"Cool." Rusty turned to leave when the ship wide speaker system announced General Quarters... again.

Bong, Bong, Bong!....

"General Quarters, General Quarters. All hands man your battle stations. Set condition Zebra throughout the ship."

Bong, Bong, Bong!....

"General Quarters, General Quarters. All hands man your battle stations. Set condition Zebra throughout the ship." *Sh-click.*

Rusty stared at Mux. "Did he say it was a drill?"

"I didn't hear."

Mux watched the speaker as if the tiny box would somehow provide additional clues, before unplugging the grounding probe to close the cabinet. He flipped the transmitter's power switch and looked at Rusty.

Rusty shrugged. "Oh well. I bet the Duke's chewing his ass right now," Rusty said. He waved before starting out for Radar 2.

"I'm sure. I'd bet the Duke is screaming," Mux said.

On one occasion, during Rusty's first month on board, General Quarters was issued and the deckhand who passed the word forgot to specify it was a drill. Every officer onboard panicked, causing a major uproar. The Captain was intolerant of false alarms. Too many false alarms bred complacency — inattention to detail — the 'little boy who cried wolf' syndrome.

Mux walked to the bulkhead and grabbed his sound-powered phones hanging on a hook. He placed them on his head and put the mouthpiece around his collar. With the cord plugged in, he spoke into the microphone. "Combat Systems. Transmitters, manned and ready." Mux gave Rusty two thumbs up and they both laughed before Rusty exited the space.

Rusty surmised Mux was the first to report in. "Transmitters" was Mux's GQ station. He beat everyone to their assigned stations, including Senior Chief and Mr. Kistner.

Rusty secured the handle on the door leading from Transmitters. He passed through Radio, into the main passageway. From there it was a twenty-foot stroll to Radar 2, which shared an adjoining wall with Mux's space.

The ship passed the second General Quarters alarm. Rusty was seconds away from entering the code to enter Radar 2 when the bridge passed the word for Flight Quarters operations. The ship grew busy, and the overabundance of drills promised to ruin the day.

"Flight Quarters, Flight Quarters, man all flight quarters stations, smoking lamp is out on the fantail. Now flight quarters!"

"Flight Quarters, Flight Quarters, man all flight quarters stations, smoking lamp is out on the fantail. Now flight quarters!" *Sh-click.*

The new Flight Quarters alarm superseded the call to GG. With a smile, Rusty walked past Radar 2 and proceeded down the hall to the helo hangar.

Air Crewmen scrambled to put their helmets and vests on. Some put on yellow vests, some red, and others green. No one paid Rusty any attention, as they'd seen him enter countless times before, during countless other launches.

Rusty reached the corner of the hangar and climbed the ladder to the flight tower. Peeking his head just above the deck, he expected to find Mr. Pratt seated in the tiny four-by-eight-foot space. But no, it was empty, and he doubted he'd see the officer during the flight evolution.

Mr. Pratt often skipped flight quarters, as he felt the crew needed his talents elsewhere. Babysitting the 'flight tower lookout' was low on the trophy-achievement list of any aspiring career officer, and Rusty suspected Mr. Pratt was chumming it up with the Executive Officer in CIC.

Rusty climbed into his seat and put on the sound-powered phones. He spoke as clean as possible into the mic. "Pilothouse. Tower. Manned and ready."

"Manned and ready, aye," was the reply. The voice sounded tiny and distant, but it was clear.

The air crew wheeled the helo out. White helmets were visible in the front widows of the helicopter; its pilots were already seated inside the helo.

The ship's loudspeaker announced **"Red Deck."**

A loud *hum* climbed to a high *whistle* as the pilots started the helicopter's turbines.

The ship's loudspeaker announced. **"Amber Deck."**

The helicopter's rotors engaged. Slowly at first, then steadily, props spun and spun and spun, eventually reaching velocities too fast for human eyes to see. With a blur, they rotated at several thousand RPMs. As the enormous blades spun, they threw airwaves and concussions outward, hurling a thudding pressure through the tower window. Its whistle-chopping sound whomped faster and faster. The chops merged to create a steady drone, a vibration not unlike a 23,000-pound bee fanning its wings. The frequency of which increased with each rotation. Rusty's chest hummed from the choppy concussion as it reverberated through the tiny space.

Rusty sounded off, yelling into the microphone. "Pilothouse. Tower. Helo rotors engaged."

"Rotors engaged, aye," the Pilothouse acknowledged.

The ship's loudspeaker announced, "Green Deck", for all hands to hear.

Propellers sent torrents of air onto the ocean's surface, forming a white mist that enveloped the rear of the ship. The helo lifted off and hovered above the flight deck. Heavy blades spun level with Rusty's tiny vulnerable glass window as the helo hovered at fifteen feet — then twenty feet — then thirty.

"Pilothouse. Tower. Helo over flight deck."

"Helo over flight deck. Aye."

Seconds later, it reclined, and leaned backwards. The large gray bird backed away from the ship and hovered over the fantail. Her intense vibrations subsided with each passing yard. As the helo drifted farther away, mist fogged the immediate surface of the ocean, rendering intense down drafts of her massive lift, making invisible air currents visible.

"Pilothouse. Tower. Helo over fantail," Rusty said.

"Helo over fantail, aye," The Pilothouse acknowledged.

The helo backed off the ship and once cleared; it turned and flew off the port side onto open waters, taking its loud *thumping* with it.

"Pilothouse. Tower. Helo away." Rusty said.

"Helo away, aye." The Pilothouse acknowledged.

With the helo gone, and no announcement to secure from Flight Quarters, Rusty remained at his post.

Outside, all seemed normal at the back of the ship — boring and as lackluster as all get out. Airman remained posted in the hangar, and Rusty leaned back in his government-issued pleather seat.

Ten minutes passed, and still Rusty waited at his Flight Quarters station for the word to secure. Having sat idle for so long, he almost forgot the ship was at General Quarters as boredom set in. He inventoried the tiny space, hoping to find something to occupy his time. But there was nothing but a chair, a window, and a few ropes rolled up in the corner near the ladder.

He kicked his feet up onto the bulkhead and leaned back in his chair. Designers engineered the tight space to allow his chair to rest on the bulkhead and to wedge his feet on the opposite wall. He placed his arms over his head, lowered his hat, and waited with closed eyes.

Thinking of Fitz, he reached for his necklace. He pinched the silver cat between his fingers and pulled the trinket out. Light reflected off the silver as he held it up to look at Fitz's sculpture.

There were tiny scratches on its surface, and he wondered if the minute detail was something she did, or if it was static from the pouring process. In either case, it was exquisite craftsmanship he thought. She should have been a jeweler or something. The thought occurred to him to pull his journal and write notes on what he could include in his letter to Fitz.

He looked at the polished, lanky cat staring back at him. Rusty's distorted reflection shined on the cat's belly.

Before Bahrain, Rusty knew everything. He was headstrong and full of answers. Everyone was "stupid," and Rusty was the "know-it-all." Bahrain was a boring dial-tone and Rusty took new experiences for granted. But Fitz showed him just how short-sighted he was. There were knowns and there were unknowns, and Rusty was not even aware of where he fell between the two.

The ship turned. It turned hard and fast. It turned back and forth like a slaloming skier.

Gonna be a lot of seasick bastards here.

Rusty peered through the rear window. The wake produced by the ship made a zig-zag pattern. Then, the ship turned as hard to starboard as it could.

The Duke is doing maneuvers again.

Still looking out the window, Rusty watched the five-inch turn and aim into the air. Pointing to the port side, the barrel raised forty-five degrees off the deck.

BOOM!..... BOOM!...... BOOM. BOOM!

The Adams fired from both mounts.

Oh crap, here we go again. I hope they don't plan on doing this shit all day.

The sudden turning of the sea sparrow rocket launcher to port, training in the same direction as the five-inch cannons, interrupted Rusty's protest.

Rusty stood up from his chair, placed his hands on the glass, and pressed his face as close to the window as possible, straining to see where the Fire Control men aimed the launcher.

"What is this shit?" he said. His timorous voice squeaked with trepidation.

The ship leaned harder. The steep angle made Rusty brace his arm against the bulkhead. He put his back to the wall, leaning against it. It was easier than trying to stand.

Rusty stared at the Sea Sparrow launcher, and he waited to see what would happen next.

On the horizon, in the background beyond the Sea Sparrow, two tiny dots moved fast — supersonic—headed port, relative to the ship's course; headed in the direction the FCs aimed their rocket launcher.

Tomcats. They are hauling serious ass! What kind of drill is this?

A Sea Sparrow rocket went off with the sound of a thousand bottle rockets, or the swoosh of a huge carbon dioxide fire extinguisher heard through concert loudspeakers. Rumbled air vibrated the glass in the tower window, and a giant white smoke plume shot from the rear of the launcher, blocking sight of everything aft of the helo flight deck. In less than a second, the twelve-foot-long rocket was out and gone. Headed down range to cause unknown carnage and destruction.

A second launch afforded Rusty little time to contemplate what just transpired. Two Sea Sparrows launched; firing both rockets in quick succession.

A thunderous noise followed the missile's sounds. They were so loud Rusty thought his head might rattle into crumbs. The CWIS let loose a barrage of bullets, firing in chorus with the five-inch cannons. Its intense rattling, hammer-drill sound was beyond deafening. It sounded like someone drilled into Rusty's head. He closed his eyes and cupped his hands over the headphones, but it was all of little use. The headphones offered some protection, but the vibration bypassed his ears and went straight to his skull. Only ten feet and a half-inch piece of sheet metal separated Rusty's head from the concussions of 3000 anti-aircraft artillery rounds being fired every minute.

The 1MC blared "Missile inbound. Port side, all hands brace for impact!"

Shit. I'm on the port side!

Rusty closed his eyes and clutched his cat. There was nowhere he could run, nowhere to hide, and nothing he could do. His fate was in the hands of chance. He thought of the irony as he froze in panic.

Seconds later, the sounds of giant fireworks exploded above the ship — crackling sounds like mortars he'd heard during Fourth of July celebrations.

It was the ship's anti-missile countermeasures. Chaff launchers blasted thousands of metal confetti flakes into the air to confuse any incoming missile's guidance systems.

Meanwhile, spinning sounds from the Gatling gun ran in a long, sustained burst of desperation.

Seconds later, an explosion rocked the ship with a deafening ***POW!***

The loudest sound Rusty ever experienced spiraled his balance. 160 decibels of over-pressure reverberated throughout the length of the ship, rendering his hearing useless. His ear drums struggled to process the sheer enormity of its explosive volume.

The once agreeable space turned foreign and hostile. Unassuming and inanimate objects became instruments of death. Matter turned against Rusty as a blast wave swept him from his feet, slamming the rag-dolled sailor against the bulkhead. He bounced off the wall and splattered flat, face down, onto the deck as the entire ship, all 8,040 tons of her, was knocked sideways, four feet to starboard.

Time slowed, and the silence was surreal, rendering objects closer and more intense. Rusty found himself placed in the moment as much as anyone could be.

The violent encounter left him bloodied, bleeding from his nose, and forced a deaf-ringing in his ears. He twisted his neck, staring in astonishment as he begged for clues outside the window, all the while struggling to understand his current state of affairs. His mind grasped for normalcy where none was found. Rusty was shell-shocked, stunned with fissioning fear, and for the longest time, all he could do was lie on the pile of rope that the blast threw him onto.

Trembling hands reached for the welded shelf as he labored to right himself. Overcome with dizziness, he laid back on the cold rope, closed his eyes, and focused on his breathing.

A feeling of impending doom, death is close.

Again, he tried to pick himself up from the deck. But, thinking he'd succeeded, the world became pixilated. His vision narrowed. Then…

18

Consciousness equals memory multiplied by experience. Without memory or the ability to perceive the world, sentient thought is impossible.

Awareness is based on persistent hallucinations of a person's past. An individual's consciousness is derived from a re-arrangement of their stored memories. This happens while minds assimilate constant inflows of experiences as they break superposition.

Abstract thoughts and freewill are determined by the physical world, not by me. No original thought exists independent of actual experience, which is subjugated by universal truths. Everything I know is based on something I have experienced since birth; as with all sentient beings living in the ***infinite hologram****. Both chaos and determinism invalidate freewill…*

Just before opening his eyes, a ringing faded in, persisting in his skull. Or were they ringing in his mind? Lightning pain shot through his chin, rousing the sailor. Half-hooded eyes cast a rolling glance around the tower. Cognizant of his surroundings, and suffering from delayed pain, he focused his thoughts, seeking guidance. He trembled, fumbling for his sound-powered phones — struggling to situate them back on top of his head. Like a hypothermic swimmer, his hands refused to follow his mind's commands. Twitchy fingers fumbled with the microphone as he tried to squeeze the transmit button.

The first of many distressing sensations gripped him in waves of panic. Hot rings originated from his naval and spread out like ripples of bitter acid. Metallic tastes filled his mouth, forcing an involuntary grimace. Iron rich blood flooded his nose and drained down the back of his throat. A heavy dose of shock suppressed physical pain as adrenaline seized his body, coating him with numbness and clammy nausea.

"Pilothouse, Flight Tower," he said. Another intense burning sensation shot through his chin. Something seemed off about his voice. It sounded muffled, congested. He spoke through clenched teeth, immobilizing his angry jaw. He touched his swollen nose, wiping it with the backside of his fist. Blood coated his fingers and knuckles.

Befuddled, the sailor stared at the microphone. He waited for clues to explain what happened, waited for a reply on the headphones, and he waited for instructions that would never come.

"Pilothouse, Flight Tower. Can you guys hear me?" he repeated, rebroadcasting his unscripted mayday. When he yelled, blood dripped into his windpipe, forcing him to choke and throwing him into a fit of coughs. Still, there was nothing. The phones were not disrupted, they were dead. The power was gone.

Should I abandon my post?

He ran his hands along the course non-skid surface and he leaned back against the bulkhead, sighing. It was forbidden "to quit his post until relieved." General order number five was a standing order, instilled in Rusty since his first day of basic training.

He swallowed, and the taste of his own blood made him more nauseated than the shock he felt. He wiped his chin and rubbed at his fingertips.

Wet.

Looking down at his fingertips…

Blood.

His head hurt, his jaw hurt, and his nose bled, all three of which had him worried the violent disruption may have hurt him more than he thought.

What do I do?

There was no protocol for his particular scenario. Nothing in his ESWS book could have prepared him for his current crisis. The universe hurled Rusty into the 'unfamiliar' — drafting him into a trial he neither solicited, invited, nor welcomed.

Struggling to reign in his panic, he sat on the deck, contemplating his options, weighing the remote risk of an ass chewing against his need to find answers, when the odd smell of burnt, 'synthetic chemicals' became apparent. Aromatic smells of melted plastic, melted rubber, and rocket exhaust infiltrated the small fight tower — along with other unidentifiable burning products Rusty would never identify.

He pulled himself up, righting his chair. The weakened soldier sat down and stared through the tiny window. Two brigades of Damage Controlmen scurried across the flight deck, hoses out. Water gushed as the teams ran, injecting torrents of saltwater into the hangar. It dawned on Rusty that he may have been unconscious much longer than he thought.

Rusty decided. He removed his phones and turned his attention to the rear of the tiny space, focusing on the ladder. Egressing had always been a drill, but on this day, it was tangible.

I'm going to abandon my post!

Fingers gripped both sides of the headphones, and he hung the device in its cradle. Using a hand to steady himself on the bulkhead, he stood to evaluate his equilibrium. Withdrawing his hand, he stood on his own strength as his eager eyes studied the ladder. He darted to it and stepped onto its top rung, readying himself to escape any potential fire raging below.

It's time.

He left, having broken the obligatory bonds of his duty station. Halfway down the ladder, Rusty stopped and scoped the scene. What he saw was chaos. Two fire teams sprayed torrents of water into the passageway leading to Radar 2, Radio, and Combat Information Center. Damage Controlmen aimed fire hoses straight into the blackened hole — irrigating the burning tunnel with thousands of gallons of water a minute.

The first hose waved a wide spray mist, used to cool the fire party. The second hose blasted a solid stream into the hole of a passageway. Black smoke spilled out into the hangar and slithered its way to the open sky. If Rusty did not find fresh air soon, he might become a casualty.

Everyone in the fire party wore large masks, and each man wore an Oxygen Breathing Apparatus. There were four men per hose — a nozzle man and three support crew members to steady the powerful water lines — eight in total.

Crewmen pointed, shouting amongst themselves through the thick black fog. The hangar soon turned darker than pure carbon, while steam and smoke embedded itself in the bulkheads, coating everything with condensate and soot. Rusty coughed and struggled to breathe. Remembering his training, the weary sailor took to his knees to crawl below the smoky layer.

One hand in front of the other, he crawled on the harsh deck. The perverse texture clawed at his knees and sanded the soft flesh of his palms. He cleared the large hangar doors. Free from the smoke, he climbed to his feet and turned around, looking back at the cloud and the obscured fire brigade.

Rusty backed his way farther out onto the flight deck. He tripped over the hard, charged hoses and fell on his ass, jolting his head, before passing out again.

Rusty did not dream. He was in a slumber too deep for his mind to process random stimuli, the ingredients of any rational hallucination. He was beyond R.E.M., unaware of a damn thing.

A sting, or was it a slap? Rusty opened his eyes to see Master Chief Greeley kneeling above him. Shouting at Rusty's face, he almost couldn't understand the Master Chief — the blast having shot Rusty's hearing to hell and all.

Aside from that one night at a strip joint in Charleston, Rusty had never blacked out — sober, anyway. The foreign feeling unnerved him. It was a feeling too close to death. This time, losing consciousness was much worse because he could not blame it on 200 proof and fruit punch.

Thick smoke floated in the air behind Master Chief Greeley's head. A vast black cloud hovered above the flight deck, extending beyond the fantail, trailing into the sky so far Rusty could not see where it ended.

Rusty offered the Master Chief no reply. Instead, he sat up and tested his balance. A self evaluation convinced Rusty he was fit to move, and he held his arm up.

Large hands scooped Rusty by his armpits, as the Master Chief helped him to his feet. Rusty wavered. He fell into Greeley's arms. Then, like lifting a large sack of potatoes, the Master Chief performed a "Fireman's Carry" and slung Rusty over his shoulders, hauling him twenty feet to the ladder which led from the flight deck to the 01 level.

The Master Chief lowered Rusty off his shoulders and laid him on the deck, while pointing to the ladder and shouting something incoherent.

Rusty understood the intent behind the shouting, even if he couldn't hear the Master Chief's voice. He wanted was for Rusty to use the ladder to get the hell off the flight deck.

His soot-covered hands held firm to the metal piping, checking the precarious support the dry-rotted netting provided. He gambled the net would handle the full weight of his body. Unbalanced, Rusty rolled across the safety netting and swung himself onto the ladder, descending to the ship's 01 level. Finding himself one deck lower, he took a knee and collapsed beside the Sea Sparrow rocket launcher. Laying on his back and with vacant eyes, he stared at the black smoke filled sky. Smells of scorched rocket fuel lingered from inside the spent launcher tubes.

Laying face up, numbed with shock, he turned his head sideways, examining the port side weather deck. The deck ran the length of the ship, allowing him to see the blackened, twisted steel that had once been the port side midship quarterdeck.

Fire and smoke poured from the former watch station. More men wearing fire fighting gear ran down the weather deck with hoses and fire extinguishers, trying to access the mid-ship station.

Something exploded..... Was it a fuel tank? Or was it one of the gas turbines?

Rusty's eyes followed the plume as it rose into the air. He watched the black billowing cloud weave through the masts and encircle the Forty's radar antenna.

He gripped the Master Chief by his wrist and yelled. "Why isn't the Forty antenna rotating?" The strain of yelling diverted blood to all the wrong places. His head throbbed like a frosty's brain-freeze, forcing him to squeeze his eyelids tight, relaxing his grip on Greeley's arm.

The Master Chief abandoned his conversation with Petty Officer Williams and ran to Rusty. "What?" Greeley asked. Rusty could just make out the Master Chief's question.

"Why isn't the Forty rotating?" Rusty raised his hand and pointed to the tall mast as he pressed his other hand against his temple.

Dismayed at Rusty's lack of awareness, the Master Chief glanced at the tall masts and back to Rusty laying on the deck. "Son, it's gone. Radar 2 was obliterated. Someone hit the whole damn superstructure. We are still trying to evaluate the damage."

He only made out a few of the words, using rudimentary lip reading skills. He never understood the Master Chief's answer and repeated the same question. "I know Master Chief, but why isn't it rotating?" he asked again.

"You'll be alright, son. Can you get to medical?"

Medical? Where the fuck is medical?

Rusty did not want to go to medical. Why would he need to go to medical? Rusty needed to see what happened, and he pleaded for answers. He had to find Mux at all costs.

The Master Chief shouted to a Senior Petty Officer and pointed down at Rusty. It was unclear what the two crew members discussed concerning Rusty's future. Rusty was confused. Disoriented.

Determination took hold, forcing him to his feet. It was a slow process, but he stood and walked to the port life-rail. The ship leaned left at a precarious angle. Rusty measured the height of the waterline near the midship.

The entire section was black. Bulkheads and metal jutted out, preventing access to the forward areas on the port side. Long curls of metal strips protruded from the hull, like enormous scorched flower petals — an exploded cigar from the Road Runner cartoons.

It was an immense hole of considerable size, and it appeared to take on water. The ship took a knockout punch, and Rusty wondered if she might sink. He took inventory in the event the Duke ordered everyone to abandon ship.

Flotsam floated in the water. Flames danced on the surface, near the mid-ship. A person drifted face down along with all the debris. The stillness of his shipmate became apparent to Rusty, and he stared in morbid curiosity. It was his first time seeing a dead body. Curious eyes fixated on the bobbing corpse while he waited for the person to move, but it never happened. It never would.

If only someone could shake that man, he would wake up. If you shake a person, they can never die. As long as you shake them, you will keep them awake.

With a blink, Rusty looked in the air. The Seahawk helicopter hovered over the burning ship, floating 400 feet above the carnage. Its flight crew, no doubt attempting to define the devastation, in order to convey the scene to higher-ranked officials who were located... elsewhere. Large swirls of black smoke blew into the blades of the helo, which sent the clouds spiraling outwards in two round vortexes.

Panic radiated through Rusty in waves. The waves came on quickly and went away slowly. They then came with more severity. The last wave was the hardest to manage. Panic mingled with anger. It was a mixed bag, and Rusty stared at his dead shipmate, struggling to assimilate his feelings about the morbid scene. But his emotions and thoughts were at odds with each other. Rage was the last emotion he thought he'd feel. He gripped the rail with a fury so strong it would have taken anyone else years to cultivate.

Minutes passed, and two jets buzzed the ship, cutting Rusty's anger in half with curiosity. The jets circled back to inspect the crippled vessel, close enough to survey the damage, while dodging the smoke plume of the burning destroyer.

With inquiring eyes, Rusty analyzed the water, trying to identify his lifeless shipmate. He scanned the body, straining to find anything to identify the person. On the left wrist was a large tacky-white wristwatch, the one his mother gave him the day he left her for boot camp.

Random debris added to the absurdity of the scene. Everything was misplaced. Singed paper, blackened pencils, pristine white cotton towels, and melted blue plastic food trays bobbed in the choppy water.

The jetsam insulted the dignity of the lifeless boy. Anger thawed to pity as Rusty surveyed the lifeless body of his murdered friend.

He fixated on Booger, seeing his own mortality reflected there. Rusty's eyes glossed over with grief. His stomach burned, radiating heat to his extremities, while his head lightened, accompanied by labored breaths. He knew one day he too would join those who crossed the ultimate threshold, making one last journey into the realm of eternity.

Somehow, Booger's death put the many philosophical perspectives of life and death into a single picture, immersing Rusty with the terror of panic. Beads of sweat raced down his cheek as he reached for his chest, searching for his necklace. It was safe. He closed his eyes and focused on his forced breaths as he caressed the smooth surface of his cat charm.

Confusion set in, offering Rusty no obvious clues to an alternative course of action. A grisly thought pierced his mind, and although it was honest, it was uninvited…

What could be done to restore his broken soul? Life is transient, fragile, and precious — an ephemeral gift from the universe, and one day the universe will want it back. Why must men harm men — robbing another soul of their most cherished belonging?

Rusty had learned the ultimate consequence of war.

19

Rusty was powerless to decide his fate. Dire circumstances called for action. Did Rusty have a say in the decisions he would make? Was it up to his freewill? It would seem the physical world made the choice for him, and it pushed Rusty into action. Was his every option a mirage of freedom? He observed his situation to see where the universe carried him — almost like an out-of-body experience. Choices needed to be made. Would he do nothing, or would he help his friends, his ship, and himself? He sought to understand the veiled conflict between the two concepts — morality and mortality. Fight or flight induced panic, mixed with nihilistic complications, overrode his desire for self-preservation. Overwhelming desire to risk his life for those in need, dared Rusty to confront the danger.

Someone projected their murderous intent when they fired missiles at Rusty's ship. They willed their intent and Rusty was left picking through the aftermath.

When at sea, a fire provides the crew with two options. Fight or swim. Emergency services could not save a Navy ship from fire. There was no one to call for help. If the crew could not save the ship, she would compel them all into the sea, cook them alive, or drown anyone unlucky enough to find themselves cornered by fire, steel, or water. The decision to fight was paramount to all other's at that moment.

It was possible to find his friends. However, in order to do so, Rusty needed the correct gear before attempting to access the damaged areas of the superstructure. The rear Damage Control Station held the Oxygen Breathing Apparatus Rusty needed to aid the rescue. With his mind settled, he willed his body to move. Operating on instinct, he staggered to the back of the ship and clambered down the ladder to the fantail.

Judging the fantail and the lack of crew members on deck, hinted at the number of missing. Rusty did a quick head count, and noticed the crew was not only absent, but the ones who gathered on the fantail looked too stunned to respond to the threat with the skills needed. The fantail looked like a poisoned ant mound, as wounded men stumbled in incoherent circles, waiting for the assault's ultimate effect.

Rusty wobbled his way through the door leading into the port side passageway. Crew members emerged from the door, followed by thin smoke that emanated from somewhere deep inside the ship's interior.

There was no time to contemplate the risks, and imperative compulsions forced him to enter the burning ship. Rusty was desperate to reach the rear Damage Control Station. The DCS was located a short distance from the fantail, but far enough to pose a mortal danger if Rusty was to be asphyxiated by the toxic smoke.

He pulled on the heavy watertight door to close it. The solid metal door was heavier than normal because of the ship's lean to port and Rusty's weakened strength.

Smoke rushed past him with a wind tunnel effect, collecting near the overhead. With the ships' power being out, the only light came from the yellow emergency battle lanterns located two feet above the deck, shining down on the glossy blue tile. The light was faint, but the lanterns lit his path.

Crouching, Rusty made his way forward, passing crew members already wearing OBAs. Some men walked, while others ran, abandoning the burning hallway, headed to the safety of the topside decks. They pointed and shouted to Rusty to evacuate the passageway.

"You're going the wrong way!" some shouted with muffled yells, their arms stretched outward, feeling in the darkness.

Others weren't so lucky and found themselves crouched without the luxury of an OBA — their eyes closed while they stumbled their way topside.

Engineers and ship planners littered the firefighting station with various esoteric controls and valves — water spigots and meters resembled the chromed mid-side of a large fire truck. Thick hoses, filled with water, stretched forward into the darkened hall, stretched onward to the point of contention. A mere fifty feet forward, up the hall, the crew battled an inferno.

Rusty grabbed an OBA hanging on the bulkhead and crouched to his knees, positioning his head below the smoke layer. He donned the OBA and slid the fresh oxygen canister into the cradle, flipping the lever to puncture the chemical oxygen canister to fill his mask with breathable air.

Alchemy.

He positioned the mask back on his face and pulled the straps to press an air-tight seal, angering his jaw. Still, the trade was worth the pain. Now, able to open his eyes and breathe, his gear would suffice for a half hour. In the darkened hall, his fingers felt for the timer on top of the breastplate. Rotating the dial, he twisted the knob to the max, setting the timer for to the thirty-minute mark.

Donned in firefighting gear, Rusty faced a decision. How to get to the Shop, and how to get to Radio. He could try getting upstairs via the helo hangar, but he knew that area was impassable, even if the Airmen and Damage Controlmen would step aside and just let Rusty run through the open flames. With limited options, he didn't know if wreckage blocked the interior halls, so he stayed below deck to confront the fire with his shipmates.

Smoke-filled air darkened the passageway. Farther forward, the smoke thickened, blackening most of the emergency lanterns, rendering them close to useless. Blinded in the blanketed light, Rusty pressed his feet against the hose and felt his way forward, using the hoses as guides against the insteps of his feet.

Smoke was less dense in the large open cafeteria, where two men crouched at the far corner of the Mess Hall, struggling to orient themselves and find their bearings. They coughed and huddled on the floor, arms extended, feeling for walls that were not there, fighting to orient themselves with closed eyes.

Rusty approached and grabbed them both by their flailing arms. "Hey, hey, hey. Let's skedaddle. Keep your eyes closed, head down, and hold my belt loop!" Rusty shouted through the diaphragm, worrying he was unheard in the chaos. "Hold your breath for a minute, and I will get you guys out."

The frightened sailors nodded. They held their breath and felt for Rusty's life saving belt loops.

"Stay low and move," Rusty shouted.

The egress train ran through the darkened smoke, fast enough to get the men out without requiring them to take renewed breaths. It took less than fifty seconds to get the men topside. Their eyes watered from the smoke and heat while Rusty escorted them to the far end of the fantail, away from the smoke, away from danger. "Stay here," he said through the vibrating diaphragm.

In the bright mid-afternoon sun, Rusty looked up to the helo hangar, re-evaluating his options. The smoke pouring from the hangar showed the lack of progress of the fire brigade in the upper hallways. There was no way through the infernal hall.

Rusty ran back to the lower port side passageway. Penetrating deeper into the ship, headed forward to follow the fire hoses. Small steps marched him closer to the fire, where the hose teams battled the inferno with extreme prejudice.

Heat and steam from the fine water mist flooded the hall — signaling he'd reached the back of the Number 2 hose team.

Fighting men yelled orders to 'advance!' and the team would advance the hose a foot or two, and then the lines would stop. The hall hissed like a gas furnace. Smoke was so thick, it was impossible to see the flames from five feet away.

Water formed on the deck. Puddling on the left side of the passageway. It was ten inches deep, near the hull bulkhead.

One man shouted something indiscernible, drawing Rusty's attention to the hose at his feet... Rusty looked down. The round hoses lay flat on the deck, deflated. There was an obvious problem, as both hoses had lost water pressure.

With his attention turned rearward to the Damage Control Station feeding the fire hoses, Rusty backtracked in double-time fashion to check the valve. It was on, but the hose was still flat. He hurried from the broken port control station to the starboard control station.

He spotted another pair of hoses hung on the bulkhead. The obvious solution was to splice the hoses and run them from the starboard DCS. A task he carried out in record time.

He pulled the hoses to the port DCS just as the two rear hose-men arrived to troubleshoot the failed hoses.

Rusty and the two men used a pair of emergency couplings to splice the hoses together. Satisfied with the connections, Rusty ran to the starboard DCS and turned the handle, opening the valves. He cranked the circular handle, and water flowed hard, charging the hoses.

I sure hope those big bastards didn't let go of their nozzles.

The flat fire hose snapped to life with instant rigidity, becoming as hard as a four-inch thick steel cable. Charged again, the two teams were back at it.

Rusty crouched as he hurried to resume his place at the rear of the hose teams. He reached for the Number 2 hose and tapped his shipmate on the shoulder. Rusty reached for the hose, intending to help steady the heavy line, but he slipped on the wet tile. His foot went right to the base of the wall, and he landed on the hose, almost jerking it from under the linemen's arms.

The startled firefighter turned to see Rusty struggling to find the proper friction to stand. Rusty floundered, sliding around on the wet tile like a shitty break dancer on greased-glass.

"We have this under control." The hose-man yelled. His mask muffled his voice the same as Rusty's. "Offer help elsewhere," he shouted.

Rusty nodded and gave a thumbs up. He made his way rearward, but thick smoke forced him to stop — unable to see a thing, because the air was too heavy.

We need ventilation!... Flashover is a risk, but no one can fight something they can't see.

With outstretched arms, Rusty jogged topside and pushed the door open, causing the heavy door to crash against the bulkhead, drawing the crew on the fantail's attention. Rusty secured the door with the hook and loop welded to the bulkhead, while a thick cloud of smoke poured from the opened hallway.

Pulling his mask off, Rusty let it fall behind his head, held over his shoulders by the dual air hoses. The cool dry air evaporated his sweat as he took to his knees and swallowed natural breaths. He wanted to rest, but knew of five more doors to open. It was his goal to create as much cross-venting as possible.

Crew members moved about on the weather decks and some huddled in small groups on the fantail. The crowd grew in numbers as men emerged from the rear accesses, scuttles, and hatches, seeking the safety of the isolated fantail. Men realized the ship was on fire, and likely sinking — some speculated on the cause of the explosion — and some were too traumatized to speak at all.

"It was the forward engine," someone shouted.

"No, it was one of the ammo storage lockers," another argued.

"You're all wrong. It was a missile," Rusty said.

"A missile? Who would have shot us with a missile? How do you know?" someone asked.

"I heard the chaff," Rusty said. "Didn't you hear them pass the word 'Missile inbound'?" Rusty looked to the port side. The water line, only a few feet from the fantail deck, looked iridescent.

"I never heard them say that," someone said, arguing.

Rusty rolled his eyes. "Well, they did. By the way, there is fuel in the water. You guys need to stay on the starboard side." Rusty's finger pointed at the water, directing the attention of the onlookers who'd gathered around him.

"Why?"

"In case it catches fire and your dumb asses get cooked, that's why," Rusty said.

"What do you think caused the fuel leak?" someone asked.

Rusty opted to ignore the interrogation. He acknowledged the group of wide-eyed sailors looking at him for answers, growing anxious. They were "chompin' at the bit" as his mother would say. It was her favorite cliché, and Rusty used it when the occasion demanded it. But the ship needed damage control, not commentary. There would be plenty of time for forensics later.

With his attention turned to the superstructure, Rusty took a mental assessment.

The ladder near the forward fan room might be accessible. I can get to the Shop from there.

As he ran the length of the starboard side deck, smoke seeped from the midship area. His pace slowed when he reached the halfway point of the ship. Chief Michaels surveyed the damaged midship where the OOD stood watch while in Bahrain.

The quarterdeck was a blackened wall of destruction. The open pass-through was transformed into a solid wall of mangled pipes, wires, and smoldering metal. Swollen, the wall bulged to the point of reaching the side of the ship, where Rusty and the Chief stood. Smoke trickled upward from cracks within the wreckage.

Chief Michaels manned a fire watch. With a carbon dioxide extinguisher in hand, he stood ready, in case flames re-erupted from the smoldering wall.

Unaware of his appearance, with soot covering his face Rusty was cooked and stood out of place against the bright backdrop of the clear blue Persian sky. Smoke damaged dungarees turned him into a human figure shaped like coal.

The Chief interrogated Rusty. "What's going on below?"

"There's a team on the port side, near the mess deck, fighting a fire near the galley. They are managing, but I don't know how bad the fire is. I couldn't see three feet. There are two teams in the hangar and that's all I know. I'm trying to vent the ship."

The Chief's gaze followed Rusty as he started off to open the forward doors. "Where are you headed?" the Chief asked.

"To open the forward fan room door and then I need to get to the ET Shop," Rusty said.

"Chances are, it's blocked. You can't get through, and besides, it's more than likely destroyed by the fire."

Rusty offered no reply to the Chief's callus comment. Instead, Rusty continued his forward route, unpersuaded. Thirty-seven steps later, he stood in front of the door with his hand near the handle. With surveying eyes, he studied the door and reached for the lever, pausing inches from the handle... Rusty ran back to the Chief. "We have a fire up here! The door is blistering."

20

"I think all the DC's are fighting fires below decks. Grab men from the fantail. I need eight men, including you," the Chief shouted.

Rusty ran to the fantail, where a large crowd assembled. He calculated there to be thirty or more men. Beside men coughing from smoke inhalation, others with burns and shrapnel wounds lay in pools of thick, coagulated, blood on the deck. Blood so thick it formed dark, violet streams which gravity steered to the port rail.

The ship's only Corpsman tended to the fallen sailors. He knelt beside one man who appeared sleeping. The Corpsman pressed his fingers to the man's throat. By the gray pallor and blue lips of the sleeping sailor, Rusty knew the man no longer felt this world.

Rusty cupped his hands to his mouth and announced: "I need seven guys on deck. We have a fire!" He took stock of the men on deck, guessing how many would shirk their duty, but was impressed at the overwhelming response. Ten men vied to fill Rusty's request.

Rusty was the first one back. Chief Michaels readied the two hoses and ran them from a fire main in the forward break room, laying the hoses side by side, ready for charging.

Without thinking, Rusty grabbed a hose and pointed it toward the blistered door. MM3 Knowles grabbed the other hose.

BM2 Mercers supplied the teams with fresh oxygen canisters and bottles of air, resembling upside-down oxygen tanks worn by scuba divers.

Rusty's shaky hands pulled his OBA mask back into position and inserted the new oxygen canister, dialing the timer for another thirty minutes.

The Chief threw OBAs and bottles filled with oxygen to the other men on the hose party. "You boys tuck your pants into your socks. Do you remember your training? If it is too hot, we will fall back." The Chief held two large Firefighting Ensemble coats. "Sorry fellas, two is all we have." He tossed them to Rusty and Knowles.

The brass nozzle was heavier than Rusty remembered from boot camp. His arms strangled the hose in a deathly tight headlock as he placed his hand on top of the nozzle. Both nozzles were as ready as they could be. Poised, Rusty looked to the Chief and nodded.

Knowles was nervous as hell. He eyed the solid gray door and shouted through his OBA mask. "I think I'm ready."

The Chief turned to the men operating the water valves. He drew invisible circles in the air above his head, ordering the hoses charged.

Sailors rotated the valve, and the hoses tensed, filling with seawater.

As a precaution, the Chief removed his over-shirt and wrapped it around his hand. Dropping to his knee, he reached and pulled the hot door lever. Wearing only his white t-shirt for protection, the senior officer lifted the hot handle and backed up as the door swung open. Flames erupted from the fresh supply of oxygen, and the fire exploded in the open air, tossing a huge flame above everyone's heads.

The Chief rolled back from the door. His knees scraped, peeling from the harsh non-skid deck.

The two nozzle men crouched, pulling the supporting linemen holding the hose closer to the ground. Unsure hands of both men urged their respective levers forward. At first, nothing but air came from the hoses. But a few seconds later, water made its way through the nozzle and flowed in torrents.

Rusty was supposed to spray a wide fan, but his hose shot a solid stream instead. As fast as he could, he rotated the nozzle to widen the pattern, and a starburst of water fanned like an umbrella. Mist saturated the air around the entire fire party; without meaning to, he coated everyone with salt water. The extra weight of water was unplanned, adding to an already strenuous situation.

The two teams sprayed the sea into the doorway while flames snaked upwards in spiraled columns. Steam hissed as hoses blasted the fire with a deluge of water. An occasional *thud* signaled the solid stream hit at the heart of the flame, dousing the hot metal with suffocating water.

Molten iron glowed orange like fresh lava, and at first, the firehoses had no effect. Large flames were too hot and the water jets turned to steam the moment they contacted the flames. Fighting fires of such intensity became a battle of attrition and the crew's only choice was to continue dousing the inferno until the fire relented.

Some short time later, the blaze lessened, but only by the smallest of margins. Still, it was enough.

The two teams squeezed into the narrow doorway. A solid stream from Hose Team Number 1 bounced off bulkheads, blasting anything and everything that resembled orange flame. But, thanks to Rusty, the entire hall became a foggy sauna. His fan ricocheted off the flames, sending a steady mist back into everyone's faces.

Rusty inched forward. Both parties remained crouched, stopping to lay the hall with a blanket of water. Over time, Rusty gained confidence in his hose and adjusted the fan to a more narrow jet, throttling back and forth as the heat increased and decreased in cyclical rhythms. His finesse at fire management turned him into a human thermostat.

Both men's mask beaded with condensate and in the dark hall, water droplets further obscured his vision. Blinded as they were, both teams fired at will and blasted everything they could. From time to time, they glimpsed the fire through the smoke, and anywhere orange flame presented itself, they doused it.

Heat from the raged inferno dropped to tolerable levels. Rusty twisted the nozzle, tightening his fan so both fire hoses emitted solid streams.

Rusty's team advanced deeper into the hall and rounded a corner. Twenty feet later, a massive wall of debris blocked his progress. The ladder he and Mux used to race was a mangled ball of blackened metal. The blast damage welded the floor to the overhead, crushing the doors of the main hallway. Through a small hole in the overhead, a faint orange glow showed fires on the next level above their heads. But the hole was too small to pass, even if a ladder was present.

Someone shouted behind Rusty's head, tugging at the hose, urging a withdrawal from the charred passageway. "Backup, Backup!" they said.

As they receded, Rusty checked the spaces off the main hall, clearing rooms as he went, blasting water over every surface that he suspected was hot.

One space was still on fire, but the fire was minimal. A cypher lock secured another space, and with the power turned off, there was no way to enter the room. Rusty tapped on the door, inspecting it for signs of heat. But the door felt cool to the touch.

The two teams extinguished the remaining flames in seconds. Blasting water into the Calibration Room, the heavy jets hurled books and files like dead autumn leaves on windy days, while soggy paper stuck to slimy bulkheads like huge spitballs.

Rusty felt another tug on the line. The support team reeled the hose as Rusty withdrew from the hall, keeping the spray going to cover their retreat.

The smoke thinned. As it did, it revealed black walls, charred from the intense heat and large blisters which swelled on all the painted metal surfaces.

Weary men emerged from the passageway, smelling like torched paint or cooked tires. As sunlight reflected off the decimated metal, the draggled damage control party glared into the fire's aftermath. The mess looked like a thousand gallons of glossy black paint exploded in the hall.

"I hope no one was in there," The Chief said with zoned-out eyes fixated on the devastation.

We never had a choice.

Matt and five other sailors jumped from the Gig Boat ladder, holding carbon dioxide extinguishers.

The Gig Boat landing was located just over the Quarter deck. Welded halfway between the main deck and the top weather deck, the small boat deck held the Duke's personal boat. Escaping from the upper decks, sailors used the small platform as a fire escape.

Matt approached the group of sooty sailors and pointed to the upper decks. "Everything's blocked and the upper levels are impassable. The only way down from the upper decks is to jump. Also, I think there's a fire up by the Crypto-Shack."

Other men jumped onto the deck, having followed Matt down the ladder.

An unfamiliar helicopter circled the ship, drawing everyone's attention. It was an Osprey, and everyone guessed it came from the USS Dallas.

Everyone was looking at the helo, assessing the need to climb topside, when someone shouted, "Hey, look! There's a ship!"

The group turned their attention west. On the horizon, a small dot sailed toward the wounded Adams. It was three miles off the starboard side.

"Is that the Dallas?" someone asked.

It was way too small to be a carrier. "No, it's a frigate," Rusty said.

Indeed, it was a frigate, and she fast approached — taking just five minutes to reach their burning destroyer.

The frigate was the USS Madison. She pulled to the port side of the Adams, allowing her damage control teams access to spray foam into the Adam's wounded hull, coating everything in a white blanket of "A-triple F." Aqueous foam covered the port side in a frothed bubble bath.

The Maddie doused the smoldering hull, while the frigate's senior officers inspected the damage from the safety of their pilothouse. Curious men pointed to the damaged midship, casting investigative glances through large binoculars, mirroring the areas of damage to all the sailors standing on the Adam's fantail.

Lieutenant Robertson stepped off the Gig Boat ladder and approached the Chief. "The Duke is with the signalman. He is talking to the Maddie."

"Where is the X.O.?"

Robertson shook his head. "The X.O. was in Combat."

The Chief wiped his face with both hands. "Is the X.O. dead?"

The Lieutenant read the eavesdropper faces as they waited for the news. "Yes. CIC is destroyed. Let's keep our shit together. We have important work to do," he said.

Rusty thought of Mr. Pratt. The Lieutenant never made it to Flight Quarters and Rusty feared he would never see the officer again. Although Rusty was not friends with the officer, knowing he would never see the man again dosed Rusty with the taste of his own mortality.

The Maddie's helo hovered in the air, floating over the fantail of the Adams. Four other helicopters circled in holding patterns to lower their baskets and lap up wounded sailors, hauling the men to safer places. The most obvious destination would be the carrier. With a ship's complement the size of a small town, it housed a sick bay large enough to render medical aid to crewmen in critical condition.

The Dallas and the Maddie sent Corpsmen to perform triage on the wounded sailors scattered across the fantail. Men, colored black with smoke and fire damage, lay on the gray-painted deck. Streams of blood flowed across the floor and collected in large red pools along the port railing. Some sailors missed limbs. Others strapped belts around their arms and legs, using them as makeshift tourniquets. Sailors, with shrapnel, lay wounded among the motionless and burned bodies of their fallen friends.

Not wanting to leave his ship, Rusty ran back to the mess decks. His desperate side-quest to find a way to the Shop was not abandoned, but the mauled decks were impassable. A black wall of metal, that was once an overhead, blocked the spaces forward of the chow line. As well, the ship's store was destroyed and there was no way past the wreckage.

A party of five Damage Controlmen surveyed the destruction. They donned full firefighting gear. Yellow jumpsuits with large oxygen tanks turned the firefighters into scuba divers in rubber chicken suits, while their round firefighting helmets, with white stickers, reflected the faintest of light sources. Tanked in fire armor, they were prepared to walk through any flame unscathed.

One man towered above the group. It seemed the Damage Control Chief thought Ocean was the best person for the job and had designated him "Team Leader."

Covered in soot, Ocean aimed the NFTI camera at the wreckage. The thermal camera scanned the charred debris, looking for hidden heat signatures behind the overhead, bulkheads, and deck. Ocean's mask reflected its bright display, illuminating his wide eyes behind the mask's thick glass.

The bright five-by-seven-inch LED screen displayed a wall of twisted metal. Blue light represented cool spots, while orange and white spots pinpointed fires burning on the opposite side of the mangled debris. Ash-covered ceiling cables dripped with gooey slime. Small stalag-tights of melted paint dripped from exposed black wires and melted rubber housings. Scorched insulation resembled a mattress in the aftermath of a house fire. Toxic fumes lingered throughout the interior of the hull, and the odors were so strong Rusty caught occasional scents through the tight seal of his mask.

He tapped Ocean on the shoulder. "Hey, Ocean! I'm glad to see you're okay."

Ocean gave no reply. Instead, he lifted his chin in an exaggerated gesture of greeting and returned to looking at the camera display.

His large hands, housed in thick flame resistant gloves, gripped a handheld Motorola radio, shouting status reports to the head of Damage Control Central. Sounds of other fire battles blared over Ocean's radio. Roaring infernos mixed with muffled yelling, rendering the messages indecipherable. Sailors interlaced a cornucopia of shouted obscenities with incoherent commands, all the while expecting compliance with the orders given from DCC.

There were no training manuals to prepare the crew for the nuanced glitches of the damage control procedures. How could the Navy prepare a crew to handle muffled radio communications in a noisy environment filled with static and grainy reception?

Rusty left the space, defeated. His worry that Mux and his division were in mortal danger motivated his need to find a path to the Shop and the radio room. He knew their chances did not look good, as the full extent of the damage had yet to reveal itself. His limited perspective prevented him from judging the scale of the ship's damage. But he would not stop trying to help his friends.

With his hands buried in his dampened pant pockets, Rusty climbed topside. A Chief Corpsman from the Dallas ran to Rusty, gripping Rusty's jaw with upturned hands as he inspected the condition of his busted chin. The Corpsman whistled at the men loading the copters. The medic turned and judo-chopped his hand toward the basket, urging Rusty to evacuate the ship.

His swollen nose was not only busted, it was broken. But as stubborn as Rusty was, he refused to abandon his ship. Ignoring the Chief corpsman, he backed away from the basket and threatened to take off running, pretending he didn't hear the Chief's order. This was Rusty's ship, and he planned on staying with the crew.

It is just what ya do... Besides, what are they going to do, put a fucking cast on my nose?

The Chief shook his head in disbelief and signaled to the helo. The pilot gave a thumbs up. As the turbine engine's pitch increased, the air-ship ascended into the sky, bringing relative peace to the fantail.

Rusty had laid low until the Corpsman finished evacuating the remaining crew. Once the coast was clear, he emerged from his hiding spot near the forward break room to find the ship was down to only the damage control party and senior officers. By all rational accounts, Rusty had no business being onboard — yet he remained with the skeleton crew.

The rear fires took several hours to combat. More fires burned below and the forward ammo locker was close to igniting. The senior Officers redirected all available firefighters to the gun mount and ammo storage depot.

Salty and drenched in sweat, Rusty fell in line with the other crewmen. A heavy hand grabbed his collar, swinging him around —

his eyes followed the arm to Ocean's face, towering over his shoulder. "You need to go topside. The space is too small for all of us. Your puny little ass'll just get in the way." The context made his general meaning clear.

Rusty's well-intentioned gesture was sincere, but futile and counterproductive. The real motive of Ocean's order was to steer his friend away from the tons of high-powered explosives. If the fire reached the volatile powder, it would destroy the front half of the ship, and Ocean didn't want Rusty near the explosion.

"What about you?" Rusty asked.

"I'm a Gunner's Mate. It's our responsibility. I'll be fine. You go topside and see if there's anything you can do to help."

Ocean smiled, and like ushering a clingy puppy, he pushed Rusty away, sending him toward the fantail. "Go on," he said.

Rusty backed up ten feet before he stumbled. He scurried outside to the darkened afternoon of early dusk, as the sun had just set. The purple fade of night's transition replaced the afternoon's bright blue sky, and evening blew the first of its cooling breezes.

Later on, during the night, the Adams found additional support. The USS Percy, a supply ship, pulled alongside the Adam's starboard deck. To stabilize the damaged ship, the Percy's crew tied heavy ropes to counter-balance the ship's list.

The Adam's Damage Controlmen positioned generators on the fantail, and large pumps diverted floodwater over the starboard side, helping to right the ship and regain her balance. Inside the destroyer, heavy watertight doors did their jobs and maintained the integrity of the ship's buoyancy.

Smoke hung in the air, as men ran around the fantail, throwing lines and setting up emergency lighting. The rear deck became a makeshift command post.

Fire hoses washed blood from the deck. Pink pools of saltwater mixed with the coagulated blood of wounded sailors drained over the side to rejoin the sea.

Three billion years ago saltwater had a Ph of 6.0 to 6.5, somewhere between the range of human blood and milk.

Shadows of shipmates moved like ghosts in the night, silhouetted against the night sky and faint moon. Rusty looked down at his open palms, observing how the ordeal blistered his palm's virgin complexion. His body knew its limitations, but events of the day pushed him to surpass those limits and its after-effects would hurt like hell.

21

Darkness. Late evening. Huge floodlights focused intense beams on the ship, producing macabre streaks which traced the hull like prison spotlights. Generators powered large pumps, while the droning of their motors reverberated off metal walls in the dense night air.

Rusty had nowhere to go. His Berthing compartment was a smoke-infested wreck — dark, dank, and poisonous from burnt synthetics. Even if his rack was dry and free of salt water, the humidity and heat would make things less than ideal for relaxation.

The emergency ladder leading to the helo hangar was tied up, still strapped to the safety net. After a fast survey of the Maddie and his own ship, Rusty investigated the upper superstructures.

He climbed the ladder, rolled over the netting, and stood facing the silent helo hanger. With the fire long extinguished, the crew moved to the forward fires, leaving the hangar unoccupied.

Sluggish steps guided Rusty to the threshold of the large sliding hangar doors. To his left, the flight tower ladder remained unscathed, tucked away in its unassuming corner of the spacious hangar. Beckoning him.

Rusty's shadows mirrored his every move, telegraphing his gestures onto the smoke-damaged walls of the hangar. He was now free to make his way to the Shop. In fact, the opened hall dared him to.

At the back of the hangar, the passageway revealed the devastation of the area leading to Radar 2 and to the other spaces of his division. The explosion blew twisted metal through the deck. The door to Radar 2 was off its hinges, laying in the middle of the hall. Its malformed shape was almost indistinguishable from the scattered debris — save for its painted label. A huge crease ran the length of its center. Riddled with holes the size of golf balls, the door was blasted like a spent shotgun target, peppered with shrapnel holes. The door was blown off Radar 2, exploding not imploding.

Beyond the door was nothing less than utter destruction. Contorted objects rendered the hall unrecognizable. One was hard-pressed to determine if the ceiling went into the floor, or the floor went into the ceiling. Cables and pipes lay twisted in the debris like black spray-painted pasta. The smell of burnt nylon, rubber, and oil overwhelmed Rusty and forced him to breathe through his mouth.

He took a step over the lip that separated the hall from the hangar bay. With his hands on either side of the doorway, he peered into the blackness. Morbid curiosity reduced his need to rescue his friends while pressing him to inspect his defunct radar room.

Hope that his friends might have survived the explosion, dissolved upon inspection of the hallway. Nothing could have survived there. If the blasting over-pressures didn't kill them, then the fire and smoke would have. Crushing pressures of compressed metal would have squashed their bodies beyond recognition.

Strange sounds welled within the passageway. Moans reverberated from the deep confines of the stricken ship. Was it imagined, or was it a trick played by the ship's fires raging on the decks below?

Low-pitched wails of ocean winds penetrated the newly deformed hallways. Haunting sounds of its steady howl denoted the finality, the passing of his friends to the "other place."

Taking another step into the charred corridor, he held firm to the doorway, steadying himself with both feet on the deck. A three-inch layer of soft muck covered Rusty's boot, and he examined his lifted leg as black tar dripped from his soles.

He stood motionless in the doorway, studying the morbidity of it all. Time stopped, frozen like the surface of the moon.

Twenty feet away lay the entrance to the Radio room and Transmitters. What was inside Transmitters? He fought back mental images.

It was not fear of harm that gave Rusty pause. Fear of finding his shipmates in a mutilated condition stopped him from advancing deeper into the gloomy passageway. He wanted to remember them as they spent life, not as they now looked in death.

A heavy breeze swept through the hanger. Salty smells broke the scent of the putrid ash encrusting the hall and the sudden gust of wind blew dust into Rusty's eyes, making him blink and look away.

In the corner of the helo hangar, a pile of Woobies sat unharmed next to the large, overturned tool chest. He stomped the gunk off his boondockers and ambled to the folded pile. Grabbing the remaining Woobies and tucking them under his arm, he made for the flight tower. As he passed the doorway, he leered at the devastated hall one last time. Anger filled his thoughts as he realized his friends were gone forever.

Rusty gripped the ladder with one arm and held firm to the blankets with the other. The salt-ridden bluejacket climbed up the rungs and made a nest of the Woobies. Kicking off his boots and stripping out of his damp uniform, he wrapped himself like a mummified cocoon and waited — listening to distant shouting voices.

His watch read 9:44 p.m. He stared through the small window, out into the night sky to the Milky Way's stars. Laying so close to the carnage, it was impossible to ignore how close his departed friends were, and the bereaved sailor mourned his loss.

Mux, I think I'll stay with you a little longer, my friend. Reality and the universe hurt you today. I don't want to leave you cold and alone. Tonight is our last night together, and I will spend it here with you. Some violence falls too hard on mortal men, and many times the universe doesn't realize its strength against the frailty of living things. Where is your disembodied spirit now, Mux? Where have you gone? This cannot be the end.

With heavy lids, Rusty sulked himself to sleep. All the while, tides rocked the ship, cradling him like a small child. Throughout the night, his Woobies kept him safe as morbid thoughts flooded his mind in waves.

Touching his broken nose, Rusty imagined the wounds on his dead friends. If they were alive, he wondered how their injuries would feel, the harsh stings of infection as it set in so many hours after being wounded. It might be better that they no longer felt anything at all.

Images flashed in Rusty's mind even as he struggled to control them. The harder Rusty fought to remove them, the more the morbid thoughts manifested, embedding images in his psyche. Corporeal manifestations consumed Rusty, and he was powerless to control them...

The next morning, a loud *bang* reverberated throughout the hangar, startling Rusty from his sleep. He jumped and stared at the ladder, expecting to see a head peeking over the edge, looking for him. But no one climbed into the tower.

Thinking of his current predicament sent a wave of depression through his body. The dull shot of grief cascaded from head to toe, suppressing his desire to move. But he needed to move.

Outside, the Adams was moving, though not under her own power. It seemed the frigate and the supply tender were towing her... somewhere.

How long did I sleep?

Thoughts of his fallen shipmates, combined with the fatigue of the previous day, made Rusty forget the raging fire near the ammo storage locker. Hell, he didn't remember falling asleep.

But, during the night, the ship never stopped fighting. It took thirteen hours for the brave crew to get the ship under control. Damage Controlmen spent the night putting out fires and pumping continuous streams of water. Some men traded their lives to save the ship, while others helped men escape other intense fires. Most men replaced normal ship-wide duties with unspoken acts of heroism, and none of the gallant crewmen assumed the role of victim.

With renewed vigor, Rusty hurried down the ladders and emerged on the scene at the rear of the ship, eager to offer additional help. After making his way to the fantail, he approached Master Chief Greeley.

"We have it under control," the Master Chief told Rusty. "If you want to do something, follow me to the focsle. We need to watch the lines in case they snap."

"Aye, Master Chief." As ordered, Rusty followed as Master Chief Greeley walked to the main starboard weather deck near the focsle.

Ten men sat ready in the starboard side break room, huddled in the shade. An additional five men sat at the front of the ship, standing by. The two groups rotated every four hours.

Everyone was tired, and most didn't speak. Ocean was in no mood for conversation. He stumbled and yawned from having been up all night, dealing with the forward ammo fire. Covered in heavy soot, he slept on a pile of rope in the forward break room. His large forearm draped over his eyes and blocked reflected sunlight from the doorway.

Out of three-hundred and sixty crew members, fifty men remained onboard. The Adams was down to a skeleton crew, as most of the ship's company were onboard the Dallas, the Maddie, and the Percy. Commissioned Officers evacuated all nonessential crewmen during the night. The Duke wanted to keep a small duty section behind in the event of a reoccurring fire, or if there were any malfunctions with the mooring lines. The remaining ship's complement comprised

Commissioned Officers and Chief Petty Officers. Rusty, Ocean, and Matt were the lowest-ranked sailors onboard.

"Does anyone know where we are going?" Rusty asked.

Master Chief Greeley glanced up from his boots. "Bahrain. We will go there and patch the hole. Then the Navy will tow the ship to Norfolk for the permeant repairs."

"Bahrain?" Rusty asked.

"Yes, it's the closest port. We should be there by tomorrow morning."

Mixed emotions ran high as Rusty walked back to the break room. His excitement at reuniting with Fitz and his friends in Bahrain wedded feelings of guilt for the catalyzing circumstances. Should he rejoice or should he mourn? Losing his friend, Mux, devastated him. Shit, he mourned them all. There was no way to separate himself from his polarizing emotions. Any elation he felt thinking of Fitz only deepened his depression with thoughts of Mux.

Mux and Palmer would never feel joy again. The world robbed them of all of life's experiences in the most profound way possible.

Once, leveraged emotions were weighed according to the intensity of pleasure versus pain. But now, pleasure and guilt were interwoven. It was an underestimated mix, and a mix he'd never experienced before. Tainted euphoria meshed with shame, releasing gut-wrenching sorrow to the point of nausea.

Survivors guilt?

Mux and Palmer were not enemy combatants, they were not soldiers in any genuine sense, and nothing could negate or offset the cost of their absence. They were good men who would never take a life. Men who joined the service to gain an education, and all they wanted was to experience the world. They never expected to be killed working on a radio or drawing on a dry-erase board in the middle of the ocean. Like everyone else, they too deserved to feel life's happiness.

Rusty had dodged fate. Had he been in Radar 2, he would have died, along with the rest of his division. Either from a raging fire or the deadly concussion of the blast. He would have become 'non-existent'. It was the only way he could describe it.

"Nothing" — a person under permanent anesthesia — forever void of experience, robbed of his very consciousness. He shuddered at the insanity of his thoughts.

Death's oblivion bridged a person's essence, as re-made awareness flowed across infinite lives. All Rusty ever knew was the 'present moment' — the "now." Death was a mirage, an illusion he would never experience. Awareness only existed in the 'now' ad-infinitum. Consciousness was a personal thing, a fingerprint. And his essence carried consciousness with him for eternity — turning his soul on and turning it off, as his body strobed in and out of the material world, the same way atoms did.

The body *was* the spirit. The body was not independent of a spirit; it was the spirit itself — they were the same. A hologram made of energy forever stuck in the present moment.

Death stills everything.

Late afternoon. Over her loudspeaker, the Madison ordered flight quarters. Her echoed sounds seemed to shrink the vastness of the glassy ocean, creating a sort of artificial intimacy.

The entire break room walked outside and looked at the frigate.

Master Chief Greeley ordered five men, Rusty included, to the fantail. It was time to gather supplies for the fourteen-hour trip to Bahrain. "They are starting a Vertical Replenishment. I need you guys to go aft to unload the supply pallets," he said.

But the Maddie never launched her helo, confusing the crew of the Adams. Instead, the Dallas sent in a Chinook helicopter. It flew in to grab the cargo staged on the Maddie's fantail. The double-bladed helicopter lowered a cable to deckhands who hooked the cable to staged pallets waiting to be hoisted.

Rusty ran to the fantail and crouched in the doorway as the Chinook helicopter skipped from fantail to fantail.

Powerful down drafts from the helo's propellers showered the waiting crew members as it hovered over the fantail. The warm air smelled like spent JP5 jet fuel. The Chinook's massive and powerful double blades chopped through the air. Each thrust of wind pulsated down, forcing a repetitive thudding into Rusty's ears.

It laid pallets on the deck and flew back and forth from the Adams to the Maddie, retrieving two additional pallets of fuel, water, and food. Also included was a large canvas sheet, which measured twenty feet by twenty feet.

Deep inside the Adam's Mess Hall, smoke damaged the spaces too much to store the emergency rations, so the crew placed the boxes close to the topside doors, just inside and away from direct sun. Everyone formed a bucket brigade to offload the stacked pallets, storing the supplies in the holding areas inside. Soon, large stacks of boxes displaced the scant space of the ship's interior, forcing men to squeeze past the tight rows of cargo.

After dropping the last pallet, the helicopter flew off to the carrier. Its thudding faded into silence with it.

The crew announced from the Madison's pilothouse: **"Red Deck. Secure from flight quarters."** *Sh-click.*

Men on the Maddie stood on the side of their ship, looking at the giant hole in the starboard quarterdeck of the Adams. The curious sailors pointed at the massive gash. Some shook their heads in disbelief.

Rusty was never one to downplay the importance of things, but during World War II, this might have been a common sight. However, this was not World War II and the sight of such a devastating missile attack set a precedent among the crew of the frigate — a novel level of fear, the new warfare of high-tech weaponry. If a state-of-the-art destroyer could find itself surprised by such an assault, what chance did *any* surface ship have?

It was a running joke that destroyers and frigates were nicknamed "missile sponges." A sarcastic descriptor for the fast attack ships of Destroyer Squadrons. But the recent attack meant anyone using the nickname deserved a blanket party.

How could this have happened? The Forty was in perfect working order when I last checked. It should have picked up the target on the radar. Could my radar have caused this?

It had to be an error in judgment. But who? Who fucked up? We deployed the Chaff. That should have prevented the ship from taking the hit. What happened?

Jets flew over the trio of ships as the convoy hobbled to the safety of Bahrain. Tomcat pilots rocked the wings of the loud fighters from right to left in a show of greetings. They performed aerobatics to lighten the mood of the weary crew members, and at any other time, Rusty would have thought it was spectacular. But no one was interested in morale boosting.

Crewmen idled on the focsle, drinking bottles of water and eating very little. The blistering sun robbed them of any reserved energy they may have held from the trials of the past twenty-nine hours. It was not possible to go to Berthing, not possible to find refuge, and not possible to find sleep. Below the deck, the smell of burnt cables and paint was too toxic to breathe. There was nothing to do but wait, think, and drink water.

A bunch of sailors from the Maddie pointed to the damaged hole, urging Rusty to investigate the commotion.

A few officers climbed above the damaged superstructure and draped the large white canvas over the gaping hole, tying it off with heavy lines. The large white canvas flapped in the wind, snapping like loose sails.

With his head so full of questions, Rusty went to the fantail to find FC2 Mattingly. Maybe he could offer answers.

Matt sat on the deck with his back pressed to a shaded bulkhead, pinching an unlit cigarette between his fingers. Rusty sat beside him, staring at the passing sea.

"What's up?" Rusty asked.

"Thinking I want to light this, but I'm scared I'll blow the ship up," he muttered. He held up the unlit cigarette, drawing attention to it.

"What do you think happened?" Rusty asked.

"I think it was an Exocet missile," Matt said.

Rusty looked at Matt. "What? You know for sure?"

"Sitting in the rear mount, I had direct communications with CIC, and that was the last words I heard before the line went dead. We locked on and shot one missile, but the other got through. I think the jet launched them from twenty miles out, and by the time they gave the order to shoot at them, it was too late. It was an Exocet missile, for sure. At least that was what they said before it hit us."

"Damn," Rusty said.

"The CWIS is good, but those missiles were traveling at six hundred miles per hour. We only had seconds to catch them both. We couldn't. Do you know how fast a missile can close a twenty-mile distance?"

"There were two missiles?" Rusty asked, floored with disbelief.

Matt pinched the unlit cigarette between his lips, bouncing it as he spoke. He removed his zippo from his front pocket. "The jet was out twenty-six miles, but he wasn't squawking his IFF code. CIC didn't want to shoot a civilian plane by accident.... Fuck it. I need a smoke."

Matt flipped the metal lid on the Zippo and snapped his finger over the flint wheel. He held the gentle flame to the end of his Marlboro. Soon after, white smoke escaped his lips. "Combat hesitated. By the time they realized it was a threat, it was too late. That's all I know. I'm sure there will be a trial or investigation or something. But that's what I know."

"Damn, could you imagine if two missiles hit us? Shit."

Matt blew another cloud of smoke into the air. Its arrested shape floated into the open sky and dissolved with the passing wind. "Yeah," Matt said.

"Exocet, huh?"

"I'm sure of it. It was with that or a pair of 'Silkworms.' The missiles came in low and skimmed the water. I know because the CWIS shot at them. We tracked their approach vectors."

"Do you know if the Sea Sparrow shot the jet that launched the rockets?"

Matt shrugged. "Maybe, but I have no way of knowing. Everything went dead when the missiles hit us. The only Fire Controlmen who would know were in CIC and right now they are too dead to tell us anything."

Ocean approached and stood at Rusty's feet. "It was a 'French Mirage.' We saw it on the screen. The XO ordered it locked on and I heard from the guys in CIC." Ocean said. "Not sure what country it came from, but it came at us from the north."

"Well, If it was a Mirage, then it couldn't have been a 'Silkworm.' Those are launched from shore." Matt said.

Rusty squinted at Ocean. "Did you guys hit it with the five-inch?"

"Not even close. It was twenty-five miles out and way too fast." Ocean said. "But that didn't keep us from trying. The Duke ordered hard to starboard, to bring our ass around, making our profile smaller, but there wasn't enough time."

Ocean grabbed the top rung of a nearby life rail, leaning his back to it. "I know it's a bad thing to say, but if it hit the rear mount, it would have blown the entire back half of the ship off. Me with it. Do you know how much ammo is back there? If we'd made that turn, we'd all be at the bottom of the sea right now."

"What good are all the sophisticated electronics if they can't identify a threat?" Rusty asked. "I have been loading the crypto codes into the IFF every single night for almost 2 years. What was the fucking point of all that, if they didn't even use the shit, anyway?"

"Beats me," Matt said.

"Dude, could you imagine if the missile hit the VLS? Things could have gone nuclear!" Rusty said.

"I don't think it works like that?" Matt said.

"Yeah, but do you know this for sure?" Ocean asked. His quizzical look matched Rusty's.

Matt shrugged. "I don't know. All I know is it didn't hit the VLS, so I guess it doesn't matter, anyway."

"It could have set off something and blown up half the gulf. We don't know," Rusty said, looking at the sky, caressing his cat necklace.

22

Early the next morning, Master Chief Greeley climbed on the Vertical Launch System and ordered the crew to "man the rails," prompting the crew to scan the ocean horizon.

On the starboard side, a thin sliver of land cut the horizon from the sky, hinting the ship was near her destination. Rusty surmised Bahrain to be about twelve miles to the southwest.

Sailors sauntered to the life rails, where each one of the tired men did their best to stand at parade rest, ill-prepared to conduct standard docking procedures. Covered in wiped-away soot, the crew did not present a sharp and squared-away state of readiness. Dirt penetrated the sharp folds of their skin — holding fast to places only warm water hoped to penetrate. The small crew of seafarers looked aged.

The sharply dressed crowd on the pier stood in heavy contrast to the draggled men of the Adams. Officers in their clean dress-white uniforms, banded in clusters along the half-mile long slab of concrete. The crew identified the official's white, black, and gold bandy-brimmed hats from five-hundred yards away.

"I bet those are Admirals," Ocean muttered.

"I wouldn't be surprised if it was the secretary of the Navy," Matt said.

The conversation distracted Rusty, but not enough to curb his claustrophobia. He felt a desperate need to get off the ship and onto dry land. There was nowhere to escape in the open sea, so Rusty fixated on the pier as his shaky hands reached for the rail. If the ship moved slower, he would have to jump. Being on land would help him relax. He needed to slow his racing thoughts, but that would prove impossible — especially on a slow crawling ship like his.

Tug boats motored out to greet the convoy. Light plumes of smoke trickled from their stacks as they took flanking positions on the sides of the huge tender ship and the sleek frigate. Rusty's crew released the lines securing the frigate and the tender to the Adams. The tugs then pulled alongside the destroyer and pressed the ship to the pier, exposing everyone to her battle-wrecked scar, which was still covered under a huge white canvas.

As the destroyer touched the large shoulder bumpers, officers pointed at the covered hole. Some turned and whispered to the person standing beside them as everyone waited to view the crime scene. A civilian woman in an expensive suit pointed at the side of the ship, urging a young man to dictate important notes on his clipboard. Now and then, cameras took photographs based on orders from high-ranked officials who pointed at areas of damage.

There were Admirals and Captains in the crowd of over seventy-five officials. The Navy dressed civilian personnel in expensive suits — suits too clean for the Bahraini desert. Someone had the idea to present the tableaux group of rented spectators to satiate the curiosity of the world media, and with so many civilians wearing dress coats, the event looked outlandish in the infernal landscape — absurd, even.

"I bet those bitches are hot," Ocean said.

Rusty squinted in the bright sun. He clenched his teeth and spoke without moving his aching jaw. "Yeah."

Line handlers tossed mooring lines to the pier as the tugs held the Adam's close to its dock.

Overpaid men in civilian uniforms ran to the forward and aft line stations, mishandling the lines in an uncoordinated effort. It seemed apparent the amateur civilians replaced the normal line handlers, all in the name of national security.

Government contractors were part of the investigative team. The group of well-groomed men hoisted the gangway into position, bridging the gap between the pier and the fantail. It was all staged and held a high production value for the media.

Once moored, The Duke passed the word by yelling to the group from the starboard break room. "Alright, you boys, time to grab your shit and get to the pier. Report to the base medical. They want to look you over. There will be a shuttle at the end of the pier to haul you there. That means everyone."

The crew watched as two Admirals came aboard. Someone yelled, "attention on deck," and the crew snapped to attention.

"At ease," one Admiral said. The Duke approached, and all officers saluted as they walked to the midship to survey the damage. It was the last time Rusty ever saw the Duke. Days later, the skipper was relieved of duty, even though the fault stopped at the Executive Officer.

Rusty traversed the gangplank and walked the pier, along with everyone else. They walked in a slow procession past the damaged hull. Rusty looked past Ocean and Matt, staring at the sizable crowd.

Meanwhile, civilian men boarded the Adams and clamored over the large white canvas. They untied the ropes, lowering the sprawling blanket to exhibit the full extent of the damaged superstructure and hull. Unveiling the wound of the midship stirred feelings of disgust among the crewmen walking past the scene. All except Rusty, who was busy looking at the crowd — looking for familiar faces, as everyone does when reading large groups of people.

Many on the pier turned away in horror. One female officer placed a hand over her mouth while averting her eyes. Some witnesses buried their faces in their palms, while an Admiral with pursed lips lowered his head in disbelief.

Melodrama.

Rusty judged the spectators, he judged their expressions, and he judged them to be over-reacting. He would soon realize the reactions of those officials were, in fact.... understated.

Once in sight of the mid-ship, Rusty turned his attention away from the crowd to observe the giant gash of the midship quarterdeck. With his new perspective, he co-witnessed the mass murder of his fellow crew members, and its effect on their bodies.

The hole was enormous. A rocket blew a twenty-two-foot hole in the port side of the superstructure. Bodies lay scattered in the debris, contorted in the wreckage, frozen as though cast in a permanent flinch. The blast incinerated some beyond recognition, while others, only a few feet away, appeared to rest in their chairs, undisturbed. CIC and Combat Systems looked like closets of broken dolls in the aftermath of a house fire. Men froze like charcoal statues. Some of their skeletons looked black like charcoal, seeming so fragile a shout would cause them to disintegrate into a pile of dust. Of all the words Rusty could find to describe the faces of death and war, only one word came to mind... vaporized.

Horror compelled Rusty to look away. But it was too late, as the scene already embedded its image forever in his memory. Debris obscured Radio, Transmitters, and Radar 2, and Rusty was relieved at having been spared seeing his close friends in their state of death.

Still, other crew members stared on in shock. The massacre was surreal.

Earlier, from their limited vantage point, the crew was kept unaware as to the extent of the damage. It wasn't until they departed the ship and walked the pier that the men could gauge the carnage with any real perspective.

Master Chief Greeley turned red. He pointed to the men on the top weather decks, who were busy managing the large sail. "Hey. Assholes! Cover that shit up!" he yelled. "Show some respect." The Master Chief's voice thundered across the bay and echoed off the other ships tied along the pier.

Every dignitary within two hundred yards heard his commanding boom, grabbing the attention of several Admirals. One of which turned and issued an order to the men with the large white sheet. "You there. We have seen enough," the gray-haired Vice Admiral said.

The onlookers parted, allowing the crew to make their way down the pier. Faces in the crowd mirrored Rusty's rundown appearance. He knew he looked like hell, and so did the rest of the ship's survivors. As he and everyone else passed, the official's clean-cut expressions blurred into a macabre carnival show. The "rent-a-crowd" resembled strange statues on display in a wax museum, with each one displaying the same incredulous expression. The incident had reduced the surviving crew of the USS John Adams to a freak show on parade for the large audience.

Rusty neared the bus. Shore patrol roped off the pier, isolating the spectators behind the line of yellow tape.

"Wonder how long they're gonna hold us in medical," Matt asked as he grabbed the handle and started up the bus steps.

"Don't know," Ocean said, looking at Rusty. "Hey man, I'm sure she will be here soon."

"Yeah," Rusty said, answering Ocean.

The interior of the bus was hot and smelled like thick rubber flooring, vinyl seating, and diesel mixed with hydraulic fluid and axle grease. Except for the desert heat, the smell and sounds of the bus reminded Rusty of early morning bus rides in fourth grade.

The low rumbling hum of the diesel engine revved as the bus surged forward. Two minutes later, the crew rolled up to the front of the hospital, and men filed out of the bus, staggering into the lobby. It was the first cold air conditioning they felt in almost three days. One man fainted.

A lady with a clipboard took everyone's name as they passed, single file, through the hospital entrance. Rusty gave her all the relevant details before being ushered through the open doors to the back rooms. He walked to a hall where nurses corralled men into stalls, like parking attendants shuffling cars at a music festival. They sent Matt and Ocean into joining stalls behind the flimsy curtains.

Rusty climbed onto a hospital bed, still wearing his unsalvageable, blackened, dungarees. A nurse walked into the room and set a stack of folded linen on the foot of his bed. "You can take off those clothes and put on the gown," she said, reaching into a cabinet to remove a light blanket, tossing it near the clean linen she'd laid on the foot of Rusty's bed.

"Thanks," Rusty said, ignoring her request to disrobe. It was his plan to bolt from the hospital, and he did not want a gown to hinder his escape. He intended to find escape, and the entire hospital exercise was an unwelcome detour.

Thirty minutes later, a familiar voice broke the monotony of the hospital's silence. "There you are!"

Rusty looked up from the blue vinyl-tiled floor to see Blume standing in the doorway.

"Someone asked me to find you," he said.

Rusty smiled. It was his first in days.

"Who would that be?" Rusty asked, making no attempt to hide his excitement.

"Who the hell do you think? Damn, you look like you need a few weeks of vacation! How are you holding up?" he asked.

The sound of Blume's voice drew Ocean from his bed. He stood behind Blume in the doorway.

Rusty asked Blume, "How did you know I was here?"

"I didn't. I knew the ship was here, and Fitz asked me to see if you were with the crew. She was worried the explosion might have killed you. She wanted to come, but I told her to stay home and that I would check to see if you were here. I didn't want her upset if you weren't on the ship."

"I meant, how did you know the ship was here?" he asked.

"Fuck man, the entire world knows what happened. It's been on the evening news. Everyone on base knew you were coming here. And they televised your ship's arrival live on Bahraini news. Hell, there are cameras on the pier right now."

Ocean sat near Rusty.

"The Iraqis are saying it was an accident or some bullshit," Blume said, scratching his forearm.

Astonished at what he heard, Rusty jumped out of the bed, pacing. "Accident?!" he asked.

Blume backed away. "News said some douche-nozzle stole a military plane and wanted to be a hero."

"So it was an Iraqi?" Ocean asked.

"Not officially. Not sanctioned anyway. They said they were going to hang the pilot, but that is all 'pillow talk.' You know how politics are. It's all over the news and everyone with a TV knows about it by now."

Matt walked into the room after hearing the conversation. "Well, that's as fucked as a soup sandwich," Matt said, having heard the tail end of the scoop as he approached Rusty's room.

"Amen, brother," Blume said. "I'm here to take you to Fitz's place as soon as the doc releases you on a medical. From what I hear, they are gonna Mac flight you all back to Charleston after the investigation. I'm sure you'll be in dry dock for a year while they repair your ship."

"I'm ready to leave. Let's go," Rusty said, jumping out of bed.

"Hang on, skippy, the doctors need to check you over. Your nose looks like you've been mule kicked by a Jarhead and your chin is bruised. I'll wait for you outside until you can get treated," Blume said. He turned to leave and addressed Matt and Ocean. "You fellas take it easy now. We are all proud and happy to have you back safe."

"Thanks man," Ocean said.

The three sailors waved as Blume walked off.

Rusty lowered his head. "Iraqi. I knew it was something like that. There aren't many countries that would shoot a missile at us."

"The pilot's lucky he didn't start a war," Ocean said.

"He may have. Who knows what might happen?" Matt said.

"I gotta get out of here!" Rusty paced the floor, dragging his feet. He walked to the door and glanced at his friends. The urge grew too great. "I'm outta of here. I'll see y'all later."

"Where are you going?" Matt asked. "You'll be UA."

"I doubt anyone would miss me. If they ask, tell them I'll be back later. They can write my ass up if they want. I don't care, because I'm heading to Fitz's house. I'll catch up with you guys later."

Ocean and Matt exchanged glances as Rusty disappeared around the corner.

Minutes later, Rusty walked out of the front entrance into the parking lot of the hospital. Blume slid off the bumper of his Mercedes. His hands pressed to the seat of his shorts, wiping dust. "So much for waiting to get checked out. I should have waited until the doctor saw you. Oh well, let's go."

The windows were down in Blume's car. Rusty consumed the warm breeze and the scent of exotic spices permeating the air. Distracted with thoughts of Fitz and the week's events, he failed to notice the large 18-wheeled truck that darted into Blume's lane, almost forcing them to rear-end the hapless semi driver. Blume honked. He threw his hands in the air and yelled, but Rusty ignored the incident. The world had grown quieter, and in the grand scheme of life, some things just weren't worth getting hung up on.

Tragedy always stripped existence to its smallest denominator, and all things previously deemed important, were deprived of meaning. Possessions, acquisitions, goals, dreams, and ambitions were at once removed by tribulation, distilling a person's aspirations to the most basic of primal needs.

Dreams and contentment are luxuries.

"They're gonna mark you UA for this, ya know," Blume said.

Rusty squinted out the passenger window. "I wish I cared about work right now. Two days ago, I saw men with their arms torn off who would give anything just to hug their kids again," Rusty said.

Blume remained silent as he slowed to a stop at a stalled intersection. He scowled at the semi driver, who was also snared by the red light.

Still, Rusty hoped his name would get lost in the confusion and no one would miss him, for a day at least. Truth was, he did not want to talk about anything. He just wanted to gather his thoughts and rehearse what he would say to Fitz.

"Well, that shit that happened on your boat? It was a shitty deal," Blume said. "I know it shook you up. Hell, it would have shaken me up too. There's nothing wrong with taking some time to get over it."

Blume accelerated through the intersection. "Don't be a tough guy. If you need to talk to someone, do it. If anyone ever ragged on a guy or called someone weak for talking to a counselor, I would beat their ass. PTSD is not something to ignore."

"Thank you, Blume. But I'm okay. I don't have PTSD," Rusty said, biting on his middle fingernail.

"I know that look, man. Marines and Rangers come to my house and I've seen it many times. Dani and I have heard a shit-ton of things you wouldn't believe. They call it the 'thousand-yard stare.' Tody has seen so much action, it's ridiculous. Being a Delta Ranger, he's been through tons of traumatic shit."

Rusty's eyes widened as he turned to Blume. "Tody is enlisted in the Army?" Rusty asked. He'd always assumed Tody was a Navy Seal.

"Yeah. Staff Sergeant Tody Sawyer is in the Delta Force. Bitch is qualified for everything the Army offers. I thought you knew. Shit, his ribbons and medals go all the way to his dick, and even he struggles with PTSD. Anyway, pay attention to what I'm saying. Trauma can fester and you won't know it," Blume said. "One day it could grow bigger than you can handle. Repression is no cure for depression."

"Thanks, Blume, I'll remember your advice."

Blume watched Rusty's reaction with incredulous eyes. "That's all I can ask for," Blume said. "I want your serious consideration to getting proper help if shit gets too real."

Minutes later, they arrived at Fitz's house, and Blume parked his car on the street. Fitz sat on the steps of her porch, holding a white piece of paper in her hand, nursing an expression Rusty could not make out. Upon seeing Rusty, she stood and waited for him to exit Blume's car.

"Well brother, this is where you get off," Blume said.

Rusty extended his hand in gratitude. "Thank you."

"Don't mention it," Blume said.

Rusty stepped out onto the sandy concrete road, stepping onto the curb as Blume sped off.

Fitz's silhouette seemed dark against the low-hanging sun as it lit her from behind. Sand whipped at her feet as she approached and met Rusty on the gritty sidewalk, holding her arms out, awaiting his embrace. Lavender perfume filled the air while the two of them basked in the golden sunlight. Her auburn hair shimmered like ember coals.

"We all saw photos of your ship on the news," she said. "I just knew Radar 2 was hit by the missile, and I worried it killed you. You're supposed to be my agent when we get older, remember?"

"I'm okay. Radar 2 *was* hit, and they hit Combat Systems. Asshole killed my entire division. Mux is dead." Rusty severed their embrace and pulled back.

Fitz looked into his eyes in horror. It took a long moment for her to process what she heard, and her mind reeled in its aftershocks. She clung to Rusty for a long while, before stepping back to wipe fresh tears from her eyes.

Rusty waited for her gaze to meet his. "I feel an overwhelming need to say this… I apologize for not waking you the morning I left," he said. "I was too afraid of dealing with 'goodbyes.' Any sort of formal departing would have added too much reality for me to handle. Besides, I never want to be anyone's terrible memory."

"There's no need to apologize and you shouldn't make a big deal of this." Fitz took deep breaths to calm herself. "Our friendship is not tainted, if that's what you are worried about. Besides, I was awake when you left. 'Goodbyes' scare me as much as they do you. I didn't want drama, either. Shit, I hate drama."

Rusty should have been stunned by her admission, but at the current juncture of his life, it took more than unpleasant revelations to surprise him. His sensitivity to astonishment felt terminally blunted. Events of the past few days distilled his desire for amazement to mundane levels.

Fitz waited for a response, but none was given. After a long moment of paused contemplation, she addressed Rusty with a softened voice. "Let's agree we'll never bring this up again. I want to think of the fun times," she said. "Besides, here you are and all feels right again."

Rusty held her hand in his, caressing her fingers with his thumbs. He pressed her cheek to his chest and everything seemed well, once more — except for feelings he tried to suppress — feelings of his lost shipmates and his best friends. The harder he tried repressing them, the louder they screamed. Guilt contaminated his feelings of contentment for not grieving enough over his fallen friends.

"I have a lot of things to sort out. My mind is floating from one thing to the next, and I cannot seem to pull my thoughts into perspective," he said, frowning. "I mourn Mr. Kistner, Palmer, Mux, and Senior Chief. I mourn everyone who died."

Rusty turned from the afternoon sun. The faint orange sky of dusk played well with the bronzed sand of the desert foreground. Dust-colored structures provided the landscape with an artistic quality — an aesthetic of chosen colors — Daliesque. Where once all Rusty saw was blighted desolation, he now saw beauty with a renewed fondness for life. However, nature's sublime beauty only added to his hurt. He knew his lost friends would never experience such splendor again, at least not in this world.

It seemed like life was even more frightening than the macabre. Life revealed itself for what it was — callus in every aspect, and this notion panicked Rusty beyond anything his nihilistic coping skills could handle. Life was given a blank check to cash in on a person's mortality at any moment, regardless of how trivial or ridiculous the reason was. Death never needed a reason.

The couple stood on the sidewalk, oblivious to the steady flow of cars and the rubber-necking Bahraini's, curious why two Americans stood on the sidewalk, sobbing and hugging.

Rusty let her go and slid his hands into his back pockets. "I'm so confused. It's like I am watching a TV that is quickly flipping through channels, and just when I understand what the show is about, the channel switches to something else," he said. "Sometimes my thoughts rest on blank channels of static and those are the moments that worry me the most — the moments vacuous thoughts are snuffed by repressed emotions. It is an actual thing, and it's weird having almost no feelings, nothing at all, and then a minute later, having feelings so intense I panic, thinking the world is collapsing in on me."

In hindsight, the ordeal made Rusty's most exciting moments feel pointless by comparison. Nothing ever measured up in his life experiences, and the attack had a profound effect on his determined future. Try as he may, he could not shake the horrific event.

Fitz placed her hand on his shoulder. "You suffered a traumatic experience. PTSD is not something you 'just get over.'" She offered a consoling hand and rubbed it up and down the small of his back. "I want to help and I'm here if you need me."

Rusty's demeanor shifted, and his hands flew into the air, pulling away from Fitz. He reproached her, shouting. "Why does everyone keep diagnosing it as PTSD? How does everyone know it's PTSD? I just keep imagining the dead faces of my friends. They haunt my thoughts," he said in an angered voice. "My ship was blown up and I would have died if somebody didn't decide to launch that helicopter. Can you believe that shit? My life was spared because they launched a fucking helicopter. Fate sure can be a capricious bitch."

He turned his back to Fitz, squeezing his eyes shut so hard they hurt. Shunning her not out of anger, but out of a need to isolate himself and his thoughts, shielding her from them. He felt the pang of sorrow as he pitied his friends and their unrealized potentials.

His worst thought was imagining the pathetic lives they led. Did they live fulfilled lives? Were their dreams unrealized, robbed of futures they would never see, stolen from them and their surviving loved ones? The only world they ever knew was the short twenty-something years of experience and most of that was spent forever planning for a future they would never know. Everything they had or ever would've had, was gone.

"I know survivor's guilt is a real thing now," he said in a mannered voice. "I will still experience happiness, even if it is beyond my reach at this moment. My friends deserved happiness too. My only consolation is knowing they will feel nothing ever again. Their pain is over."

Fitz lowered her hand and motioned for him to follow her inside. "Maybe you need time to sort your thoughts," she said, circling around to re-establish eye contact.

Rusty was not one to take aggression out on others, especially those he cared about. "Are you going to play shrink?" Rusty asked.

"I might just. I'm a 'colossal' listener." Fitz waved her hand toward her house, motioning Rusty to come inside, bribing him with the promise of domesticating comfort. "Besides, you don't want to stay outside all night."

"How should I feel?" Rusty asked. His look of desperation was so moving, it made Fitz's lips tremble, and her eyes water.

Coping with the sorrow, she wiped away her tears and smiled. "I cannot tell you how to feel, only you can do that. There is no right or wrong way to grieve."

To Rusty, death's erasure was the universe's way of keeping his friends from being tortured by immortality. Blissful or not, experiencing endless awareness would be agonizing. Death only affected the living who are left chasing the deceased toward eternal oblivion; a poignant reminder to cherish every waking instant.

Fitz grabbed his hands. She rubbed her thumbs over his blistered palms. "With all the tranquility creation can provide, your friends have found peace."

As if cued by her words, the sound of chimes filled the air, announcing the first evening breeze as comforting wind swept over the dusty lot, offering cooled air.

While watching clouds float across the dusk-scape, he brimmed with all the glory and splendor being alive offered. Awareness consumed Rusty's soul, and never had he experienced such an emotional rejuvenation. The sense of awakening was overpowering, and the grandeur of his surroundings was indescribable. Fitz was the catalyst for his surreal enlightenment, and although he did not know why, he suspected she was the yin to his yang, in the vast duality of being.

Their glossy eyes met. "Come. Let me fix you," she said, urging him to follow her inside.

Fitz back-stepped into the door, holding Rusty's hands in hers — pulling him in. Rusty spotted the crumpled paper she'd been holding. For a moment, he rejected the urge to grab it, watching as strong winds blew it in random directions. The letter danced in circles like a dead leaf. It floated over the front steps of her porch, and just before being blown away for good, Rusty stomped on it. To her objection, he released Fitz's hands and knelt to retrieve it. After reading it, he crushed the soft paper in his balled fist and closed Fitz's door behind them.

Dearest Erica,

You had your misgivings when you said it was a bad idea to get involved. Making commitments during a time when our lives are filled with so much change, to build upon so much instability was ill-advised. You were right.

Standing on a precipice, I have traversed the point of no return and find myself on the side of serenity, looking back. Our paths split here. I have no regrets about this, as I feel the past two weeks have been the best, even in the lowest of moments.

As a dear friend, you have given me my most unparalleled experience and I thank you for the wisdom it has brought me. With tender reflections, your memory will accompany me, carried beside me, forever floating along the surface of my thoughts. I cannot forget the time we've shared, nor will I try.

I wish you all the best, and I hope the universe provides you with a life fulfilled. You are a beacon in a world of darkness, and you deserve nothing less than everything you strive for.

Maybe someday, if fate intervenes, the universe might allow us to meet again.

With warm regards,
Rusty